eight

photojournalism

NO GLOSS. NO SPIN. NO BULL. QUARTERLY.

Cover photograph: Mikhail Evstafiev (Vol.1, No.1).
Top: Qilai Shen (Vol.1, No.3), Bottom: Francesca Yorke (Vol.1, No.4)

ei8ht
photojournalism

GET INSPIRED

- Subscribe today and every quarter you'll see the world through fresh eyes.
- Experience the texture of lives and places as distinctive as they are inspiring.
- Receive an insight into the people, events, emotions and environments that have driven the most dedicated photographers in the field to look beyond the surface, and bring it home to you.

GET CLOSER

- Challenging, incisive photo stories from the hottest talent worldwide
- Fresh and engaging commentary by leading journalists
- Personal perspectives on contemporary issues
- Interviews and reviews of important new books
- Worldwide gallery listings of photographic exhibitions
- Inspiring reference for everyone interested in communicating reality

GET IT

- Put yourself first. Subscribe immediately – let us bring the world to you
- It's quick and easy. Complete and return the form opposite, call us on +44 (0)20 7636 0399, or subscribe online at www.foto8.com

"Great mag. I am looking forward to my next issue already."

Subscribe now from £27* (inc. p&p) – Saving 20% on 2004 price, and see more

ei8ht

SUBSCRIBE

online: **www.foto8.com**

by phone: **+44 (0)20 7636 0399**   by fax: **+44 (0)20 7636 8888**

or by post to: foto8 Ltd FREEPOST 26 LON20566 London, W1E 8EA England
(no stamp is required for postage within the UK)

YOUR DETAILS

name

delivery address

city   country   zip/postcode

e-mail   telephone

DELIVERY DETAILS if different from above or tick for gift subscription ☐

name

delivery address

city   country   zip/postcode

e-mail   telephone

ARE YOU A ...?

☐ professional photographer   ☐ amateur photographer   ☐ photography collector

☐ journalist   ☐ art director   ☐ picture editor   ☐ other

☐ tick if you do not wish to receive information on products or services that foto8 ltd feels may be of interest to you

FOR OFFICE USE ONLY

DIRECT Debit

ORDER all prices include p&p.

☐ **Please start my subscription with the current issue, Vol.2, No.3**
☐ **Please start my subscription with the next issue, Vol.2, No.4 (Feb 2004)**

☐ **1 year (4 issues)** UK £29.00, Europe 46.00† euros, Rest of World £38.25
☐ **2 years (8 issues)** UK £53.55 (save £6.00), Europe 86.50† euros (save 8 euros),
Rest of World £72.25 (save £6.00)

Previous Issues £8.00 each (11 euros) inc. p&p - see overleaf for contents

V.1 N.1 ☐   V.1 N.2 ☐   V.1 N.3 ☐   V.1 N.4 ☐   V.2 N.1 ☐   V.2 N.2 ☐

£/euros [   ]   **total** (subscription price + back issue order)

PAYMENT

☐ **Cheque enclosed** UK sterling or Euros, payable to foto 8 ltd
(cheque payment for uk and eu subscribers only)

☐ **Credit Card:** Visa/Mastercard/Eurocard/Delta/JCB/Solo/Switch card

[   ]   issue# [   ] (Switch only)

valid from [   ] until [   ]   Signature:

☐ **Direct Debit – receive an extra £2.00 saving!** (UK ONLY)

originator's ID no. **705314**   ei8ht

to the manager of...

address of your bank   bank/building society

country   city   zip/postcode

name(s) of account holders

Bank/Building Society account no. [   ]   Bank sort code [   ][   ][   ]

Signature: Date:

1 2 3 4 5

Please allow 28 days for delivery of your order

VOLUME 33 • NO 2 • APRIL 2004 • ISSUE 211

WEBSITE NEWS UPDATED WEEKLY
WWW.INDEXONCENSORSHIP.ORG • CONTACT@INDEXONCENSORSHIP.ORG
TEL: 020 7278 2313 • FAX: 020 7278 1878

SECRETS & LIES
URSULA OWEN

'Political language is designed to make lies sound truthful and murder respectable, and to give an appearance of solidity to pure wind.' This is George Orwell, who became what Martin Jay calls 'the saint of liberal democratic honesty', in 1946.

Democracy, more than any other political system, depends on a modicum of honesty. We in the democratic West condemn governments that force people to live behind a curtain of official lies. Yet sections of our own media regularly exaggerate and invent (p68), our politicians are adept at evasion and half-truths, our advertisers and public relations gurus manipulate images and ideas in order to manipulate people (p101). We have become accustomed to living in a world where the truth is hard to pin down.

What is more, there is in our time unease about the notion of a perfect truth, especially in politics. Events are always complex, the argument goes, so how can there be a single truth about anything (p54)? Yet it is lying in politics that surely disturbs the most, as the Spanish election showed. We elect our politicians to represent us and, though we accept that they will keep some secrets, we do not want them to lie to us.

So what does it mean to say that truth is important to our democratic way of life? Are there ever necessary lies (p91)? Or virtuous lies? And in what circumstances do we lie to ourselves (p42)? In the pages that follow, *Index* explores these questions and many more. For instance, what happens to trust in a society where public life does not require that words should mean what they say? A recent poll in the UK asking how much people trusted politicians and journalists to tell the truth showed that only 14 per cent of the sample trusted the tabloid press, 20 per cent leading Conservative politicians and 25 per cent ministers in the current government. Interestingly, in the light of the Hutton Report, 81 per cent of the same sample trusted BBC journalists. In another poll designed to show who was winning the war of words over weapons of mass destruction, 54 per cent were inclined to believe the BBC and only 21 per cent supported the government.

In due course, we shall have to decide whether the prime minister sincerely believed in weapons of mass destruction in Iraq, whether he lied about them to lead the country into war, or whether he was led by the US and the intelligence community into an unnecessary war. ❑

IN THIS ISSUE

<< Mordechai Vanunu

The man who blew the whistle on Israel's nuclear secrets is due for release after 18 years inside, 12 of them in solitary confinement **page 12**

Last of the nomads >>

The last reindeer herders of Siberia threatened with extinction by oil and gas exploitation **page 32**

<< Spooks in the spotlight

John le Carré, master of spy fiction, takes a cynical look at the real thing **page 78**

You just don't get it! >>

The smartest advertisers flatter, cajole and co-opt their audiences into the game. That's the way to sell things, stupid! **page 101**

CONTENTS

INDEX FREEDOM OF EXPRESSION AWARDS

The fourth Annual Freedom of Expression awards were held on 22 March at City Hall, London. The awards honour those who have made outstanding contributions to the promotion of free expression and draw attention to and support for their work. This year the awards were expanded to cover music, books and film.

The judges were Monica Ali, Geoffrey Hosking, Mark Kermode, Ann Leslie, Caroline Moorehead, Nitin Sawhney, and Ursula Owen and Judith Vidal-Hall from *Index*. Jonathan Freedland hosted the ceremony and Helena Kennedy made the keynote speech.

Kaveh Golestan's widow Hengameh (right) and his son Mehrak with Lucy Young, widow of Hugo Young. Kaveh was killed in 2003 by a landmine in northern Iraq

Mende Nazer (right) with novelist and judge Monica Ali. Mende was abducted and sold into slavery at the age of 12. Slave *tells the story of her survival and escape*

INDEX MUSIC AWARD
Daniel Barenboim & Edward Said

INDEX FILM AWARD
Lee Hirsch for Amandla!

INDEX BOOK AWARD
Mende Nazer & Damien Lewis for Slave

INDEX WHISTLEBLOWER AWARD
Satyendra Kumar Dubey

INDEX / GUARDIAN HUGO YOUNG JOURNALISM AWARD
Kaveh Golestan

CENSOR OF THE YEAR
John Ashcroft

INDEX SPECIAL AWARD
Mordechai Vanunu

Meir Vanunu, who received a special prize on behalf of his brother Mordechai, imprisoned for 18 years for blowing the whistle on Israel's secret nuclear programme

TALKING ABOUT MY FATHER

MEHRAK GOLESTAN

Being here tonight evokes very bittersweet emotions within me. On the one hand I am very privileged and honoured to be accepting this award on my father's behalf, and yet at the same time it saddens me that it has to be this way and that he cannot receive it himself.

Before working as a cameraman, my father worked as a photojournalist. During the course of his career, my father had been interrogated, persecuted by the Iranian authorities and placed under house arrest on no fewer than three separate occasions due to the content of his work.

The first instance was when he produced *Recording the Truth*, a documentary film about censorship in Iran in 1991. I remember being quite young at the time and not fully understanding what was happening around me, only that it was very serious.

At the time this was happening, *Index* was following the story and publishing articles about my father's situation. I have a vivid recollection of picking up an issue in which there was an article about my father and I remember thinking to myself, 'Wow, this has got to be serious, it's in the papers and magazines!' It was important for me to read a completely objective version of the events as it helped me come to terms with what was happening around me.

In her introduction, Ursula Owen mentioned that we need people who are willing to speak freely and take a stand, as it is they who strengthen individual human rights and make democracies possible. I believe that we also need publications like *Index on Censorship* and awards such as these that celebrate freedom of expression, as they are just as vital to the vision of a free world.

Previous speakers touched upon the issue of journalists working 'embedded' with military forces [as in Iraq], and how this affects their independence. At the time when my father was killed by a landmine, he was working as part of an independent team. While being 'embedded' is by no means a guarantee of safety, I believe it is far less likely that my father's team would have entered a minefield had they been accompanied by trained military forces.

So why did they choose to work alone? My father was not a rash man, nor was he pig-headed or stubborn. My father simply chose to work independently as he had a vision of recording the truth in its purest form. It is a vision that I believe is shared by all who are present here tonight. ❑

Mehrak Golestan *is Kaveh Golestan's son*

IN THE NEWS

FATTY FOODIES In March, the US House of Representatives overwhelmingly approved a 'cheeseburger bill' that will block lawsuits blaming the food industry for making people fat. The Personal Responsibility in Food Consumption Act was passed one day after health officials announced that obesity was close to surpassing tobacco as the leading cause of preventable death in the US. 'We're talking about protecting the single largest private-sector employer in the US that provides 12 million jobs,' said Republican representative Ric Keller.

SMOKING PORN Professor Stanton Glantz of the University of California, San Francisco, recommends that crowd-pleasing films such as *Seabiscuit* and *Chicago* should be given adult ratings because they include smoking scenes that could influence children. His survey of 775 US movies found that 80 per cent of films rated PG-13 featured incidents of tobacco use, including *102 Dalmatians*, *Secondhand Lions* and *What A Girl Wants*. 'What we're asking for,' said Glantz, 'is that smoking be treated by Hollywood as seriously as it treats offensive language.' Films about smokers such as Winston Churchill and Cochise would be exempted.

WHEN A DRUG IS NOT A DRUG French wine producers are up in arms over a ban on domestic advertising that forms part of the government's tough campaign against drink-driving and alcoholism. In January, a Paris court caused uproar when it ordered a Burgundy producers' association to cease advertising its products under what is known as the Evin law, the first time France's national drink has been targeted. 'They are comparing wine to a drug,' said the association's president, 'when it is an item of culture.'

BIG BROTHER An Arab version of the *Big Brother* TV show, set in Bahrain, was evicted from the schedules 10 days after it first aired, following protests by 1,000 people, mainly Islamist activists. Heralded as an example of perestroika, the format was adapted by Saudi-owned MBC TV so as not to offend Muslim sensibilities. Out went booze, canoodling and bathroom filming, replaced by segregated sleeping areas, a separate women's lounge and a prayer room. But the 12 contestants,

M.ALₑ

Mohamed Ali

Press conference in Baghdad. In March, US overseer Paul Bremer closed the Shia paper Al Hawza for 'inaccurate reporting'

who included a salsa dancer from Jordan, a Bahraini actress and an Iraqi musician, still managed to offend their elders. In the first episode, only one female contestant wore the traditional black robe, or *abaya*, while the body language spoke volumes. Meanwhile, the German version of *Big Brother* suffered a setback when animal rights activists complained at the number of dead goldfish surfacing in the bowl kept on set.

BRASS NECK Tina Turner, 64, must have seemed a dead ringer to play the Hindu goddess Shakti in Merchant Ivory's new film *The Goddess*. A personification of female power and energy, Shakti is depicted wearing a necklace of men's skulls, an accessory that wouldn't look out of place around the neck of the high-octane rock-and-soul diva from Flatbush. But on a recent scouting trip to India, film-maker Ismail Merchant and Turner – who has been a Buddhist for 20 years – were met by Hindus protesting that the singer's status as a 'sex icon' would denigrate the nature of the goddess. 'In India,' said Shaunaki Rishi Das of the Oxford Centre for Hindu Studies, 'the Bollywood actresses, even if they may not be totally pure in their lifestyles, know how to play the game well enough.'

BREWING UNREST President Chandrika Kumaratunga banned all beer advertising in state-controlled media in March after Buddhist groups agitated against the 'pollution' of Sri Lankan society by 'unbridled Western decadence'. The ban, which follows government efforts to 'discourage' Valentine's Day messages in February, was introduced when Sinhalese nationalists deplored the effects of television beer ads during the island's international cricket fixtures.

DON'T CUT IT LIKE BECKHAM The Chinese Football Association (CFA) has banned its under-17 team from sporting David Beckham-style haircuts. 'Dyed hair, long hair and weird hairstyles are all strictly prohibited in the training camp and all players must cut hair short,' the CFA's Feng Jianming told players. 'You must learn how to behave as a true man before becoming a soccer star.' Beckham, a pop-culture idol in China, is featured on billboards and television commercials.

PICK OF THE PUPS A St Petersburg-based firm, Prosperiti, is marketing plastic toothpicks bearing the image of President Vladimir Putin with the saying 'Our future, a strong Russia' against a background of the Russian flag. Also available is a toothpick packet with a picture of Putin's black Labrador, Koni, with the saying 'Our Koni, heroine-mother'. Koni gave birth to eight puppies last year. 'This is such a direct violation of the law on elections,' said Dmitrii Krasnyanskii, deputy chairman of the city's election commission.

STINKING GAG The BBC was forced to apologise to the Albanian ambassador after comedian Jo Brand offered to fart the country's national anthem during the *EastEnders Christmas Party*, broadcast by BBC1. Brand's comments sparked a storm of protest from Albanians living in Britain. A spokesman for Brand said: 'She did not mean to cause offence.'

JESUS V THE ZOMBIES With the ultra-violent *Passion of The Christ* suffering box-office eclipse in the US from *Dawn of the Dead*, its controversial director Mel Gibson went on to receive mixed reviews across Europe. Pope John Paul II lent his episcopal seal: 'It is as it was,' he reportedly said after a private screening last year. But the Jewish-born Archbishop of Paris, Cardinal Jean-Marie Lustiger, who was expected to comment on the movie's alleged anti-Semitism, simply observed that Christ's passion 'is not a spectacle to be watched'. 'The faithful follow the Stations on foot,' he added, 'they are not sitting in an armchair.' *Passion* was distributed in France by Quinta, whose owner, Tarak Ben Ammar, is a Tunisian-born Muslim, further enriching the controversy the film has aroused among the People of the Book. Of more critical reviewers, *La Repubblica* characterised Gibson as a 'Taliban', while *Le Monde* observed: 'Mel Gibson is to cinema what George Bush is to politics: a dangerous zealot who doubts nothing and from whom we can fear the worst.'

OSAMA NEWS A struggling artist, known only as 'Pierre', was given a three-month suspended sentence in Montpellier, France, after trying to run over a pedestrian he said he had mistaken for the head of Al Qaida. Lawyer David Mendel said his client was the victim of a temporary hallucination, triggered by media coverage of the Madrid bombings which had killed nearly 200 people days earlier. 'It wasn't bin Laden,' said Mendel. 'If it was, we would have won US$5 million.' Meanwhile, Canada's CBC television offered a glimpse into the private life of the terror boss in a documentary about a family that had lived in the bin Laden compound in Jalalabad for several years. 'He has issues with his wife and he has issues with his kids, financial issues,' said Abdurahman Khadr. 'You know, the kids aren't listening, the kids aren't doing this and that. It comes down to the fact he's a father and a person.'

WHOSE JACKPOT? In its first decision on an Internet-related issue, the World Trade Organisation (WTO) ruled in March that a US policy prohibiting online gambling violates international trade laws. The ruling, reported by the *New York Times*, was welcomed by foreign online casino operators as a victory that could reverse laws that ban their businesses. The Bush administration has promised to appeal against the decision and a number of members of Congress said they would prefer an international trade war or to withdraw from the WTO altogether rather than have US policy dictated from abroad. ❏

Compiled by **Michael Griffin**

MORDECHAI VANUNU
PETER HOUNAM

THE ISRAELI WHISTLEBLOWER REACHES THE
END OF HIS 18-YEAR PRISON TERM IN APRIL.
THE JOURNALIST WHO ORIGINALLY EXPOSED
THE STORY REFLECTS ON 12 YEARS OF SOLITARY
CONFINEMENT AND THE FICTION OF ISRAEL'S
NON-NUCLEAR STATUS

Almost 18 years ago, I flew halfway around the world – to Sydney in Australia – to meet a man who had taken a momentous decision. Mordechai Vanunu, a former worker at Israel's Dimona nuclear research centre, had decided to blow the whistle on his country's biggest secret.

Although Israel refused to acknowledge it, Dimona manufactured nuclear weapons in an underground factory in the Negev Desert. I had learned Vanunu was willing to talk and that he had taken photographs inside the most sensitive section of all, the area separating out plutonium from uranium fuel rods. My assignment held out the hope of puncturing Israel's duplicity: a public posture that it would not be the first to introduce nuclear weapons into the Middle East while clandestinely producing them on a large scale.

Arriving in Sydney, Vanunu immediately impressed me as a careful and honest witness. He was candid about what he knew and what, as a technician, he didn't. He said he had become alarmed at the quantity and sophistication of the weapons being produced. What compounded his concern was that the Israeli public and the Knesset (parliament) were being kept in ignorance.

Had Dimona been producing just a handful of atomic bombs – enough *in extremis* to deter an enemy threat – I doubt if Vanunu would have become a whistleblower. But in the 1980s, the activity in the hidden complex where he worked had changed and become much more sinister. Apart from producing plutonium, the plant had begun making tritium and lithium 6. Morde knew this meant something far more significant: Israel was developing neutron and hydrogen bombs. Coupled with public disclosures that Israel was developing ballistic missiles, it was evident to him that the country was becoming a fully fledged nuclear power with the capacity, if not the inclination, to wage an offensive war far beyond its borders. Nor was this a small-scale operation. He knew that scores of warheads had been fabricated (we eventually calculated between 100 and 200).

Given that this had no public mandate in Israel, Vanunu believed, and still believes, it was irresponsible, dangerous and immoral. He believed that disclosing what he knew would help the peace process in the Middle East. By speaking to a newspaper with international reach like the *Sunday Times*, it never occurred to him he was being a traitor to his country and a spy, as he would later be branded. His aim was to generate public debate in Israel on the issue of weapons of mass destruction, something that the media had never dared do previously.

After debriefing him in Sydney for nearly two weeks, I flew with Vanunu to London for his story to be checked by experts. He realised the danger of what he was doing, but we had no idea that Mossad, the Israeli secret service, was then on our trail. I have since learned that a hit team was already under orders to follow him. At the same time, they were instructed to do nothing in London that might damage the harmonious relationship between Britain's prime minister, Margaret Thatcher, and Shimon Peres, her opposite number in Jerusalem.

After nearly three weeks of further debriefings here, Vanunu became irritated with his *Sunday Times* minders. He was also upset that the paper had delayed publication of the story to seek further verification. He began to take walks on his own and, one fateful day in Leicester Square, he casually fell into conversation with a US tourist who called herself Cindy.

They dated two or three times and Cindy suggested a holiday in Italy. On 30 September 1986, they flew to Rome. As is now well known, it was a terrible mistake. He had walked full tilt into a honey-trap, sprung by Mossad, and these were his last moments of freedom.

Cindy, a well-trained Mossad agent, took him to an apartment where two men grabbed him and manhandled him to the ground, clasped handcuffs on his arms and legs, and injected him with a sedative. That night he was smuggled on to a boat off the coast of La Spezia and taken to Israel. Tied to a stretcher, he was landed on the beach at Tel Aviv and taken to an interrogation centre. Someone thrust a copy of the *Sunday Times* into his hands, showing his story spread across three pages. It must have given him some satisfaction that his story was out, but there were other emotions: what were they going to do with him? Kill him and dispose of him quietly?

If it had not been for the international publicity generated by his disappearance, I suspect Vanunu would have been tried in secret and locked away without anyone except his family knowing of his fate. A brother was visited by agents and told that he was safe but that he would never see him again.

However, faced with having to disclose he was in Israel, the authorities produced Vanunu in the Jerusalem District Court and charged him with treason, espionage and breaches of the Official Secrets Act. The trial was held in camera but I was able to give evidence in his defence. I tried to tell them this man was not a traitor or a spy. He did not sell secrets to a foreign power and he was not spying for one. I said he had acted out of principle to expose something that was harmful to his country. Any action he had chosen to take in Israel would have led to his arrest and, by talking to me, he had placed the facts openly before everyone, including the Israeli public. I added that Israel had not been made militarily weaker and, arguably, was strengthened by his disclosures.

I was asked at one point if I was aware Vanunu had converted to Christianity in Australia. I could see no relevance in this but answered that he had never made a secret of it. I was taken aback when the prosecution responded: 'So you knew he had turned against his family and his country.'

The court adjourned and, later in 1987, sentenced him to 18 years' imprisonment. Whether the stigma of his conversion affected the decision is not known but it has always inflamed the Israeli press. Few joined the campaign to help him and the numbers have remained low.

Vanunu spent nearly 12 years in solitary confinement. For the first two and a half years, his cell had no natural light and a fluorescent tube remained on 24 hours a day. With just occasional visits from some of his family, most of whom have rejected him, his mind began to go, as evidenced by his letters to me.

In 1997, after much lobbying and campaigning, and the support of a couple of Knesset members, he was allowed to leave solitary confinement. His mental health improved quickly and today he is well and optimistic about his release. But as we became aware last year, the notion that he would be freed unconditionally on his scheduled release date of 21 April 2004 was not a foregone conclusion.

Reports began to circulate in Israel last year that the authorities might prevent his having contact with anyone who could not be trusted. These reports were given added weight in January this year when we learned that

Jerusalem 1986: Vanunu reveals details of his kidnapping on the way to court. Credit: AP

the Ministry of Defence was seeking ways to keep him in administrative detention under a little-used emergency law dating back to the British Mandate. If that failed, he might be kept under house arrest and barred from leaving the country.

In late February, however, a spokesman for Ariel Sharon announced that Vanunu would not be placed under administrative or house arrest. The Defence Ministry said some monitoring mechanism would be established – probably surveillance and telephone tapping – and that he would not be given a passport. By early March, a small degree of common sense appeared

Mordechai Vanunu, July 2002: in Israel's Supreme Court. Credit: AP / Zoom 77

to prevail, but the threat of a passport ban remains. Vanunu wants to settle in the US with a couple who have legally adopted him. But wherever he lives, the only damage he could do is to remind the world that Israel's nuclear policy is based on a lie, make life uncomfortable for Israel and its allies, and expose the double standards of the West in what is supposed to be a uniform stance against nuclear non-proliferation.

Meanwhile, Israel has been left free to demonise him. Had Vanunu been, say, an Iraqi or an Iranian whistleblower with evidence of nuclear secrets in these countries, who had come to the *Sunday Times*, been abducted and tried for treason in Baghdad or Tehran, it is hard to imagine the world's leaders would have remained silent, as they have done in this case. They would, rather, have fêted such a person as a hero. Yet here was a man who had been locked away for most of his adult life after being kidnapped – a blatant offence against international law as well as the domestic law of the UK and Italy. Yet neither the UK nor Italy did anything in response. My only consolation is that in one important respect neither the kidnapping nor the imprisonment succeeded: the *Sunday Times* published the Vanunu story and, 18 years on, we are still talking about those disclosures.

Vanunu is a victim of a gross act of censorship for which Israel has gone uncensured. A victim, too, of the extraordinary duplicity of the West in turning a blind eye to Israel's nuclear capacity in the interests of preserving Israel's close relationship with the US. An open admission that Israel has a nuclear weapons programme would bring into play the Symington Amendment to the US Foreign Assistance Act, which forbids US military aid to countries illicitly acquiring nuclear weapons. Israel is still the biggest benefactor of US military aid.

Vanunu has survived a terrible ordeal and triumphed over his enforced idleness for nearly 18 years; Dimona has not fallen idle. The reactor is still operating and so is the plutonium separation plant, the supply of which is the reactor's main purpose. One can calculate that Israel has made at least another 100 to 200 nuclear weapons since 1986 of ever greater sophistication. It has taken delivery of three submarines from Germany capable of launching nuclear-armed cruise missiles. It has three-stage missiles with a range of many thousands of miles. It has thermonuclear weapons, every one of which is capable of destroying an entire city.

Vanunu's crime is to have embarrassed Israel by exposing its policy of nuclear ambiguity: a policy that has enabled its nuclear build-up to continue unhindered. ❏

© **Peter Hounam** *was an investigative journalist on the* Sunday Times Insight *team when the Vanunu story was published. He currently works in TV, and is a freelance journalist*

MADE IN AMERICA
NOAM CHOMSKY

A CENTURY OF US INTERVENTION
AND SUBVERSION CULMINATES IN
HAITI'S LATEST COUP

Those who have any concern for Haiti will naturally want to understand how its most recent tragedy has been unfolding. And for those who have had the privilege of any contact with the people of this tortured land, it is not just natural but inescapable. Nevertheless, we make a serious error if we focus too narrowly on the events of the recent past, or even on Haiti alone. The crucial issue for us is what we should be doing about what is taking place. That would be true even if our options and our responsibility were limited; far more so when they are immense and decisive, as in the case of Haiti. And even more so because the course of the terrible story was predictable years ago – if we failed to act to prevent it. And fail we did. The lessons are clear, and so important that they would be the topic of daily front-page articles in a free press.

Reviewing what was taking place in Haiti shortly after Clinton 'restored democracy' in 1994, I was compelled to conclude, unhappily, in Z Magazine that 'It would not be very surprising, then, if the Haitian operations become another catastrophe,' and, if so, 'It is not a difficult chore to trot out the familiar phrases that will explain the failure of our mission of benevolence in this failed society.' The reasons were evident to anyone who chose to look. And the familiar phrases again resound, sadly and predictably.

There is much solemn discussion today explaining, correctly, that democracy means more than flipping a lever every few years. Functioning democracy has preconditions. One is that the population should have some way to learn what is happening in the world. The real world, not the self-serving portrait offered by the 'establishment press', which is disfigured by its 'subservience to state power' and 'the usual hostility to popular movements' – the accurate words of Paul Farmer, whose work on Haiti is, in its own way perhaps, even as remarkable as what he has accomplished within the country. Farmer was writing in 1993, reviewing mainstream commentary and reporting on Haiti, a disgraceful record that goes back to the days of President Woodrow Wilson's vicious and destructive invasion in 1915 and on to the present. The facts are extensively documented, appalling and shameful. And they are deemed irrelevant for the usual reasons: they do not conform to the required self-image, and so are efficiently despatched deep into the memory hole, though they can be unearthed by those who have some interest in the real world.

They will rarely be found, however, in the establishment press. Keeping to the more liberal and knowledgeable end of the spectrum, the standard version is that in failed states such as Haiti and Iraq, the US must become engaged in benevolent nation-building to enhance democracy, a noble goal but one that may be beyond our means because of the inadequacies of the objects of our solicitude. In Haiti, despite Washington's dedicated efforts from Wilson to FD Roosevelt while the country was under Marine occupation, 'the new dawn of Haitian democracy never came'. And 'not all America's good wishes, nor all its Marines, can achieve [democracy today] until the Haitians do it themselves' (HDS Greenway, *Boston Globe*). As *New York Times* correspondent RW Apple recounted two centuries of history in 1994, reflecting on the prospects for Clinton's endeavour to 'restore democracy' then under way: 'Like the French in the nineteenth century, like the Marines who occupied Haiti from 1915 to 1934, the American forces who are trying to impose a new order will confront a complex and violent society with no history of democracy.'

Apple does appear to go a bit beyond the norm in his reference to Napoleon's savage assault on Haiti, leaving it in ruins in order to prevent the crime of liberation in the world's richest colony, the source of much of France's wealth. But perhaps that undertaking, too, satisfies the fundamental criterion of benevolence: it was supported by the United States, which was naturally outraged and frightened by 'the first nation in the world to argue the case of universal freedom for all humankind, revealing the limited definition of freedom adopted by the French and American revolutions'. So Haitian historian Patrick Bellegarde-Smith writes, accurately describing the terror in the slave state next door, which was not relieved even when Haiti's successful liberation struggle, at enormous cost, opened the way to the expansion to the West by compelling Napoleon to accept the Louisiana Purchase. The US continued to do what it could to strangle Haiti, even supporting France's insistence that Haiti pay a huge indemnity for the crime of liberating itself, a burden it has never escaped – and France, of course, dismisses with elegant disdain Haiti's request, recently under Jean-Bertrand

Incendie de la Plaine du Cap . Massacre des Blancs par les Noirs. 1794

Haiti 1794: slave rebellion that freed the island from French rule.
Credit: Archives Charmet, Bridgeman Library

Aristide, that it at least repay the indemnity, forgetting the responsibilities that a civilised society would accept.

The basic contours of what led to the current tragedy are pretty clear. Just beginning with the 1990 election of Aristide (far too narrow a time frame), Washington was appalled by the election of a populist candidate with a grass-roots constituency just as it had been appalled by the prospect of the hemisphere's first free country on its doorstep two centuries earlier. Washington's traditional allies in Haiti naturally agreed. 'The fear of democracy exists, by definitional necessity, in elite groups who monopolise economic and political power,' Bellegarde-Smith observes in his perceptive history of Haiti, whether in Haiti or the US or anywhere else.

The threat of democracy in Haiti in 1991 was even more ominous because of the favourable reaction of the international financial institutions (World Bank, Inter-American Development Bank) to Aristide's programmes, which awakened traditional concerns about the 'virus' effect of successful independent development. These are familiar themes in international affairs: American independence aroused similar concerns among European leaders. The dangers are commonly perceived to be particularly grave in a country such as Haiti, which had been ravaged by France and then reduced to utter misery by a century of US intervention. If people even in such dire circumstances can take their fate into their own hands, who knows what might happen elsewhere as the 'contagion spreads'?

The first Bush administration reacted to the disaster of democracy by shifting aid from the democratically elected government to what are called 'democratic forces': the wealthy elites and the business sectors, who, along with the murderers and torturers of the military and paramilitaries, had been lauded by the current incumbents in Washington in their Reaganite phase for their progress in 'democratic development', justifying lavish new aid. The praise came in response to ratification by the Haitian people of a law granting Washington's client killer and torturer, Haiti's former president 'Baby Doc' Duvalier, the authority to suspend the rights of any political party without reasons.

The referendum passed by a majority of 99.98 per cent. It therefore marked a positive step towards democracy as compared with the 99 per cent approval of a 1918 law granting US corporations the right to turn the country into a US plantation, passed by just 5 per cent of the population after the Haitian parliament was disbanded at gunpoint by Wilson's Marines when it refused to accept this 'progressive measure', essential for 'economic development'. Their reaction to Baby Doc's encouraging progress towards democracy was characteristic, worldwide, on the part of the visionaries who are now entrancing educated opinion with their dedication to bringing democracy to a suffering world – although, to be sure, their actual exploits are being tastefully rewritten to satisfy current needs.

Refugees fleeing to the US from the terror of the US-backed dictatorships were forcefully returned, in gross violation of international humanitarian law. The policy was reversed when a democratically elected government took office. Though the flow of refugees reduced to a trickle, they were mostly granted political asylum. Policy returned to normal when a military junta overthrew the Aristide government after seven months, and state terrorist atrocities rose to new heights. The perpetrators were the army – the inheritors of the National Guard left by Wilson's invaders to control the population – and its paramilitary forces. The most important of these, FRAPH, was founded by CIA asset Emmanuel Constant, who now lives happily in New York – Bill Clinton and George W Bush having dismissed extradition requests, because, it is widely assumed, he would reveal US ties to the murderous junta. Constant's contributions to state terror were, after all, meagre: merely prime responsibility for the murder of 4,000–5,000 poor blacks.

Recall the core element of the Bush doctrine, which has 'already become a de facto rule of international relations'. Harvard's Graham Allison writes in *Foreign Affairs*: 'those who harbour terrorists are as guilty as the terrorists themselves', in the president's words, and must be treated accordingly, by large-scale bombing and invasion.

When Aristide was overthrown by the 1991 military coup, the Organization of American States declared an embargo. George Bush Sr announced that the US would violate it by exempting US firms. He was thus 'fine-tuning' the embargo for the benefit of the suffering population, the *New York Times* reported. Clinton authorised even more extreme violations of the embargo: US trade with the junta and its wealthy supporters sharply increased. The crucial element of the embargo was, of course, oil. While the CIA solemnly testified to Congress that the junta 'probably will be out of fuel and power very shortly' and 'our intelligence efforts are focused on detecting attempts to circumvent the embargo and monitoring its impact', Clinton secretly authorised the Texaco Oil Company to ship oil to the junta illegally, in violation of presidential directives. This remarkable revelation was the lead story on the Associated Press wires the day before Clinton sent the Marines to 'restore democracy', impossible to miss – I happened to be monitoring AP wires that day and saw it repeated prominently over and over – and obviously of enormous significance for anyone who wanted to understand what was happening. It was suppressed with truly impressive discipline, though reported in industry journals along with scant mention buried in the business press.

Also efficiently suppressed were the crucial conditions that Clinton imposed for Aristide's return: that he adopt the programme of the defeated US candidate in the 1990 elections, a former World Bank official who had received 14 per cent of the vote. We call this restoring democracy, a prime illustration of how US foreign policy has entered a noble phase with a saintly glow, the national press explained. The harsh neo-liberal programme that Aristide was compelled to adopt was virtually guaranteed to demolish the remaining shreds of economic sovereignty, extending Wilson's progressive legislation and similar US-imposed measures since.

As democracy was thereby restored, the World Bank announced: 'The renovated state must focus on an economic strategy centered on the energy and initiative of civil society, especially the private sector, both national and foreign.' That has the merit of honesty: Haitian civil society includes the tiny rich elite and US corporations, but not the vast majority of the population, the peasants and slum-dwellers who had committed the grave sin of organising to elect their own president. World Bank officers explained that the neo-liberal programme would benefit the 'more open, enlightened, business class' and foreign investors, but assured us that the programme 'is not going to hurt the poor to the extent it has in other countries' subjected to structural adjustment, because the Haitian poor already lacked minimal protection from proper economic policy, such as subsidies for basic goods. Aristide's minister in charge of rural development and agrarian reform was not notified of the plans to be imposed on this largely peasant society, to be returned by 'America's good wishes' to the track from which it veered briefly after the regrettable democratic election in 1990.

Matters then proceeded in their predictable course. A 1995 USAID report explained that the 'export-driven trade and investment policy' that Washington imposed will 'relentlessly squeeze the domestic rice farmer', who will be forced to turn to agro-export, with incidental benefits to US agribusiness and investors. Despite their extreme poverty, Haitian rice farmers are quite efficient, but cannot possibly compete with US agribusiness, even if it did not receive 40 per cent of its profits from government subsidies, sharply increased under the Reaganites who are again in power, still producing enlightened rhetoric about the miracles of the market. We now read that Haiti cannot feed itself, another sign of a failed state.

A few small industries were still able to function – for example, processing chicken parts. But US conglomerates have a large surplus of dark meat, and therefore demanded the right to dump their excess products in Haiti. They tried to do the same in Canada and Mexico too, but there illegal dumping could be barred. Not in Haiti, compelled to submit to efficient market principles by the US government and the corporations it serves.

One might note that the Pentagon's proconsul in Iraq, Paul Bremer, ordered a very similar programme to be instituted there, with the same beneficiaries in mind. That's also called enhancing democracy. In fact, the record, highly revealing and important, goes back to the eighteenth century. Similar programmes had a large role in creating today's third world while the powerful ignored the rules, except when they could benefit from them, and were able to become rich, developed societies; dramatically in the case of the US, which led the way in modern protectionism and, particularly since World War II, has relied crucially on the dynamic state sector for innovation and development, socialising risk and cost.

The punishment of Haiti became much more severe under the present administration. Aid was cut and international institutions were pressured to do likewise, under pretexts too outlandish to merit discussion. They are extensively reviewed in Paul Farmer's *Uses of Haiti*, and in some current press commentary, notably by Jeffrey Sachs (*Financial Times*) and Tracy Kidder (*New York Times*).

Putting details aside, what has happened since is eerily similar to the overthrow of Haiti's first democratic government in 1991. The Aristide government, once again, was undermined by US planners, who understood, under Clinton, that the threat of democracy can be overcome if economic sovereignty is eliminated, and presumably also understood that economic development will also be a faint hope under such conditions, one of the best-confirmed lessons of economic history. Current planners are even more dedicated to undermining democracy and independence, and despise Aristide and the popular organisations that swept him to power with perhaps even more passion than their predecessors. The forces that reconquered the country are mostly inheritors of the US-installed army and paramilitary terrorists.

Those who are intent on diverting attention from the US role will object that the situation is more complex and that Aristide, too, was guilty of many crimes. Correct, but if he had been a saint the situation would hardly have developed very differently, as was evident at the time of his restoration in 1994, when the only real hope was that a democratic revolution in the US would make it possible to shift policy in a more civilised direction.

What is happening now is awful, maybe beyond repair. And there is plenty of short-term responsibility on all sides. But the right way for the US and France to proceed is very clear. They should begin with payment of enormous reparations to Haiti (France, the colonial ruler until dislodged in

1804 after the slaves' revolt, is perhaps even more hypocritical and disgraceful in this regard than the US). That, however, requires construction of functioning democratic societies in which, at the very least, people have a prayer of knowing what's going on. Commentary on Haiti, Iraq and other failed societies is quite right in stressing the importance of overcoming the democratic deficit that substantially reduces the significance of elections. It does not, however, draw the obvious corollary: the lesson applies in spades to a country where 'politics is the shadow cast on society by big business', in the words of America's leading social philosopher, John Dewey, describing his own country in days when the blight had spread nowhere near as far as it has today.

For those who are concerned with the substance of democracy and human rights, the basic tasks in the US are also clear enough. They have been carried out before, with no slight success, and under incomparably harsher conditions elsewhere, including the slums and hills of Haiti. We do not have to submit, voluntarily, to living in a failed state suffering from an enormous democratic deficit. ❏

Noam Chomsky
This article first appeared on Znet at www.zmag.org

NEWS FROM PATAGONIA
ANDREW GRAHAM-YOOLL

'WE BELIEVE THIS SYSTEM HAS A FUTURE
AND THAT COMMUNITY FM IS THE GENUINE
MEANS OF EXPRESSION FOR THE POOR AND
EXCLUDED IN OUR COUNTRY AND LATIN
AMERICA' – NÉSTOR BUSSO

Argentina's discredited Supreme Court recently delivered a historic decision in favour of community radio when it declared that a law passed during the last military dictatorship was unconstitutional. Néstor Busso, head of the Forum for Argentine Community Radio (Farco), hailed the ruling as 'a victory'. He said: 'For 10 years we have been fighting for the cancellation of that clause [section 45, law 22,285]. We even filed an appeal with the Inter-American Committee for Human Rights [part of the Washington DC-based Organization of American States]. Now we are pressing the Federal Broadcasting Commission (Comfer) for a new law.'

The Supreme Court's 4 September 2003 ruling upheld an appeal against a 1981 law that bars community radio from applying for a broadcast licence on the grounds that only commercial enterprises are eligible for legal status. The original case was filed 10 years ago by a small radio cooperative in Villa Santa Rosa in Córdoba, central Argentina, the Carlos Mugica cooperative – named after a priest who was murdered in the mid-1970s. It had applied for a licence for its FM station La Ranchada (The Shacks) and was refused by Comfer.

The military thinking behind the old law argued that commercial ownership made it easy to identify directors and prevent infiltration by guerrillas; cooperative and community broadcasters were suspect. However, the strongest reason for retaining such a law is that the award of radio licences is deeply enmeshed in political cronyism.

In the 20 years since the dictatorship, congress has considered reforms to the current law – some of whose sections date back to 1948 and the first government of General Juan Perón – to control the national network of AM stations. Each of these bills died on congressional shelves, and Comfer did nothing to change the system of licences as favours for political allies. Although a more democratic arrangement was to be enshrined in the constitution under the August 1994 reform, the idea was quietly dropped by politicians who had an interest in keeping the old law. And since licences can be granted by presidential decree, the executive has not much need of laws.

As a result, Busso describes an FM system that is surviving on the edge of disaster and is an easy target for politicians anxious to get dissident voices silenced. However, FMs are relatively easy to set up and the number of illegal FMs operating in Argentina and run on shoestring budgets continues to grow.

With the exception of some stations in Patagonia that have programmes in the Mapuche Native Indian language, most FMs broadcast in Spanish. As yet there are no specific community FMs dedicated to feminist, ethnic or nationality groups; the law is strict in its ruling that Spanish is the only language to be used and that existing stations must be of public interest. Some, whose legality is precarious, seek protection through membership of Latin American regional bodies. Busso's Encuentro Radio, which broadcasts from Viedma in Rio Negro, northern Patagonia, is part of the Latin American Educational Radio (ALER) system and uses advanced digital technology. Busso describes the present law as a convenient form of censorship; in October 2002, it was reported as discriminatory to the World Association of Community Radio Stations, as well as to ALER.

The more established form of censorship in most of Argentina's provinces for FM station operators who fall out of favour has been a beating, a bullet or a bomb. This still happens at regular intervals. President Nestor Carlos Kirchner, who took office in May last year, for instance, never liked criticism during his 12-year governorship of Santa Cruz in Patagonia province. Unidentified persons among his aides were known to have ordered one FM owner's car to be destroyed and his house set on fire. This was in Rio Gallegos, in the provincial capital. On another occasion, a power cut was caused in an area where two opposition FMs operated. The effect was immediate: on the one hand, the critical voice was silenced; on the other, the neighbourhood suffering the power cut blamed the FM owners, not the government.

According to Busso, Farco, which has 70 member radio stations and a similar number considered 'associates' or 'contacts', has to deal with all these cases. 'We give legal advice and have led the field with lawsuits against the government to get the law changed. I think we are going to get on much better with the Comfer authorities from now on,' he adds. In December, he

*FM 88.1, Buenos Aires: Villa 31 Retiro's very own shanty radio.
Credit: Andrew Graham-Yooll*

travelled to Geneva for the UN 'information society' summit (WSIS) and is working as regional representative.

'Financial viability is our main problem,' says Busso. 'We try to sell advertising locally, but it is limited to advertisers within the broadcasting range – usually about 15 to 20 miles. Some FMs raise funds in the community, or lease out spaces to religious groups. But in spite of the poverty, our success is enormous. Farco has a training programme and we advise broadcasters on how to manage their station. The right to communication is a fundamental human right. The plurality of voices is essential to democratic society and it is important that the actors here are basically the poor. This testifies to our success. We believe this system has a future and that community FM is the genuine means of expression for the poor and excluded in our country and Latin America.'

However, Argentina's radio administration is in a shambles, the combined result of political interests, the legacy of old dictatorships and provincial governors who run their territories as private fiefdoms. Comfer is supposed to establish a broadcasting regulatory guide, but mainly occupies its time in imposing fines on television programmes that use bad language – a profitable activity. And it, too, is also an area of political pillage. Directors appointed by each government go in looking clean, but are soon corrupted by the riches available: mainly the opportunity to have their own licence and give political friends and associates one. Central control has been more concerned with morality than with democratic use of the air; and the laws are flouted daily. New laws that would take account of the reality of FM radio have yet to make it to through Congress.

Meanwhile, of the myriad FM stations operating in Argentina, only 300 or so are properly licensed; 200 of these were licensed by President Carlos Menem in his last week in office in December 1999. These are the exception: approximately 1,500 more stations operate with 'precarious' or provisional licences. The Roman Catholic Church has control of about 200 of these, municipal authorities another 150. About 1,000 FMs are completely illegal and have no legal recourse. Out of that total, some 200 are facing legal action by the government, but usually continue to broadcast until they are raided by police (often acting on behalf of a politician who wants the frequency for himself or for his group).

Under former president Fernando de la Rúa (December 1999– December 2001), an FM clean-up was promised but, as previously, the promise came to nothing. During that time, Comfer announced a reform of the criminal code to crack down on illegal radio. It estimated that there were 6,000–7,000 illegal FMs, although the figure was thought to be exaggerated and circulated largely to support the reform. However, by the time de la Rúa fell, the economic crisis had hit and nothing was done until May 2003 when outgoing president Eduardo Duhalde signed a decree that ordered the current status quo to be maintained for 10 years.

It was also during the de la Rúa presidency that the newspaper *Clarín* waged a campaign for 'legality' in radio ownership. Reasonable enough – except that it aimed to wipe out the small stations and community radio that were siphoning off considerable audiences from *Clarín*'s commercial stations. If people were listening to the local shack – and there is a wide range of services on offer from medical help to job counselling, from help for drug users to the highly competent FM La Colifata (Radio Daft) run by the main state mental asylum in central-south Buenos Aires – they were not hearing *Clarín* and its advertising support was at risk. The campaign was intrusive and insistent but, like most proposed changes in Argentina's broadcasting set-up, came to nothing in the end. ❏

Andrew Graham-Yooll *is editor of the* Buenos Aires Herald

KIDSVILLE

You have to climb a wobbly metal winding staircase to get to the second-floor 'studio' of FM 88.1 in the shanty town known as Villa 31 Retiro on the edge of Buenos Aires close to the River Plate.

This is where Juan Romero, aged 39, and 'the kids' from the slum broadcast illegally 16 hours a day from 8am every morning. The programmes are news and commentary in the morning, with music magazines and phone-ins for teenagers most of the rest of the day. A religious group leases some afternoon space, but the sect's attempt to run the station all night met with Romero's opposition. 'I said they could use it, but they would have to work with the kids. They said they had their own staff, so no deal. The station is run by the kids, for the kids of the slum, and they are not going to be pushed out. We have a brilliant programmer aged 14. She started with us when she was nine.'

Romero, a former private security agent for a bank and a five-star hotel who was sacked when his employers discovered he lived in the slum, set up FM 88.1 with his severance pay in 1998. 'It was more than we expected. I discussed how to spend it with my children, and instead of buying a little house on a plot of land out of town my son suggested the radio for Villa 31.'

The FM's 'number' was taken from another station that operated in the slum about seven years ago. 'That station was called Carlos Mugica – like the Córdoba cooperative, but no connection – after the murdered priest whose parish the slum was. That radio ran for a few months and then all its equipment was stolen, so they folded. We had done a couple of programmes there with the kids so the taste for radio remained,' Romero explains.

FM 88.1 is completely illegal and Romero lacks the 400 pesos (cUS$130) to pay for the registration as an *asociación civil*, a not-for-profit association, which could help to get a proper FM licence in the future. His only income is about US$30 a week from selling food in the shanty market.

'We lead a very uncertain existence. One of the front-runners for mayor of Buenos Aires in the 14 September elections last year told his workers in the slum that he would close this radio as soon as he took office. It was a relief to see him lose. The politicians don't like us because we refuse to deal with them. They're trouble, and once you get in with the slum *punteros* ['pointers', neighbourhood political representatives], you're finished. You begin to depend on their handouts and then they demand support.'

The station has two main rules, no truck with shanty politicians, and all-out war on drugs in the slum. Its campaign against drugs in the shanty began when Romero's best friend died of Aids. 'That shocked me and my obsession now is no drugs. The slum only makes it into the papers because of drugs and murders. As if drugs and murders only happened here and not in the posh flats across the tracks.'

Villa 31 Retiro is on former railway land, alongside what was once the Central Argentine Railway, built by the British and 'nationalised' in 1948. The strip of land between the edge of the wide river and the railway is about one mile long and, according to Romero, 5,000 families live there, many of them illegal immigrants from the border countries of Bolivia, Chile and Paraguay. 'The government says there are 3,000 families; this denies about half the population.'

Juan Romero.
Credit: Andrew Graham-Yooll

The slum land, if it were to be cleared for development, would probably command top real-estate prices in the city, given its place overlooking the wide brown river. A long line of city mayors have said they want to 'set up a real urban plan for the slum', with properly marked properties and ownership deeds. 'I've heard that ever since I arrived here,' says Romero.

The radio station is on the second floor, above the empty 'cultural centre' on the first which used to be used for the children's activities, and the family home on the ground floor, built by Romero and his children. It is one of the taller buildings on the edge of the slum, staring at the new long-distance bus terminal. The streets between the shanty homes are sometimes wide enough for a car; more often they are paths in a warren much like a medieval city. The better homes are made of bricks and concrete, but many of the newcomers simply settle under pieces of tin and board until they can buy something better. ❏

AGY

LAST OF THE NOMADS

HEIDI BRADNER

They call it the 'land of the second sun', a landscape that is lit even at night by the radiance of the moon and stars reflected from the crystal-bright snow. Theirs is also the land of the midnight sun of the Arctic summer. For much of the year, they follow the seasonal migration of their reindeer over 1,000 miles of tundra – the Yamal Peninsula in Siberia, above the Arctic Circle.

Having survived the depredations of civil war, revolution and forced collectivisation under Stalin, Russia's Nenets are today threatened from another direction entirely: from the vast natural gas reserves beneath their feet.

According to Unesco, the Yamal Nenets, 'living on the edge of the world', now number around 35,000 at most and are 'nearly extinct'. Their language – part of the Finno-Ugrian group spoken by Finns, Estonians and Hungarians, one of Europe's indigenous languages – may once have been spoken by the whole of northern Europe, and is equally at risk.

Almost alone among other nomadic minorities of the region, the Yamal Nenets have preserved an ancient way of life to which the reindeer is central, providing for all their needs including shelter, food and clothing. Under cover of Communist Party membership and as wage slaves providing meat for the Soviet economy – Russia has over two-thirds of the world's reindeer – they maintained the essence of their culture and continue to bring their children back from compulsory education in the towns to the freedom of the tundra and the annual trek. Contact with the outside world is maintained through radio and newspapers, which are highly prized.

But now the Yamal Nenets fear the depredations that will come with Russia's development of one of the world's largest natural gas deposits. It lies directly beneath their migration route and, since the mid-1990s, workers from Gazprom, the Russian national gas company, have been working on the roads, railways and pipelines that will export the precious gas across the tundra to an energy-hungry world. Already the herders are finding deer wounded and infected by rusting debris left near oil and gas sites; their infections are usually fatal. In Russia's frantic rush to industrial wealth, there will be little concern for the delicate ecological balance of this remote region; even less for a tiny minority of nomads. ❏

JVH from information supplied by Heidi Bradner

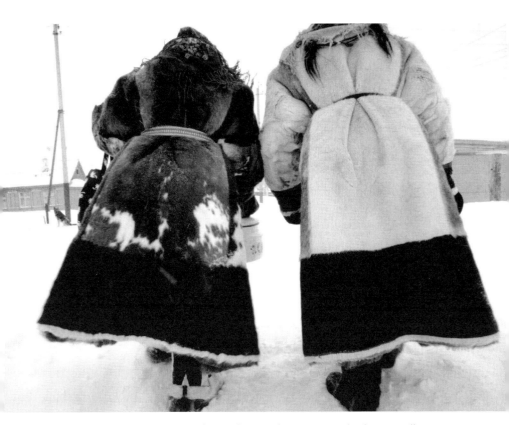

Stocking up on supplies on the annual visit to Yar-Sale, the main village on the Yamal peninsula. Nenet woman wearing their warmest hand-sewn reindeer garb carry off their new teapot

Above: Vera and the reindeer, providers of shelter, food, clothing – and transport. Nenets women move with caravans of four to 12 sledges roped together and pulled by deer trained for the task. They carry their entire home and family, including the food that will feed them for the next nine months

Left: Masha and Haptco, an orphan deer raised by the family, inside the family's summer choom. *The teepee-like* choom *is formed of reindeer hides stitched over a wooden frame. In winter, a double layer of hides helps keep out wind and sub-zero temperatures*

Opposite: Nenets women work together to construct their home for the night. The choom *and all the work involved is entirely their responsibility*

Top: Tanya enjoys freshly slaughtered reindeer meat. The fresh warm blood and meat of the reindeer,
eaten raw, provide vitamins in place of fruit and vegetables, unavailable on the tundra

Above: spring ends, summer begins and the winter sledges lie in the wilderness
packed and ready for next season

Below: the generations – babies and elders – travel together. Arkadi and his grandchildren pack the sledges to continue the journey

Bottom: herding reindeer. The daily task of choosing the deer for that day's transport. The lassos are braided by Nenets women from deer sinews that can withstand the extreme cold better than conventional rope

*Anatoli and his son Ivan round up three calves who
have been separated from the herd*

THE LYING GAME

**FROM PUBLIC RELATIONS TO SPIN
TO THE LIE DIRECT, THERE IS A
WORLD OF UNTRUTH OUT THERE.
INDEX LOOKS AT THE MANY
VARIETIES OF SUBTERFUGE**

*Madrid, 12 March 2004: Spain's PM Jose Maria
Aznar, hand on heart, 'I cannot tell a lie . . .'
one day after the attack on Spanish trains that left
192 dead and 1,400 injured. Credit: AP / EFE,
Manuel H de Leon*

THE LIES WE TELL

STANLEY COHEN

HOW MUCH DO WE BELIEVE THE LIES WE TELL TO OURSELVES AND OTHERS?

Plain lying, we assume, is a far simpler matter than denial. In some states of mind and political states, however, the difference between obvious lying and paradoxical denial becomes blurred. This is the terrain of self-deception and bad faith. What can it mean to 'lie to yourself' – the conventional (and bizarre) meaning of self-deception? A lie is 'a statement intended to deceive a dupe about the state of the world, including the intentions and attitudes of the liar'. The liar, that is, intends to cause the dupe to adopt an understanding about the world and/or the mind of the liar that the liar believes to be false. The distinction between truth and deceit refers to the intentions of the liar, not the nature of the world. In *Deceit, Delusion and Deception*, W Peter Robinson nicely identifies the 'prototypical, fully fledged lie as a proposition (P) asserted by S (sender) to an addressee (A) such that (1) P is false, (2) S believes P to be false, and (3) in uttering P, S intends that A shall come to believe P'. Despite its ungainly appearance, this is a helpful tool to weed out those denial statements (surely the majority) that are 'merely' fully fledged lies.

But what about self-deception? If this means *lying to yourself* rather than to others, it looks similar to prototypical denial. The notion of self-deception, though, must suppose inner dialogues or many-sided conversations just like these: the roles of liar and dupe are indeed played or thought out by the same person (the 'I' and the 'me'). These are more like ongoing internal reality negotiations, which – like external negotiations between real, different people – can include denial, lying, delusion, illusion and deceit. In this looser sense, self-deception is imaginable. So is self-delusion: the liar begins to believe that her lie is not a lie, but true. In order to live with yourself, you allow yourself to be 'taken in' by your own deceptive style. So internal denial is similar to self-deceit or self-delusion.

But how much do people 'really' believe the lies they tell to themselves and others? There are perpetrators of dreadful atrocities who not only deny culpability, but insist (and convince others) that they were morally right: 'they started shooting . . . we are the real victims . . . they deserved what they got . . . this was the will of God'. This self-righteousness may be only a tactical ploy, a rhetorical gesture, a pretence. Such people know that they are lying, and don't for a minute believe their own clichés. Alternatively, however, they (and their audiences) may be convinced that this is the truth: the self is the text. It takes long practice, cultural learning, indoctrination, routinisation or conversion to enable people to believe their own lies and not see themselves as deluded. You become sincere when, in David Riesman's classic definition, you start believing your own propaganda. Remember that the truth or falsity of such narratives does not tell us whether they are fully fledged lies, empty rhetorical chat or utterly sincere beliefs. More likely, from the lips of a Serb soldier talking to the CNN, they are a mixture of the three.

YOU BECOME SINCERE WHEN YOU START BELIEVING YOUR OWN PROPAGANDA

But assume that he does mean what he says – either after assuring himself that he does or because he has never questioned his beliefs. Is this self-deception or sincerity? And is it better (less dangerous) that soldiers, press officers and politicians believe their own rhetoric than know that it is only rhetoric? Do they start believing, then become cynical, or begin to believe what they were cynical about?

In any talk about deceiving ourselves by hiding the truth 'from' ourselves, terms like 'deceive' or 'hide' surely negate the idea that denial is an *unconscious* process. Freudian theory does not require us to be, at every stage, totally unconscious of what we are doing. Thus we knowingly choose not to make enquiries that might confirm some hidden cognition: 'I just don't want to know what he gets up to at those conferences.' Nor are we unconscious when we profess not to recognise what we are doing or protest against the (quite correct) name that someone gives to this: 'It's not that I'm actually *leaving* you.' But the master force must be unconscious to allow us to go on thinking that we are doing something quite different from what we acknowledge to others as well as ourselves. Protected thus by denial – we are not responsible for this evasion of the superego's judgement – we not only avoid anxiety, but enjoy the forbidden.

This looks pretty close to self-deception. According to a standard account, people in states of self-deception defensively avoid 'spelling out' what they are doing: 'The self-deceiver is one who is in some way engaged in the world but who disavows the engagement, who will not acknowledge it even to himself as his,' says Herbert Fingarette, noting that this is like

Jean-Paul Sartre (left) and Sigmund Freud.
Credits: Archives Charmet / Bridgeman Art Library; Rex

Freud's 'splitting of the ego'. Even if they have a clear personal self-identity, people act in ways they know to be morally unacceptable, but do so in pursuit of isolated projects disengaged from the rest of the self. This type of disavowal – the act has no connection with who I really am – may be sincere, and hence self-deceiving. It is critical in the perpetuation of atrocities. I might engage in an even more radical form of denial: the person who did (or observed) all those horrible things in Vietnam *was not me*.

Self-deception is a way to keep secret from ourselves the truth we cannot face. As Sisela Bok notes in *Secrets*: 'To see the self as deceiving itself has seemed the only way to explain what might otherwise seem incomprehensible: a person's failure to acknowledge what is too obvious to miss.' But this explanation is troubling: 'Exactly how can one be both insider and outsider thus, keeping secrets from oneself, even lying to oneself? How can one simultaneously know and ignore the same thing, hide it and remain in the dark about it?' Without this simultaneity – knowing *and* not-knowing the same thing at the same time, being in the light *and* in the dark, keeping a secret *and* ignoring it – both self-deception and denial lose their paradoxical character. Yet there is no way to 'show' any of this. If I am told that I am deceiving myself or in denial, I have no convincing way to deny this. All my denials are further proof of the depths of my denial, the force of my resistance, or the falsity of my consciousness.

The Freudian solution is appealing because the topology of splitting – 'portions' of the mind – keeps these dualities in place. This is just what Sartre famously ridiculed: 'the hypothesis of a censor, conceived as a line of demarcation with customs, passport division, currency control, etc, to re-establish the duality of the deceiver and the deceived'. His alternative, *bad faith*, is a form of denial that consciousness directs towards itself – but it is not 'lying' to oneself. The person practising bad faith is, to be sure, hiding a displeasing truth. But this is not a falsehood – simply because you are hiding the truth from yourself. There is no duality of deceiver–deceived; every-thing happens within a unified single consciousness: 'It follows . . . that the one to whom the lie is told and the one who lies are one and the same person, which means that I must know in my capacity as the one deceived. Better yet, I must know the truth very exactly *in order* to conceal it more carefully.'

This makes sense. But Sartre now becomes his most opaque. Bad faith, he insists, is not something one is infected with; it is precisely not a 'state'. Consciousness 'affects itself' with bad faith: 'There must be an original intention and project of bad faith.' But just what sort of project can this be in the world of social suffering? Sartre insists that knowing the truth 'very exactly' and concealing it 'more carefully' do not happen at different moments, but 'in the unitary structure of a single project'. If the project is neither unconscious nor a deliberate and cynical attempt (obviously doomed) to lie to oneself, then just what is it?

One result is the refusal to spell out one's engagement in the world. Jon Elster interprets this as the deliberate refusal to collect threatening informa-tion. Thus the dictator tells his underlings that he doesn't want to know any details; he knows that something unsavoury is going on, but his self-imposed lack of detailed knowledge allows him later to tell himself and others that he had no knowledge of what was happening. Hence the ability of millions of Germans to overlook the extermination programme: they must have known that something terrible was happening, but as long as they remained ignorant of the details, they could say later, 'We didn't know.' This is not a hard or paradoxical form of self-deception to explain, 'because we do not have to impute to the self-deceiver a knowledge of the facts that he does not want to know, only a knowledge that there are such facts'. We have all, I believe, dabbled in this particular project of bad faith.

Comparing the tragic view that we are all doomed to perpetual self-deception (we cannot help being false to ourselves) with the thesis that self-deception is impossible (because this would entail the same person both knowing and not-knowing the same thing in the same respect), Elster can only conclude: 'Between the two stands common sense, which tells us that men sometimes but not always deceive themselves.' Common sense also tells us that 'sometimes but not always' we slip into modes of defensive denial without our conscious awareness that this is happening.

The psychic world is complex enough to accommodate both denial as unconscious defence and self-deception as bad faith. Let us imagine that both Freudian and Sartrean homunculi are present, each getting to work on different material at different times. In one part of your mind, without an invitation and without you even being aware of her presence, sits a rather benign Freudian aunt. She may be smiling, but she is working hard all the time – and without much conscious help from you – to protect you from the psychic costs of living with threatening and unwelcome knowledge. She doesn't want you ever to feel too anxious. She helps you by means of all sorts of weird folk techniques (projection, dissociation, reaction formation), but her favourite trick is to nudge you into denial. She works so quickly that you don't realise what you had noticed. Literally without you knowing it, any 'troubling recognition' – feeling, fantasy, fact, the realisation of what you have done or seen – disappears. Later, every now and then, you get a quick, anxious flash, an intimation of the denied knowledge. This, of course, your aunt immediately helps you to deny yet again. 'It's all in your mind,' she chuckles, and goes back to her knitting.

In another part of your mind, stands a rather stern and malignant Sartrean uncle. You are aware of his presence almost all of the time. He works too hard at his job – which is to save you from the moral costs of acknowledging and taking responsibility for your own (stupid) decisions, amoral fantasies, selfish impulses and nasty actions. With your collusion, he has drawn you into the project of bad faith. You are contemplating doing something (or have already started) which is morally dubious or contrary to your self- and/or public image. You are too terrified, however, to face the abyss of your own freedom, the knowledge that you can choose. So you give each other a knowing wink – and out you pour the sad tales about 'no choice', 'compulsion', 'unconscious motivation', 'just obeying orders' and 'didn't know what was happening'. He half listens while smoking his pipe.

You eventually turn into your uncle – and never do anything authentic for the rest of your life.

Careful management is needed to sustain the convenient fiction that those in charge knew nothing of what was going on. The key to successful conspiracy, as IF Stone noted, is that the higher-ups do not ask what's going on, and the lower-downs do not tell them. The powerful need reassurance that they are kept *fully uninformed*. Middle-level conspirators manufacture 'genuine' deniability by hiding the truth from top people whose later denials are better if they are true. These key people are protected in advance by being designated (however implausibly) as having no need to know. They do not need to turn a blind eye: there is nothing to not-know.

When Watergate was first being investigated, one official asked Nixon's campaign finance chairman what Gordon Liddy intended to do with huge amounts of cash. The answer was: 'I don't want to know and you don't want to know.' This cliché expresses the denial paradox (how can you decide not to know something if you don't know what that something is?), but is also a simple (too simple?) way to ensure later deniability. The president's most loyal supporter, John Mitchell, told the Ervin Committee that he kept quiet in front of Nixon, not to spare him from having to decide, but to let him make a decision as to whether he wanted to be informed for the record – and then face the consequences of a denial that was obviously untrue.

It would have been better for Oedipus had he really been able not to know what he said he did not know. ❏

Stanley Cohen *is the author of* States of Denial: Knowing About Atrocities and Suffering *(Polity Press, Cambridge, 2002) from which this is adapted*

THE PHOTO NEVER LIES

STANLEY COHEN

THERE IS NO INNOCENT EYE. THE
PHOTOS OF A STARVING SOMALIAN CHILD
AND THE REPORT OF A MASSACRE IN
ALGERIA COME FROM AND BRING WITH
THEM POINTS OF VIEW

Curiously, we know more about visual representation than about verbal reception, the meaning attributed to what is perceived. Famous war photos and images, like that of a starving African child, are often taken to 'speak for themselves'. This assumes some degree of congruence – if not full symmetry – between the intentions of the sender and the perception of the viewer. A far more fateful assumption is that, despite each viewer's idiosyncratic sensibility, there is a common vulnerability to the raw sight of extreme human suffering: truths no one could deny, universal feelings of pity.

But, of course, none of this is self-evident. I tell a friend that I was 'deeply moved' by an exhibition of war photographs. She goes to the exhibition, but she is not moved at all. 'It left me cold,' she says. Our views and tastes are so similar that this complete divergence is puzzling. I will conclude with an allegory of the puzzle: a review written 25 years ago by a youngish female New Yorker of a collection of photos taken by another youngish female New Yorker.

The photographer is Diane Arbus, the first 'art' photographer who left an impression on me. When I first saw her work at the beginning of the seventies, I was stunned, totally mesmerised. Her photos have always stayed with me, her people gazing at the absent camera as I gazed on them. I knew nothing about Arbus then, but I deeply identified with her work. I could sense that she was tuned in to the denial problem. Her subjects (pejoratively and wrongly called 'freaks') make two powerful but contradictory demands: to acknowledge their utterly disturbing difference from us and also their common humanity with us. They were not attractive people; you would be embarrassed to be seen in public with most of them; you could not easily 'identify' with them. But they could move you; you had to admire their fortitude.

Untitled (6) 1970–71. Credit: The Estate of Diane Arbus, LLC

I was astonished then to see Susan Sontag's hostile review in 1973 of the retrospective exhibition, two years after Arbus's suicide. *Every one of her* reactions was the opposite of mine. I forgot about the review and only read it again 25 years later. I now disagree even more. She describes Arbus's 112 photos as 'assorted monsters and borderline cases – most of them ugly; wearing grotesque or unflattering clothes; in dismal or barren surroundings'. I wouldn't use the term 'monster' even ironically; about a quarter of the photos, anyway, are of quite 'normal' people, not freaks in any sense. Look at *Woman with a veil, Woman on a park bench, Woman with a locket, Four people at a gallery opening,* the nudists and the topless dancer. None of them is remotely monstrous. And what are 'borderline cases'?

Maryland, USA, 1970: Albino sword-swallower at a carnival.
Credit: The Estate of Diane Arbus, LLC

Sontag's literal descriptions are recognisable; we both saw the same photos. But from this point of view, the divergence is total. I will give four examples.

Arbus's work does not invite viewers to identify with the pariahs and miserable-looking people she photographed. Humanity is not 'one'. Her message is anti-humanist.

In my view, Arbus's photos not only clearly 'invite', but also instantly achieve this identification. And she does this, most extraordinarily, with the full awareness 'that it's impossible to get out of your skin into somebody's else's . . . that somebody else's tragedy is not the same as your own'. True, some of the people look miserable, but many do not at all. One of the twins on the cover looks altogether content; two sets of *Untitled* mentally handicapped young women are laughing; most of the nudists look stupid but happy; two of the transvestites are smiling; the lovely *Jewish Couple Dancing* are radiant with happiness. Arbus saw and showed something quite stunning: 'Most people go through life dreading they'll have a traumatic experience. Freaks were born with their trauma. They've already passed their test in life.' They have reached a strange tranquillity; the awful has already happened. I see this in the photos every time, but Sontag never does. Yes, I agree that Arbus is non-political. But 'anti-humanist'? Surely the message is altogether more 'humanist'.

The ambiguity of Arbus's work is that she seems to have enrolled in one of art photography's most visible enterprises – concentrating on victims, the unfortunate, the dispossessed – but without the compassionate purpose that such a project is expected to serve. Arbus's work shows people who are pathetic, pitiable, as well as horrible, repulsive, but it does not arouse any compassionate feelings.

The photographs may not elicit *Sontag's* compassionate feelings. But such feelings hit me instantly and remain just as strong 25 years later. I don't see the slightest trace of 'ambiguity'.

Far from spying on freaks and pariahs, catching them unawares, the photographer has gotten to know them, so that they pose for her . . . A large part of the mystery of Arbus's photographs lies in what they suggest about how her subjects felt after consenting to be photographed. Do they see themselves, the viewer wonders, like that? Do they know how grotesque they are? It seems as if they don't.

Bronx, New York, 1970: Jewish giant at home with his parents. Credit: The Estate of Diane Arbus, LLC

Is Sontag saying that she would have *preferred* these subjects to have been spied on and secretly photographed? Her rhetorical 'mystery' about how people see themselves is preposterous and degrading. These are not wolf-people from the forest: they are social beings; they see and know other people; they have mirrors; they have brothers and sisters, parents and children, and neighbours; they watch cinema and television. Sontag's supposition that they are unaware of their supposed ugliness is grotesque. So too is her meaningless accusation that Arbus's work 'excludes sufferers who presumably know they are suffering, like victims of accidents, wars, famines and political persecution'.

In so far as looking at most of these photographs is, undeniably, an ordeal, Arbus's work is typical of the kind of art popular among sophisticated urban people right now: art that is a self-willed test of hardness. The photographs offer an occasion to demonstrate that life's horror can be faced without squeamishness . . . Arbus's work is a good instance of a leading tendency of high art in capitalist countries: to suppress, or at least reduce, moral and sensory queasiness. Much of modern art is devoted to lowering the threshold of what is terrible.

For myself, I have never found looking at these photos an 'ordeal'. By 'lowering the threshold', I assume Sontag means including in the definition of human people who are ugly, deformed, sexually weird or perform very badly on IQ tests. If so, then we must be eternally thankful for Diane Arbus and other sophisticated urban capitalists.

I have listed my disagreements with Sontag not to denigrate her critical faculties as compared with mine. On the contrary, there is absolutely no doubt that she is far better informed than I am about aesthetics, photography and Arbus. I cite this as a painful example of how people living within the j4 same moral world see the same images in radically different ways.

Aesthetic relativism, though, does not mean that there can be no universal response to suffering. I once thought that I had found an ur-image, something impossible to deny. This was Don McCullin's unforgettable 1969 photo of an emaciated albino boy in the Biafran War. This image has stayed with me for 30 years.

McCullin's camera – which he likened to a toothbrush: just something that does the job – gave us eyes not easily blinded, or even turned. If only for an instant, we have to look. Reviewing McCullin's work in *Photographs of Agony*, John Berger describes how this happens: these photos 'bring us up short'; they are literally 'arresting'; we are 'seized by them'; 'the moment of the other's suffering engulfs us'. The result may be *despair*, which takes on some of the other's suffering to no purpose, or *indignation*, which demands action. We sense a radical discontinuity as we leave the frozen 'moment' of the photo to go back into our own lives.

This discontinuity is not, however, our personal response or responsibility: *any* reaction to such photographed moments is bound to be felt inadequate. Those moments of agony exist by themselves; they *must be* discontinuous with other moments in our lives. We know, however, they are meant to evoke shock, acknowledgement, concern and action. This is how we are supposed to feel. But, argues Berger, as soon as we sense the discontinuity as being our own moral inadequacy, and either shrug it off as just being part of the human condition, or perform a kind of penance by giving money to Unicef, we deflect the issue inwards. We worry about our own moral inadequacy or our psychic tendency to deny – instead of turning to a political critique of the atrocities. ❏

SC
Adapted from States of Denial

THE AMBIVALENT VIRTUES
OF MENDACITY
MARTIN JAY

HOW EUROPEANS TAUGHT
AMERICAN POLITICIANS TO
LEARN TO LOVE THEIR LIES

'*Un*truth and Consequences' screamed the headline on the cover of the 21 July 2003 issue of *Time* magazine, which dealt extensively with the still burning question: 'How flawed was the case for going to war against Saddam?' Once again, it seemed that an American president was in danger of losing his credibility and being excoriated for the sin of telling lies to the American people. Only a short time after his predecessor had been impeached for perjuring himself about his sex life, George W Bush was struggling to parse his way out of the discrepancies between his statements about the imminent threat of Iraqi weapons of mass destruction and what the evidence now seemed to show. Once again, outrage against political mendacity coursed through the American public sphere.

Not surprisingly, a political culture that takes as one of its founding myths the refusal of its chief Founding Father to lie about the felling of a cherry tree and that fondly calls its most revered leader 'Honest Abe' has been especially keen on rooting out mendacity from the political sphere. In fact, American culture has been on a dogged quest for perfect legibility, fuelled by a yearning for full disclosure that stretches from the Puritans' anti-monastic insistence on 'holy watching' to the widespread acceptance of psychoanalysis as a therapy of unconstrained candour. Not for us, Americans have prided themselves on believing, are the Machiavellian machinations of Old World politics with their haughty disdain for the transparency of democratic decision-making. Not for us are the even more dangerous deceptions of totalitarian ideology based on the imposition of the Big Lie on a supine populace no longer able to tell the difference between truth and falsehood. We are determined, as the reigning cliché now has it, 'to speak truth to power'.

In the academy, ever since Harvard picked its familiar motto, a comparable assumption has ruled that truth, or at least the quest for it, is an unimpeachable value. Interestingly, that motto was originally *Veritas pro Christo et Ecclesia* (Truth for Christ and his Church), but was shortened to the one word *Veritas* to allow other, more profane purposes to be served by that quest. When the secularisation of intellectual life undermined appeals to divinely revealed truth, this often came to mean a surrogate faith in the scientific method, however that might be defined, as a viable alternative. With the growth of departments of political science, often adopting the approach that came to be called behaviouralist, the appeal to honesty in political practice could be reinforced by a comparable attempt to study politics in a disinterested and neutral way. At times, in fact, some came to believe that technocrats with the tools of political science at their command would be the best leaders of a polity that wanted to avoid the untidiness of ill-informed opinion and untested prejudice. Truth in politics, it was argued, would be achieved by transcending the cacophony of competing voices and allowing those with the skills and knowledge to cut through to the core of problems and deal with them effectively.

At the heart of this project is a desire to strip political language of its irrational, emotive and ornamental excrescences and find a way to express ideas, arguments and motivations with full clarity and univocal meaning. If common men and women looked up to anyone now, it was the technical expert rather than the literary stylist.

No more rhetorically powerful expression of this distrust of the dangers of unchecked rhetoric can be found than the celebrated essay by George Orwell that quickly established itself as a touchstone of political truth-telling on both sides of the Atlantic, 'Politics and the English Language' of 1946. Widely anthologised, incessantly taught in schools, and cited with numbing frequency, Orwell's essay claimed that a debased, impure, inflated, euphemistic, pretentious, cliché-ridden language was more than a symptom of political decline, it was one of its main causes. 'In our time,' he lamented, 'political speech and writing are largely the defence of the indefensible . . . Political language – and with variations this is true of all political parties, from Conservatives to Anarchists – is designed to make lies sound truthful and murder respectable, and to give an appearance of solidity to pure wind.' Avoid stale figures of speech, unnecessarily long words, the passive voice, foreign phrases and abstruse jargon, he urged, and perhaps the wind would die down.

When *Nineteen Eighty-Four* added a brilliant exposition of the ways in which totalitarianism depended on the deliberate lies of Newspeak and

Doublethink, Orwell's reputation as the saint of liberal democratic honesty was augmented.

Orwell has been subjected to considerable scrutiny, not all of it flattering, which has uncovered some of his own less attractive biases; but his critique of linguistic obfuscation and its political consequences has become itself a standard trope in political rhetoric. For both the right and the left, his legacy has been a ready source of epithets against their allegedly deceitful opponents. In the words of Hannah Pitkin, he stood for the 'truth of witness' in which it was incumbent on the reporter to tell the facts of the story as they are.

But what has also occurred is a growing undercurrent of uncertainty about the wholesale embrace of the values of linguistic purification and unvarnished truth-telling, at least in the political arena. Much of that uncertainty has been fuelled by receptiveness to ideas from Europe, which permeated at least a portion of the American consciousness in the latter decades of the twentieth century and which remain potent into our own. Broadly speaking, these involve what has been called 'the linguistic turn', which includes, *inter alia*, a new respect for rhetoric, an acceptance of the necessity of hermeneutic interpretation and a willingness to tolerate the inconclusive deconstruction of univocal meaning. Because truth itself seems so difficult to attain, the value of truth-telling – truthfulness or veracity – is implicitly called into question, as inherently aesthetic notions of language as more a tool of imaginative fabulation than a means of referencing the real world come to the fore. Although many of these ideas have been associated with the so-called post-structuralist thought that emanated from France in the 1970s, variations on them can be discerned still earlier among that generation of Central European émigrés who so enriched American intellectual life during the Nazi era, and who have continued to exert considerable influence well after they passed from the scene. As survivors of the widespread cynicism that pervaded the Weimar Republic, 'the German Republic of Imposters', as it has been called, they understood what might ensue once politics became thoroughly discredited, but they had also learned that the antidote was not self-righteous moralising. I want to concentrate on three in particular, who in very different ways have helped us reach a more complex understanding of the relationship between political life and mendacity: Leo Strauss, Theodor W Adorno and Hannah Arendt.

Truth or lie? George W Bush 'fulfilling his military duty' in the Texas National Guard at some unspecified time during the Vietnam War. Credit: AFP

Their inclusion in the canon of political theorists has had an impact beyond the halls of the academy. This effect is now most self-evident in the case of Strauss, a number of whose neo-conservative followers have gained considerable influence in the highest reaches of American government during the presidency of George W Bush. Perhaps most widely remarked of these is Assistant Secretary of Defense Paul Wolfowitz, who did his doctoral work under Straussians at the University of Chicago, and is a major architect of the new recklessness in American foreign policy. One of its chief cheerleaders is William Kristol, the editor of *Weekly Standard*, who served in the administration of Bush's father as adviser to Vice-President Quayle.

Wolfowitz, in particular, is relevant because of his now notorious admission that the Bush administration's hype of Saddam Hussein's weapons of mass destruction was designed to elicit the strongest possible popular support for a cause whose real motivations, still not very clear, lay elsewhere. For in this moment of candour he betrayed one of Strauss's most salient assumptions: that the masses need to be manipulated into following their best interests by an elite who are privy to the deeper truths of reality. Strauss, that is, was a believer in the possibility of knowing the truth, including the truth about the type of government that is objectively the best. Implicitly drawing on his experience of exile, Strauss argued that persecution had forced ancient thinkers to mask their true intentions in ways that required deciphering by disciples with the skills to read between the lines. It was for them, as he put it in his 1939 essay on 'The Spirit of Sparta or the Taste of Xenophon', 'a matter of duty to hide the truth from the majority of mankind'. The tradition of esoteric teaching had withered, Strauss claimed, in the Enlightenment, although its decline was already under way when Machiavelli made explicit the techniques of statecraft that the ancients had known must be kept as the private knowledge of rulers alone. The disappearance of the tradition, he lamented, roughly coincided with the 'victory of higher criticism and of systems of philosophy which claimed to be sincere but which certainly lacked moderation'. Liberal notions of an egalitarian public sphere in which transparency and sincerity were the premises of enlightened political opinion were the sorry outcome of this betrayal.

Strauss, as might be expected, has been an easy target for defenders of rationalist liberalism as well as egalitarian democracy. And I am certainly not inclined to offer a defence of his explicitly hierarchical politics based on an allegedly natural order whose self-evidence neither he nor his disciples have satisfactorily demonstrated. But what has to be acknowledged is that his animadversions on the dangers of sharing truths with the uncomprehending masses have given legitimacy to the old Platonic idea of the 'noble lie' – the *gennian pseudos* – to an important segment of the conservative intellectuals of our day. They, of course, would be disinclined to express their scorn for egalitarian democracy explicitly, but it takes no great exegetical skill to read between the lines of their texts – and observe their political actions – to come to this conclusion.

A very different, and much more oblique, defence of mendacity in politics, however, emerges if we turn to the next figure in our triumvirate, whose political agenda was very far from Strauss's. Underlying Adorno's radical politics was always a firm belief in the ultimate value of an enlightened democracy with citizens able to cast off the spell of ideological mystification.

If Adorno can be said to have contributed to the critique of traditional American notions of political honesty, it would only be indirectly, through his questioning of the premises of the conventional wisdom about language and truth-telling. Adorno never developed a sustained analysis of language, although it has been possible to piece together his thoughts from disparate sources in his vast oeuvre. What stands out is his distrust of easy notions of communicability, which assume the transparency of the current universe of discourse and the ability of individuals to judge freely for themselves what is fed them by the mass media. In the words of a recent student of the history of the idea of communication, 'there was no more formidable critic of the commercialised culture of sincerity'.

Although agreeing with Orwell that stale clichés are the enemy of clear thought, Adorno differed from him in stressing the value of difficulty and complexity, which defeated the effortless absorption of pre-packaged ideas. He also questioned Orwell's desire to purify language of its ornamental excrescences, in particular foreign words. With a sombre awareness of what a similar campaign had meant in the context of the country from which he had escaped, Adorno wryly noted that 'German words of foreign derivation are the Jews of language'. That is, linguistic purification went along with cleansing of a far more sinister kind.

Adorno's suspicion of the agenda behind purifying language of alien intrusions was of a piece with his critique of what he called 'the jargon of authenticity' in a book of that name published in 1964. Adorno's ire was directed at the German existentialists, most notably Heidegger and Jaspers, who elevated the values of genuineness, authenticity and original meaning to normative status above the content of what was believed or meant. In their hands, mere commitment, speaking from the heart, becomes an antidote to nihilism, no matter the cause to which the commitment is dedicated.

Already in *Minima Moralia*, written in his exile years, Adorno had seen the political implications of the jargon, which were frighteningly regressive and xenophobic. The supremacy of the original over the derived, he warned, 'is always linked with social legitimism'. Along with the striving for ultimate, original meaning went a suspicion of ambiguity and rhetoric, which meant a denigration of sophistry in both philosophy and politics.

The same loss is suffered when clarity becomes a fetish, either in philosophy or politics. In an essay entitled 'Skoteinos, or how to read Hegel', published in 1963, Adorno defended the notorious difficulty and opacity of that most obscure philosopher's style. 'Someone who cannot state what he means without ambiguity is not worth wasting time on,' wrote Adorno, contemptuously characterising the current orthodoxy.

Adorno, to be sure, never praised mendacity as an actual virtue in politics, nor abandoned his hope in an emphatic concept of truth that would survive all ideological attempts to assume its mantle in the present. But by alerting us to the ways in which those attempts often hid other agendas, he made us aware that simple appeals to clarity, communicability, authenticity and integrity could become obstacles to precisely what they purported to defend. Truth, he followed Walter Benjamin in arguing, was best understood as intentionless, rather than the product of subjective positing.

The third figure in our triumvirate, Hannah Arendt, is also the one who most explicitly addressed the role of lying in politics. Personally hostile to both Strauss and Adorno, she also disdained their belief that philosophers such as Plato or Hegel had anything to teach those who were active in the realm of politics. The idea of the 'noble lie', she argued, was not only wrong, but also a misreading of the text in *The Republic*. Although learning much from the Heidegger and Jaspers excoriated by Adorno as adepts of the jargon of authenticity, she steadfastly resisted their emphasis on the primacy of philosophy. Instead, she attempted to build a firewall between politics and philosophy, at least if the latter were understood as the search for eternal, universal essences rather than contingent, plural appearances.

In two essays in particular, 'Truth and politics' of 1967 and 'Lying in politics' of 1971, Arendt drew radical conclusions from her idiosyncratic political theory for the issue of mendacity in the public realm. Occasioned by two controversies over lying, the first by her own work on Adolf Eichmann's trial, the second by the leaking of the Pentagon Papers, these two essays provide a more fundamental challenge to the American quest for full disclosure in the public realm than anything written by Strauss and Adorno. Ironically, the first essay was stimulated by the charge that Arendt had unwisely told the truth about the role of Jews – or, more precisely, of the Jewish Councils – in enabling the Holocaust to the detriment of current political causes. Without denying that she was dedicated as a scholar to truth-telling, Arendt was moved to ponder the problematic effects of that practice in the political arena: 'No one has ever doubted that truth and politics are on rather bad terms with each other, and no one, as far as I know, has ever counted truthfulness among the political virtues. Lies have always been regarded as necessary and justifiable tools not only of the politician's and the demagogue's but also of the statesman's trade.' ('Truth and politics')

Indeed, lying itself was not considered a cardinal sin until modern times; Plato, for example, thought ignorance and error worse than deliberate mendacity: 'Only with the rise of Puritan morality, coinciding with the rise of organised science, whose progress had to be assured on the firm ground of the absolute veracity and reliability of every scientist, were lies considered serious offences.'

Rational notions of truth, Arendt argues, no longer hold much sway in the modern world, but have been replaced by belief in the truth of facts, which is much more of a challenge to the political realm: 'Factual truth, like all other truth, peremptorily claims to be acknowledged and precludes debate, and debate constitutes the very essence of political life. The modes of thought and communication that deal with truth, if seen from the political perspective, are necessarily domineering; they don't take into account other people's opinions, and taking these into account is the hallmark of all strictly political thinking. Political judgement is the ability to incorporate other opinions, not the search for the one true opinion. Philosophy is an exercise in searching for a singular truth; politics is the interplay of plural opinions.'

There is another consideration, Arendt continued, that makes lying itself a central dimension of political life. A lie 'is clearly an attempt to change the record, and as such, it is a form of *action* . . . [the liar] is an actor by nature; he says what is not so because he wants things to be different from what they are – that is, he wants to change the world'. One of the main reasons truthfulness is not a genuine political virtue is that it doesn't produce a desire for change, although, of course, it can contribute to undermining a status quo built entirely of lies. There is, Arendt went on to argue, a tendency in the modern world towards the systematic, organised mobilisation of lying to create wholly fictitious political worlds, thus the adoption of the Big Lie in totalitarianism.

There is, however, a limit to the capacity of those who organise mendacity to keep truth entirely at bay. Thus facts, as past events which cannot be entirely effaced, stubbornly resist the construction of a world of total untruth. And there are ways in which institutions such as the judiciary, which is inside the political arena, and the academy, which is outside, do provide a check on the capacity of political mendacity to build a world entirely out of thin air. But to the extent that politics deals with the possible future, depends on opinions rather than hard facts, traffics in contingencies instead of eternal verities, mobilises rhetoric rather than deductive logic, and is based on plurality rather than singularity, lying cannot be entirely expunged from its precincts. Thus, when it came to responding to the outcry against the mendacity revealed in the Pentagon Papers, Arendt, who had doubts about the foolishness of our intervention in Vietnam, was in a bit of a dilemma.

The Pentagon Papers, Arendt conceded, introduce something new into the debate about lying in politics. In addition to lying for the sake of their country's image, those responsible for American intervention were also active problem-solvers who prided themselves on the rational, unsentimental nature of their actions. But to impose their new reality entirely required the wholesale destruction of stubborn facts, which not even totalitarian leaders such as Stalin and Hitler could accomplish, despite their will to do so. Ultimately, the architects of American foreign policy had to face the consequences of their deceptions.

But, ironically, the reason for their downfall was less their reliance on mendacious image-making than their mistaken attempt to apply reason to politics rather than learn from experience. In the end, Arendt's attempt to distinguish radically between politics and truth-telling rationalism was thwarted by the complexities of the case before her. Still, her insight into the fatal affinity between politics and mendacity, if added to those we have

Watergate Lying Game, Washington DC 1973: spot the liar.
Credit: Magnum / Marc Riboud

WANTED

JAMES McCORD

DWIGHT CHAPIN

H. R. HALDEMAN

JOHN MITCHELL

JOHN ERLICHMAN

MAURICE STANS

EUGENIO MARTINEZ

G. GORDON LIDDY

CHARLES COLSON

HERBERT KALMBACH

JOHN DEAN

ROBERT MARDIAN

JEB MAGRUDER

RICHARD M. NIXON

BERNARD L. BARKER

VIRGILIO GONZALEZ

DONALD SEGRETTI

FRANK A. STURGIS

E. HOWARD HUNT JR.

HUGH SLOAN JR.

already encountered in Strauss and Adorno, makes a suggestive case against any simple-minded critique of lying in the public realm.

For even if one rejects the idea of the Platonic 'noble lie' as the elitist contempt for the idea of an enlightened public that it is, it is hard to dismiss the insights that Adorno and Arendt both supply into the ways in which language necessarily defeats any attempt to be utterly transparent and univocal in the messy realm of politics. Moreover, if we acknowledge that plural opinion rather than singular truth means that there will always be different interpretations of what is and what should be, we can relax our expectation that the conventional norm of political speech is limpid truth-fulness and that lying is an aberrant deviation. It is perhaps better to say that spin, exaggeration, evasion, half-truths and the like are as much the stuff of political discourse and the struggle for power as straightforward speaking from the heart. As we have come to know from experience, memoirs of statesmen acknowledge the duplicity of their negotiations, politicians give coyly evasive answers to probing journalists, laws are deliberately written with ambiguities that only lawyers can love, campaign promises are given with fingers crossed, and so forth. Although it is certainly the case that the balance between truth-telling and fabrication, with all the grey area in between, is historically variable, historians would be hard pressed to identify any polity of whatever kind in which perfect veracity was the norm.

The fear that images have replaced substance or that the aestheticisation of politics is a new departure ignores the extent to which politics, rhetoric and theatricality have always been intimate bedfellows. It also underesti-mates the extent to which the logic of politics is dealing with promises and plans about the future rather than statements about what is currently the case, with what should or ought to be rather than simple matters of fact. In addition, it fails to see that persuasion often works in politics through the power of narratives. And insofar as such narratives always find their end point in a putative future, either to be realised or avoided, they contain an even stronger imaginative moment, a moment of fabulation, than is the case with those dealing only with the past.

All this is not to say, of course, that truth-telling and wariness about falsehoods should simply be banished from the political realm, which is nothing but a contest of competing lies. Strauss and Adorno, as we have seen, hold on to an emphatic notion of truth, which stands apart from normal political life, while Arendt admits that at least factual truth is an inherent part of any political discourse. It would indeed be dangerous to allow cynicism to undermine entirely the indignation that should accompany any disclosure of outright deception.

What it does suggest, however, is that rather than seeing the Big Lie of totalitarian polities as met by the perfect truth sought in liberal democratic ones, there is a truth based on that quest for transparency and clarity in language that we have seen endorsed by Orwell and his earnest followers. We would be better advised to see politics as the endless struggle between lots of little lies, half-truths and competing narratives, which may offset each other, but never entirely produce a single consensus. Although it is certainly the case that veridical discourses, such as the judicial where participants are sworn to 'tell the truth, the whole truth and nothing but the truth', do intersect with politics at crucial moments – as Bill Clinton can well attest – they never entirely subsume it. In fact, the great irony of the goal of absolute truth and truthfulness is that it mirrors the Big Lie and total mendacity of the totalitarianism it is designed to thwart. Both enforce orthodoxy. Lots of little competing fabrications, ironically, may ward off that enforcement more effectively than any attempt to establish and defend a single, universally shared truth.

These lessons have begun to permeate, albeit still against considerable resistance, the American political consciousness. So perhaps the last word should go to another defender of the virtues of mendacity from abroad, Oscar Wilde. In his famous essay of 1889, the imagined dialogue called 'The decay of lying', Wilde has one of his interlocutors denounce with mock horror the effects on American culture of our exemplary founding anecdote: 'It is not too much to say that the story of George Washington and the cherry-tree has done more harm and in a shorter span of time than any other moral tale in the whole of literature.' And then he added: 'and the amusing thing is that the story of the cherry-tree is an absolute myth'. ❏

Martin Jay is Sidney Hellman Ehrman professor of history at the University of California, Berkeley

FOURTH-RATE ESTATE
JULIAN PETLEY

WAS JOURNALISM EVER THE
DEMOCRATIC WATCHDOG AND
CHAMPION OF FREEDOM ITS
ADVOCATES CLAIM?

Traditionally, journalism has long been regarded as a 'fourth estate': a central component of democracy and a means whereby the power of the state can be monitored and, if necessary, limited. According to classic liberal theory, as expounded most famously by Fred Siebert, Theodore Peterson and Wilbur Schramm in *Four Theories of the Press*, 'the underlying purpose of the media was to help discover truth, to assist in the process of solving political and social problems by presenting all manner of evidence and opinion as the basis for decisions'. In order properly to fulfil this purpose, the media needed to be free from government controls or domination, since its prime duty was 'to keep officers of the state from abusing or exceeding their authority. It was to be the watchdog over the workings of democracy, ever vigilant to spot and expose any arbitrary or authoritarian practice.'

In this familiar vision of things, the journalist is a crusader after truth, championing free expression and exposing corruption, oppression and abuses of official authority. Expressions of this view are legion. For example, in 1821 James Mill called the freedom of the press 'an indispensable security, and the greatest safeguard of the interests of mankind', and the great CP Scott argued that journalism 'implies honesty, cleanness, courage, fairness and a sense of duty to the reader and the community . . . Neither in what it gives, nor in what it does not give, nor in the mode of presentation, must the unclouded face of truth suffer wrong.'

Meanwhile, in his classic study of newspapers, *Dangerous Estate*, Francis Williams called the press 'a minefield through which authority, great and small and at every level of policy and administration, must step warily, conscious always that a false step may blow it up'. Most recently, this view has found powerful expression in David Randall's *The Universal Journalist*, in which he argues that the job of the journalist is, above all, to question, and then to:

- discover and publish information that replaces rumour and speculation
- resist or evade government controls
- inform, and so empower, voters
- subvert those whose authority relies on a lack of public information
- scrutinise the action and inaction of governments, elected representatives and public services
- scrutinise businesses, their treatment of workers and customers, and the quality of their products
- comfort the afflicted and afflict the comfortable, providing a voice for those who cannot normally be heard in public
- hold up a mirror to society, reflecting its virtues and vices and also debunking its cherished myths
- ensure that justice is done, is seen to be done and investigations carried out where this is not so
- promote the free exchange of ideas, especially by providing a platform for those with philosophies alternative to the prevailing ones.

Now, however admirable these sentiments may be, and however strongly they accord with the way in which many individual journalists do indeed see their role, they are hard to square with the daily reality of most of the British press. Consider, for example, the majority of papers' attitudes to refugees and asylum seekers, their collusion in the clipping of the coinage of civil liberties post-9/11, their support for a legally dubious invasion of Iraq, their outright dismissal of Clare Short's revelation of the illegal bugging of the UN by the secret services, their aggressive stance towards the BBC in its struggles with the government in the Gilligan/Kelly affair and their hostility toward whistleblowers such as Katharine Gun and David Shayler. All of these, and many more, suggest that we need seriously to reconsider the extent to which the British press is, or was, a 'fourth estate'.

For a start, it would be quite mistaken to assume that all newspapers are, or ever have been, driven by anything remotely resembling liberal, let alone progressive, values. As James Curran has clearly shown in *Power Without Responsibility*, the repeal of the stamp duty and of other 'taxes on knowledge' in the nineteenth century was not motivated by governmental conversion to the cause of press freedom; it stemmed, rather, from the growing realisation among politicians and other members of the establishment that if entrepreneurs and industrialists could be tempted to enter the newspaper market then this could kill off the hated radical press far more effectively than taxes had ever done – by tempting away its readers, by raising the cost of newspaper production – which mass-market papers could offset via advertising revenues – or by a combination of the two.

That the powers-that-be intended the press to be used as an agent of social control and regulation rather than as a means of popular enlightenment and empowerment is evident from the historical record. Thus, for example, in 1832 we find Bulwer Lytton arguing that: 'We have made a long and fruitless experiment of the gibbet and the hulks. Is it not time to consider whether the printer and his types may not provide better for the peace and honour of a free state than the gaoler and the hangman. Whether, in one word, cheap knowledge may not be a better political agent than costly punishment.' Later, Gladstone was to declare that: 'The freedom of the press was not merely to be permitted and tolerated, but to be highly prized, for it tended to bring closer together all the national interests and preserve the institutions of the country.' But perhaps the clearest indication of the motives of the reformers is provided by Thomas Milner-Gibson, the president of the Association for the Repeal of the Taxes on Knowledge, who argued in 1850 that repeal would create 'a cheap press in the hands of men of good moral character, of respectability, and of capital' which would give them 'the power of gaining access by newspapers, by faithful record of the facts, to the minds of the working classes'. It is thus hardly surprising that the modern British press, unlike that of many Western democracies, should have always been so overwhelmingly conservative, not to say reactionary, in character.

Furthermore, it would be equally mistaken to regard the media as a whole, and the press in particular, as the detached observers of the political process that liberal theory and professional journalistic ideology suggest. The spheres of journalism and government have never been hermetically sealed off one from another and have increasingly overlapped as journalists and politicians have grown ever more mutually reliant. Newspapers, in particular, have very definite political and economic agendas and are thus keen to involve themselves actively on the political scene. This, however, is almost never acknowledged by journalists themselves, with the exception of the *Guardian's* press correspondent, Roy Greenslade (author of the excellent *Press Gang: How Newspapers Make Profit from Propaganda*), and the same paper's David Walker, who noted in a recent issue of *Journalism* that 'the power held by journalists and the media organisations for which they work is unperceived or assumed away. The occupational myth of the English political specialist is the dented sword of truth in a Manichean world where a lonely battle is fought for honesty', and pointed out in his contribution to

LIBERTÉ DE LA PRESSE

Revolutionary Paris 1797: freedom of the press French style.
Credit: Lauros / Giraudon / Bridgeman Art Library

Media Power, Professionals and Policies that 'the exercise of "investigative journalism" rarely extends to the relationship of journalists with each other, with politicians or proprietors'.

The relationship between journalists and politicians is, in fact, much more collusive than either side would like to admit, and has become even more so with the growth of the media into ever more vast corporate entities. The old-fashioned press barons such as Beaverbrook and Rothermere certainly used their papers to pursue specifically political objectives such as Empire free trade, but owners today are far more likely to be corporations than a single proprietor and their activities tend to consist in using their media to fawn on politicians who favour them, attack those who don't and publish stories that further their business interests. As Steven Barnett and Ivor Gaber point out in *Westminster Tales*, modern media barons such as

Rupert Murdoch 'take a more instrumental view based on their analysis of which party will best serve corporate interests and commercial ambitions'. From this there follows 'a growing interdependence of media entrepreneurs and political parties for their own respective self-advancements'.

The classic liberal argument, as we have seen, tends to assume that it is governments that should be the sole object of press vigilance, since, in its view, they are the main seat of power in society. But in the world in which we now live, corporations and other vast private interests have taken over many of the functions previously performed by the state. And among these private interests, media corporations loom ever larger and more powerful. As James Curran has put it: 'The issue is no longer simply that the media are compromised by their links to big business: the media *are* big business.' Those concerned with questions of press freedom today need to concern themselves not only with state-originated forms of censorship such as the Official Secrets Act and the current barrage of anti-terrorism measures but also market-generated forms of censorship such as overweening proprietor power, cross-media concentration, the commodification of information, the privileging of media investors over media audiences, the growth of corporate values at the expense of public service ones, the interdependence of governments and media owners, and so on. As John Keane points out in *The Media and Democracy*: 'Market competition produces market censorship. Private ownership of the media produces private caprice. Those who control the market sphere of producing and distributing information determine, prior to publication, what products (such as books, magazines, newspapers, television programmes, computer software) will be mass produced and, thus, which opinions officially gain entry into the "marketplace of opinions".'

Such sceptical thoughts about the British press as a fourth estate are given considerable impetus by Bruce Page's recent book *The Murdoch Archipelago*. What distinguishes Page's book is its intensely detailed focus on Murdoch's relationship with political authority – in Australia, Britain, America and China – and on its consequences for journalistic standards in his media. Page's thesis is that Murdoch's activities need to be understood in terms of a 'politico-business model', and that Newscorp's core competence is 'swapping approval with the controllers of the state'.

In this vision of things, the function of political journalism is not to act as a watchdog but, on the contrary, 'consists of maintaining sympathetic relations with authority'. The result is the publication of 'pseudo-newspapers' and, at worst, as when the Murdoch press helped Thatcher to cover up the Westland affair or amplified her government's attack on the Thames TV documentary *Death on the Rock*, a pernicious form of 'anti-journalism' and 'privatised government propaganda' in which 'official lies simply flow in, to be parroted out'. Page's detailed accounts of the intimate workings of the Thatcher/Murdoch axis recalls former editor of *The Times* Charles Douglas-Home's extremely candid remark that 'Rupert and Mrs Thatcher consult regularly on every important matter of policy, especially as they relate to his economic and political interests. Around here, he's jokingly referred to as "Mr Prime Minister", except that it's no longer much of a joke. In many respects he is the phantom prime minister of the country.'

The reason for such comprehensive abandonment of the ideals of the fourth estate can be summed up in one word: self-interest. Murdoch routinely uses his media to support governments that support his business interests. So, for example, in the mid-1990s the Labour Party in the UK let it be known that it would drop its traditional hostility to Murdoch's expansionism, and thus, in the 1997 and 2001 general elections, the *Sun* supported Labour. Murdoch is then handsomely repaid in the 2004 Communications Act, which enables him finally to make significant inroads into British terrestrial television, with the consequence that, during and after the invasion of Iraq, the Murdoch press not only acts as a cheerleader for Blair but savagely attacks as 'disloyal' any media outlet daring to voice criticism of the war. The corollary of this kind of mutual back-scratching is, of course, a ferocious hostility to governments and political parties that Murdoch deems inimical to his business interests – witness his Australian papers' pivotal role in the destabilisation of the Gough Whitlam government in 1974–5 and, in Britain, the remorseless hostility of his papers towards the European Union and pre-Blair Labour.

One of the most striking aspects of Murdoch's relationships with political parties is their bare-faced promiscuity. He may be a neo-liberal ideologue who believes passionately in the virtues of the market, but Page's detailed recounting of his global wheeling and dealing convincingly demonstrates that, when calculating which parties his media will support, their ideological complexion counts for nothing compared with whether or not their media policies are Murdoch-friendly. Particularly significant, in this respect, are Murdoch's dealings with the Chinese.

In 1993, eager to colonise the potentially vast Chinese television market, Murdoch took a controlling stake in Satellite Television Asia Region (Star

TV). Within months, he was playing the familiar role of the Great Liberator, arguing that 'advances in the technology of communications have proved an unambiguous threat to totalitarian regimes . . . Satellite broadcasting makes it possible for information-hungry residents of many closed societies to bypass state-controlled television channels.' However, Murdoch has done everything possible, including indulging in the most craven forms of self-censorship, to ingratiate himself with China's communist leaders. Thus, after acquiring Star, he immediately threw BBC World off the satellite because its coverage of the Tiananmen protests had annoyed them. Similarly, *The Times*'s Jonathan Mirsky quit when the paper repeatedly refused to run articles in which he revealed that dissidence in China was widespread; and when Murdoch discovered that HarperCollins, a company he owned, was intending to publish a book by former Hong Kong Governor Chris Patten critical of the Chinese gerontocracy, he insisted that the contract be terminated. As he put it: 'Let someone else annoy them.' He also invested US$5.4 million in the *People's Daily*, and HarperCollins published the English translation of Deng Rong's hagiography of her father Deng Xiaoping.

In March 2001, James Murdoch, who was then running Newscorp's Asian operations, told a Los Angeles business conference that negative media portrayals of the Chinese regime were 'destabilising forces' and 'very, very dangerous for the Chinese government'. However, as Page argues: 'A good thing about Murdoch's Chinese activities is that no democratic politician who agrees to examine them can entertain honest doubt about the character of the operation.'

Page concludes that 'Dictatorship and state monopoly do not repel him, provided Newscorp can cut a deal with the system. Outfits like the BBC, however, under any political or economic system, are competitors that it is important to undermine.' Murdoch is much less exercised by real totalitarians than by those he calls 'liberal totalitarians'. These turn out to be anybody who stands in the way of his amassing ever more media power: the Australian Broadcasting Commission, the Independent Television Commission, the BBC, the Office of Fair Trading, the Federal Communications Commission, and so on – in other words, all those responsible for 'structures devised by democratic states and intended to limit abuses in news media'.

The paradox is, however, as Page all too clearly demonstrates, that Murdoch has repeatedly run rings round the 'liberal totalitarians', acquiring *The Times* and the *Sunday Times* in spite of regulations aimed at limiting the concentration of the UK press; establishing Sky in Luxembourg, outside the jurisdiction of British regulators, even though it was aimed at British audiences; taking over British Satellite Broadcasting to form BSkyB, thus establishing a monopoly satellite broadcasting system in complete contravention of rules that, if the political will to enforce them had existed, could have prevented this from happening; changing his nationality from Australian to American in order to buy Fox, thus thumbing his nose at the rules that prevent non-Americans from buying American media companies; relentlessly lobbying British politicians and civil servants to ensure that BSkyB is effectively immunised from any obligation to carry a majority of EU-produced programmes under the Télévision Sans Frontières directive; and effectively bribing the present Labour government to formulate, and then force through in the face of considerable cross-party opposition, a communications bill expressly designed to further his own interests. As Murdoch's political relationships across the world have all too clearly demonstrated, 'market dominion in modern states is unsustainable without political protection or collaboration'.

Page concludes that the positioning of Murdoch's papers is motivated above all by corporate tactics, and that this leaves an indelible stain on their journalism, one that clearly marks it out as quite different from the kinds of journalism to be found elsewhere: 'the politically neutral BBC, the liberal *Guardian*, the illiberal *Daily Mail* and the conservative *Wall Street Journal* all resemble each other more than any of them resemble Newscorp media output. All, in utterly dissimilar ways, have worked within the constitution of the state to consolidate their independence from it. Newscorp is about eroding the boundaries between the state power and media operations.' Of course, politicians are equally culpable for having allowed, and indeed, in some cases, encouraged, the development of this situation, but as Page points out, as often as not, 'fear moves them as fully as admiration'. None the less, whatever their motives, they now, Page argues, find themselves revolving with Murdoch's media 'in a dance of folly which has at least the potential to be a dance of death for democracy'. Were this entirely cynical, self-interested, instrumental view of journalism to spread to the press as a whole, the idea of the press as a fourth estate (never, as we have seen, an entirely convincing one in the first place as far as the British press is concerned) would need to be put to sleep once and for all. ❏

Julian Petley is chair of the Campaign for Press and Broadcasting Freedom and professor of film and television studies at Brunel University

LIES, LIES & DAMNED PR
MICHAEL FOLEY

It is becoming increasingly popular to view the suspicion in which many journalists hold the public relations industry as a form of childish disorder that hacks should grow out of; they should embrace the real world where hacks and flacks cooperate and work together.

Increasingly in the US and the UK, public relations modules are being tacked on to journalism courses for fear that journalism itself will not attract sufficient numbers. And while journalists still debate whether they and what they do constitutes a 'profession', the public relations practitioner is joining institutes and presenting business cards with so many initials after their names they look like typing exercises. While the media is being attacked for its lack of accountability, PR people are busy debating codes of conduct named after cities as if they were international treaties.

It suits the PR industry to suggest that there is no real difference between journalism and its own branch of activity, or that the relationship is a symbiotic one. But there is a difference: one serves the public interest, the other a private interest. If that sounds pompous it is probably because journalism has not been doing its job very well and has surrendered control of the agenda to the PR industry.

Journalists too readily accept and publish stories of dubious provenance: they take short cuts. Although there can be no excuse for bad journalism, journalists are facing new pressures with fewer resources. Print journalists are filling more pages, more supplements and colour magazines, and often an online breaking news service before starting on the newspaper. On TV, there are 24-hour news programmes to be produced; on radio, it's hourly news bulletins.

Into this chaos step the public relations people with their promise of exclusives, interviews and instant stories, but all at a price that emasculates the copy. The public interest is no longer paramount, it is the private. If a client does not want a question asked, it is not to be asked. According to PR executive Julia Hobsbawm, 75 per cent of entertainment stories and 50–80 per cent of news and business stories emanate from public relations. She adds: 'It is understandable that journalists can resent their reliance on us.'

Public relations learned its first lessons in war, and in the battle between public and private interest the latter has the big artillery. We know PR companies will lie for their clients. One of the world's most successful companies, Hill and Knowlton, spread the lie that babies were thrown out of incubators in Kuwait by the invading Iraqi army; we know it was a lie, as it was to suggest that Bosnians were willing to kill their own people for gain – another PR invention; we know that pictures are doctored; and we know that PR companies establish fake lobby organisations, seemingly working in the public interest, to promote a private cause.

Earlier this year, the *Observer* reported on one such organisation that had duped a number of famous women into supporting a campaign to promote a cervical cancer-screening test. The paper revealed that the organisation had been clandestinely set up by a PR company to promote a pharmaceutical company that stood to make millions if the National Health Service in the UK accepted its product. The *Observer* stated: 'Our investigation reveals increasingly covert methods that health care and pharmaceutical firms are using to push their products in this multi-million pound market. From hiring ghost writers to getting favourable articles published in medical journals to setting up allegedly independent campaign groups, the whole purpose of this strategy is to obscure the involvement of drug corporations that stand to make a fortune from selling their product to the public.'

The rich and powerful now call their PR consultants as quickly as their lawyers. When a famous chef was found guilty of possession of child pornography in Ireland last year, he came out of court with his PR man, who arranged for pictures and issued statements on the spot.

This is not simply an old hack's rant. The increasing power of public relations and the consequent decline in journalism has contributed to a collapse in public trust. The confusion of public and private makes it difficult for the public to judge the information it is given. With the increased sophistication of PR in public life, the journalist's only defence is to assume every time that the bastards in politics, business or public life are lying until proved otherwise. This cannot be good for our civic culture. ❑

Michael Foley is a lecturer in journalism at the Dublin Institute of Technology and was formerly with the Irish Times

SPOOKS IN THE SPOTLIGHT
JOHN LE CARRÉ

ONE OF THE WORLD'S MASTER SPY
NOVELISTS TURNS HIS ATTENTION TO THE
REAL THING – AND IS NOT IMPRESSED

TIM SEBASTIAN Britain's intelligence services endured a harsh spotlight in the Hutton inquiry, in particular for the now notorious claim that Iraq could launch its weapons of mass destruction in 45 minutes. The boss of MI6, Britain's external security service, appeared before Hutton on a voice-only link, and strongly defended that 45-minute claim, though it came from a single source. Do you see much signs of intelligence these days?

JOHN LE CARRÉ I felt I had a great feeling of sympathy for them, and a great sense of sadness about the way they had been treated. I think they had very poor intelligence in Iraq, but there were very good reasons for that. By 2001, the Americans were declaring publicly there were no weapons of mass destruction in Iraq, and Iraq was therefore not a major target on the list, and the customers in Whitehall were not screaming for Iraq. Then suddenly . . .

TS The 'customers' being the government?

JLC The customers being the people who in our democracy give the secret services their remit. The secret services don't write their own tickets, they get a remit, from the Foreign Office, the Ministry of Defence, the ministry of this, the ministry of that. That's how they make up their priorities.

TS You're saying they were told to come up with evidence of weapons of mass destruction?

JLC I'm saying once the decision had been taken to go to war, which we believe is somewhere around two years ago or even longer, they were given a crass order to get in there and find the reasons for going to war. We weren't really looking for reasons, we were looking for excuses.

I question the word 'claim': it was an 'intelligence claim' that was put in. It wasn't a claim, it was excellent intelligence. Now, can you imagine a situation, though, in Whitehall, in our community, our political community, where the secret service steps forward and says, 'No, we thought something quite different, we've been misrepresented.' It's more than their survival is worth, they can't possibly do that. So you get this disembodied voice coming over the mike saying everything in the garden is lovely. I don't believe everything in the garden was lovely at all, I think it was absolute chaos.

TS When you look back at your own time in intelligence, how would you have fitted in with these people?

JLC I was a very lowly worm and mostly I worked in the field rather than behind a desk.

TS You said you didn't alter the world, but you were involved in the daily battles to stop the other side.

JLC That's right, I was the cold warrior, and we did not do all the things I write about, but some, in different ways and probably not as well as I've described. But there was one rule, one law, and that was to do with the objective truth. Now, you must understand that in the intelligence community one is constantly tempted by the fabricators, by mercenaries. These are all people with intelligence themselves, it's a big, hot, rich market.

TS People tell you anything you want to hear?

JLC People tell you anything you want to hear; in addition, there are people who will tell you things they want you to hear. Those would-be liaison services who wanted to give you loaded intelligence – in this situation, let's say, for argument's sake, Israeli intelligence, or Greek intelligence, or whatever. On top of that, you have the horror story of the pushy young officer, out in the field, who thinks his swans are geese, and is perhaps going to massage his own intelligence when he sends it back to head office. And so for all these reasons, they have their ears very much pricked up for all kinds of false intelligence. And they have their own analysts; then they have the customers, whom I was describing, to whom they submit their intelligence; and finally you have the JIC [Joint Intelligence Committee] at the top of the ladder. Now for [Sir John] Dearlove to claim that this was a single source, and that a single source by itself is an authentic one, and that that's a perfectly normal intelligence practice is, in a word, nonsense. Nothing of that importance could be handed to the JIC without a full authentication and with collateral.

TS Do you think they're a bunch of liars?

JLC No, I'm not saying they're a bunch of liars. Contrary to what you were saying, they have no PR present. Often, if they get some embarrassing defector, or somebody going public on them, they're like hares trapped in the searchlights: they do not have a smooth talker who can come forward. [John] Scarlett's the nearest they got to it; and, heavens above, if that's the best they can do, what a pity.

TS The spooks do not enjoy the limelight, as you suggested, because limelight will bring with it accountability. Is that what's at stake here?

JLC Yes, they are in a half-world, they don't like the limelight, they don't like identifying themselves; it's really against their nature to start talking about sources. The two great things you never messed with were the sanctity of your relationship with the source and his or her identity; and the truth itself, as close as you could get to it. Now, our secret services, our intelligence community, has no front office as far as the public is concerned. At the time of Stella Rimington [the former head of MI5], little by little the spooks put a toe in the water of public relations, very uncertainly, and they still have no status. When Bush appears and makes one of his questionable announcements about weapons of mass destruction, George Tennett is standing right behind him, looking as if he would sandbag him at any moment. But there is nobody standing behind Blair when he makes the similar claim, or claims that someone is picking up material in Africa – or whatever else finally took us to war.

TS Do you miss the certainties of the Cold War?

JLC I think paradoxically that I miss the ambiguities of the Cold War. What I fear is that by a dismal combination, particularly the united states of industry, the corporate media and government, we have actually reduced politics to such simplistic terms that the ambiguities are disappearing. We had shades of opinion about communists; we ought to have the same about the terrorist threat. I don't have any nostalgia for the Cold War. I have, simply, a terrible anxiety about the present situation.

I recognise that the contributions that many people made to the Cold War are being dissipated now. At the end of the Cold War a golden age

Michael Hordern (left) and Richard Burton in The Spy Who Came in from the Cold *(1965). Credit: Rex*

really did beckon. If there had been a Marshall Plan, if there had been a possibility that America would move towards the Eastern, Russian, world they had been so hostile to, if we had been constructive, if there had been a real rallying voice, then I think something could have been achieved. Instead of that, we've seen America go into isolation, America become unilateralist, become a hyperpower, abandon its international treaties and, I think, seriously threaten the stability of the world.

TS A novelist who steps out of fiction and writes about daily events – you lose your protection, don't you?

JLC You lose your protection and I was very careful: I wrote only once about this war, and that was on 15 January of this year [2003].

TS It caused a huge stir.

JLC It caused a huge stir, a very gratifying stir, and attracted an astonishing amount of correspondence, particularly from the United States, practically all of it positive. The burden of most of the letters, many from people whom I have never heard of and will never hear of again, I expect, was saying: 'Thanks for saying it for us.' Because the real scandal of what happened, in my view, in the United States, was that a bunch of crazies – which is my perception of them – had taken over power in the United States, but the opposition to that ceased to be vocal. Everything, particularly after the Patriot Act [*Index* 2/2003], everything that looked like criticism, was being suppressed, and the media fell in with that. To me that is a terrible betrayal of their duty.

TS You would have liked to have got rid of Saddam but not under the banner of hypocrisy that you said America had used. How would you have got rid of him if not this way?

JLC I would have begun quite differently. First of all, I'm not sure that it was ever necessary to get rid of him. I think that by the time the UN inspectors had done their job, which we now know they did, Saddam was getting no younger; a middle class was emerging in Iraq which was very well capable of administering Iraq. Now many of those people were Baath Party people, but they were not really convinced supporters of Saddam. So I think a gradual transition would have been perfectly possible; it would have been possible by other means to impose democracy on Iraq.

TS But it wouldn't have happened, would it?

JLC It may have happened and it may not have happened. But it is not the duty of the West to go round imposing democracy on other countries that have no tradition of it and will find their own way to popular representation. I'm not sure that chaos on this scale is the right prerequisite for finding democratic balance.

TS You attribute Bush's motives basically to oil?

JLC I attribute his motives basically, I think, to a desire for power. In this respect, he was driven by this extraordinary group of neo-conservative theologians who were behind him. I think that oil and geopolitics play a huge part, but this messianic tone, this fundamental Christian voice that we are now being driven by is beyond oil; it is actually something as spooky as a crusade. And it seems to me to be leading down a terrifying cul-de-sac. It is quite impossible for people of limited political sophistication – us Westerners – to mess with all the shades of Islam, to keep countries in being through our very simplistic Western eyes.

TS Wasn't the war simply a response to 11 September?

JLC The war was a fabricated response to 9/11; seven out of 11 Americans still believe that Saddam had something to do with the Twin Towers. That is a monstrous failure of the American forces of enlightenment, particularly the media. The war was planned long before Osama provided the excuse for it. Thereafter, we may be expecting other campaigns in other places: the great 'axis of evil' has yet to be addressed in full. I think that all of this has to be stopped somehow. I'm not of the left or of the right; this is, simply and as best as I can make it, a detached judgement of what is happening to us. I'm as much concerned about our own security as about that of the East.

TS But you cringe, you say, when you hear 'the prime minister, Blair, lent his head prefect's sophistries to the colonial adventure'.

JLC Indeed I do. For me he is, politically speaking, bankrupt, derelict. I think to have taken that decision to go to war with Bush, with or without United Nations approval, and to come back and withhold that truth when he was addressing Parliament and the British people, was an unforgivable act. In my view, it was an immoral thing to do, to attach that to his role, as minstrel for the American effort and, at the same time, give away British foreign policy, give away British defence policy.

TS How much choice did he have?

JLC I think every choice. I think the worst part of the story is that the tail could have wagged the dog.

TS It tried, didn't it?

JLC I don't know, certainly he didn't take Bush to the wire.

TS He took him to the UN.

JLC Kicking and screaming he took him to the UN. But I think if he had actually said, with the support of the Foreign Office: 'This is going too far, we can't get involved in this, I cannot even begin to try and bring you, Europe, into this situation' – if Blair had had the courage to do that, or the vision, what you will . . .

TS You're saying he didn't believe what he said he believed, that he was insincere?

JLC I'm saying that he decided to go to war and then kept pretending that the option was open.

TS Which is worse?

JLC I think it's very bad indeed. And I think that this whole charade, the Hutton inquiry, overlooks the fact that in principle Gilligan was right, the BBC was right – and we're going to need the BBC more than ever.

TS That the dossier was embellished?

JLC That the dossier was embellished; that presentation is vastly important when you're selling intelligence to the ordinary man in the street. It's how you address it, how you emphasise it, what the headlines are. Every journalist knows that, every PR person knows that: the presentation is part of the truth. At the moment, we're making choices, and they're the wrong choices; we don't have to be fighting these wars. I think we shall be buried, our generation, with Kipling's quote on our coffin: 'A fool lies here who tried to hustle the East.' ❑

John le Carré was interviewed by Tim Sebastian for HARDtalk, BBC Television

THE BIG LIE
JASPER BECKER

MEMORY AND FORGETTING ARE
NOT AN ISSUE IN CHINA: THEY
ARE STILL LIVING THE BIG LIE

Immediately after Japan's defeat in 1945, Chiang Kai-shek's Nationalist Party announced that Japan had killed 1.75 million Chinese; by 1949, the Chinese Communist Party (CCP) declared that 9.32 million Chinese had died; by 1995, Chinese President Jiang Zemin had increased the toll to 35 million victims. In a race to claim victimhood, the CCP wants to be second to none because it instils a sense of virtue, justice and moral ascendancy.

As nationalism has replaced communism as the basis for ideology, the big lie in China handily covers up the plain fact that the greatest crimes against the Chinese people were committed by the CCP and not by foreign aggressors. You won't find it in books, films or articles published in China, but over 30 million people died in a man-made famine between 1958 and 1962. The Great Leap Forward is now mentioned only in inverted commas and in coy terms noting that these were 'unusual times' in which 'economic mistakes' were made. More generally, every local and national history book is edited to make sure there is only the mention of 'three years of natural disasters' or 'three years of hardship'.

In the 40 years of Mao's leadership, he was probably responsible for the death of over 100 million Chinese. The figure would include those killed during various internal purges, the deaths in the civil war, the murder of millions of 'landlords' and 'rich peasants', the persecution of minorities like the Tibetans, the imprisonment of over 40 million in labour camps and the tens of million who died during the Cultural Revolution. No real tally has ever been drawn up in the way, for instance, that the list of Japanese victims has been compiled.

In a great act of forgetting, one is permitted only to talk of the Cultural Revolution as the '10 years of chaos'. But when the party made its official resolution on history and declared that Mao was 70 per cent correct, the Great Leap Forward was not included in his errors. The party issued clear instructions on how to handle the past in such internal publications as *How to Record the Annals of a Place*, one of a series of handbooks for cadres to use when writing the history of their county or work unit. Its instructions apply equally to those censoring histories, plays, novels, films and even what is published on the Internet. The book makes it clear that there may be no talk of a famine.

The extremely efficient way the censorship system works in China has a number of consequences. It becomes impossible to investigate what any leader like Jiang Zemin did or did not do during such key periods. Most Chinese people have been born since the famine and, indeed, since the Cultural Revolution. They have not the slightest idea what happened and, when told, are frankly incredulous that such things could have happened in China.

The sense of shame that acceptance of the extreme cruelty perpetrated by Chinese would entail also runs counter to the whole artfully constructed narrative of Chinese history, which is now universally accepted at home and abroad. It is why Mao Zedong is today never mentioned in the same breath as Pol Pot, Stalin or Hitler, and is successfully being marketed as an amusing pop icon by 'dissident' Chinese artists and many others. There are films and novels about the suffering of the Chinese intellectuals, especially young people, sent to the countryside during the Cultural Revolution, but the main effect of these seems, once again, largely to point to the sense of the Chinese as victims.

The real point about the Cultural Revolution, namely that Mao used it to destroy his enemies within the party who had ended the famine by introducing some market reforms, has been lost. The particular viciousness of this campaign claimed many victims among small-time officials in the countryside as well as senior officials and their families, and it provoked a civil war between different factions.

This is forgotten. It would be too embarrassing for men like Jiang Zemin, who was in the thick of it as a propaganda official in Wuhan at the height of an armed confrontation during the Cultural Revolution between those for and against Mao. Even the new incoming generation of leaders such as Hu Jintao and his cohorts, who were members of Red Guard factions at universities such as Qinghua, or were in middle schools and in charge of gangs that took part in brutal murders of their teachers, are excused the need to explain themselves.

The willingness of the rest of the world to go along with this artificial version of history stems from another Big Lie, this one connected to President Richard Nixon's 1972 visit to China and Henry Kissinger's diplomacy

China, July 1930: the face of famine that the Great Leap Forward failed to change.
Credit: Getty Images

that successfully enlisted China in an anti-Soviet coalition and used China to help extricate the US from Vietnam. According to the accepted version of history, this daring piece of diplomacy helped usher in Chinese reforms and led to vast improvements in human rights.

In reality, as soon as Mao died in 1976, his followers were arrested in a military *coup d'état* led by the 'capitalist roaders' faction, whose numbers included Deng Xiaoping. Deng immediately began to introduce market reforms that started with agriculture and have since spread to every other sector. This seizure of power had nothing to do with Nixon or Kissinger and would almost certainly have happened anyway. In the mid-1970s, the majority of the population was at starvation levels not far short of those in

The lie that killed 30 million: propaganda poster for the Great Leap Forward 1958–1964. Credit: Stefan R Landsberger Collection / www.iisg.nl/landsberger

the Great Leap Forward. By underestimating the dire state of the Chinese economy, Kissinger made a series of concessions he need not have made.

The willingness of a wide range of China experts such as Edgar Snow and Han Suyin to propagate the Big Lie by declaring that there was no famine in China during the Great Leap, and that China's communes were actually remarkably successful in feeding the population, considerably strengthened China's hand in negotiations with the West.

The new leadership, having hidden China's urgent need for outside help, resisted all pressure to introduce any political reforms. In the past 30 years, there has not been any change in the Chinese political system or indeed any constraints placed on the power of the state. Every year it executes over 10,000 people in summary trials, many of whom have been trying to demand basic rights such as freedom of association, the right to form trade unions and freedom of speech.

EVERY YEAR CHINA EXECUTES OVER 10,000 PEOPLE IN SUMMARY TRIALS

Every visiting Western politician, anxious to win contracts, now acquiesces in the fiction that there has been a vast increase in political freedom in China. In fact, the average Chinese peasant has no more political rights than a serf in pre-revolutionary Russia. He needs permission to marry, to have children, to leave the village and to farm land allocated to him but to which he still does not have title. The status of rural Chinese is so low that their incomes have not risen for nearly 20 years. Many of them work on building sites or factories and are simply never paid. Each year they go home for Chinese New Year owed some US$20 billion in unpaid wages and they are still the most highly taxed people in the world. No wonder some Chinese are getting rich so quickly.

The willingness to tolerate the Big Lie in China meant that when the Chinese did demand political reforms during the protests of 1989, the party could first send tanks against unarmed protestors, then blatantly deny that anyone had died in Tiananmen Square – and subsequently dare anyone to say otherwise. The 'incident' has now so efficiently been covered up in China that most Chinese under 25 are completely ignorant about what happened and convinced that outside pressure for political reforms is another form of US imperialism and foreign bullying.

To some extent, the pace of reform is, as the party claims, China's internal affair. We should not belittle the real change that is going on any more than we should ignore the argument that the Chinese have to deal with these things in their own way. Yet China is a major power and a permanent member of the UN Security Council and it is using its power to defend other brutal regimes.

The need to gain China's support has ensured that it has escaped all censure for training and financing Pol Pot and the Khmer Rouge, just as China's support has ensured that the Khmer Rouge have so far escaped trial for crimes against humanity. Nor, without China's support for North Korea, should we now be negotiating to buy off possibly the most brutal regime in recent history.

Emulating the propaganda used by the Chinese in the Great Leap Forward, North Korea's Kim Jong Il has deliberately allowed at least

3 million of his 222 million people to starve to death and has murdered at least another 1 million in labour camps. North Korea blames its famine first on 'three years of natural disasters' – floods, droughts and tidal waves – and then on the sudden end of Soviet aid after 1991. China claimed there was no food because thousands of Soviet engineers working on big industrial projects left in 1960 and it had to export grain to pay back Soviet debts.

The same ghastly stories of cannibalism, public executions of 'criminals' accused of stealing a pound of grain, of a government encouraging people to eat 'food substitutes' made of sawdust and of careful campaigns to hide the evidence from the outside world have emerged from North Korea. Equally disturbing is the UN's collaboration in amplifying these lies. After nearly nine years in the country and annual appeals for emergency aid, UN officials have repeatedly denied seeing anyone who has perished from hunger and routinely mouth the government's excuses for what amounts to a form of genocide.

Not only has Kim Jong Il been able to follow China's script, he remains securely in power only thanks to China's unwavering support. While the Chinese media paint a positive picture of North Korea and attack the US for provoking a crisis, the Chinese authorities are hunting down and forcibly expelling North Koreans trying to flee the country for safety on the grounds that these are 'economic migrants'. China is routinely praised for its help in solving the North Korean nuclear crisis; had it allowed North Koreans to flee their country, Kim Jong Il's regime would have collapsed by now. ❑

Jasper Becker is a journalist based in Beijing

NECESSARY LIES

CAROLINE MOOREHEAD

THE WORLD OF IMMIGRATION IS SURROUNDED
BY LIES: THE NECESSARY LIES WOULD-BE
MIGRANTS FEEL COMPELLED TO TELL IN HOPE
OF A SAFE HAVEN; THE FALSEHOODS AND
MISINFORMATION OF NEWSPAPER HEADLINES

On the night of Saturday 14 September 2002, a freak storm hit the southern coast of Sicily. Hailstones the size of tennis balls made dents in parked cars, and locals said later that they had never seen or known anything like it. At about 11pm, while tourists were still dancing in a café on the beach at Realmonte, just along the coast from Agrigento, cries were heard coming from the sea. A few minutes later, a number of young Africans pulled themselves up on to the beach. When they could speak, they told the dancers that their boat had sunk on a reef about 100 yards offshore, and the tourists, looking out to sea, saw a boat tipped on its side among the waves, with people clinging to its sides.

Local fishing boats were too small to make much headway against the surf, and by the time the police had been called, and Agrigento had sent out naval boats and a powerful searchlight, the boat had sunk further into the water. During flashes of lightning, onlookers watched horrified as first one and then another of those clinging to its sides slipped under the water. Over the next few hours, 95 of the Africans on board were rescued and brought to shore. Some 30 others drowned. By morning, when the storm had passed, and the beach was again peaceful and sunny, there was not much left for anyone to see, except for fragments of clothing washed up at the water's edge, and bits of a lifejacket, soon taken away by those who collect the rubbish at Realmonte.

Capsized boats, the *carrette di mare* or sea chariots as the Italians call them, 10–12 metres long and painted in bright blues and yellows with Arabic writing, are not new along Sicily's coasts, where over the past few years tens of thousands of asylum seekers have arrived in search of new lives. Boats built for a dozen passengers arrive laden with 100 or more and even without a storm many founder.

In the calm days that followed, more bodies kept popping to the surface on Realmonte's beach, bloated and purple, their skin flailed away by the sharp volcanic rock of the reef. One of the bodies was that of a young girl, who the police doctor judged to be no older than 15.

Most of the dead had no names, the survivors being unable, or unwilling, to say who they were. As for the survivors, the *extra communitari,* as the Italians call the African and Asian migrants who reach their shores, they too, seemed to have no names, or only first names, for when questioned they would say little about themselves. Most were happy to talk, but only about the horror of the journey, the lack of food and water, the nightmare moment when the boat hit the reef. But as to who they were, or where they came from, they would say nothing. Those who answered questions changed their stories the next day. It was only after a while that they began to say that they were Liberians and even then the Sicilians, who heard them speaking French, suspected that they came not from English-speaking Africa but from the francophone countries. Among those rescued was a portly, fair-skinned man, with pockets stuffed full of dollar bills. He refused to speak at all and the Sicilians, who have grown used to *scafisti,* traffickers, concluded that he must have been silenced by the Mafia, known to control much of the people-smuggling business coming from Tunisia. Those trafficked into Sicily are known to be carefully coached to give nothing away, and to get rid of all documents so that they cannot be sent home or their traffickers traced. Passports, identity cards, scraps of letters and photographs are often found along the beaches, washed up by the waves, among the debris that litters the sand.

Over the next few days, the bodies of the drowned were taken to cemeteries up and down the coast, where they were given slots in the tall walls that house the dead. On each was put a placard: 'Liberian citizen. Drowned.'

The question for the Sicilians was what to do with the living, all of whom applied for asylum. Some were taken into hostels, to await a summons to the Ministry for the Interior in Rome where they would be interviewed to see whether they were eligible for refugee status, and with it permission to live and work in Italy. Others vanished quietly during the night, and were assumed to have entered Italy's thriving black economy. But something about the violence of the storm and the horror of the shipwreck had touched the hearts of the people of Realmonte, and two young couples, a brother and sister and a married pair, were offered a flat in the

21 November 2002, Lampedusa, Italy: flotsam and jetsam after the storm, all that remained of migrant hopes. Credit: Franco Origha / Getty Images

village by the local chapter of the Red Cross after it became known that the two young women were pregnant. Realmonte felt protective about these two girls, both still teenagers. And when they gave birth, in the spring, its citizens gave them prams and cots, cooked meals for them and tried to teach them how to care for their babies.

But then the mood changed. The trouble started when the midwife let it be known that the girl claiming to be with her brother was, in fact, having sex with him. Word quickly spread around the village. Was it possible, the villagers asked themselves, that the two were not in fact brother and sister, as they had claimed? And if not, why had they not said so? They felt there was something distasteful in such a lie.

The shipwreck had in fact made ripples all along Sicily's southern shore. Up in San Biagio Platani, a small town set high among summer pastures, a local doctor and his wife invited 15 of the young Africans to settle while they waited for their summons to Rome. Five of them were women and when one was found to be pregnant the local people, as in Realmonte, looked after her. Jobs were found for the men. But by spring the relationship between the people of San Biagio and their African guests had turned a little sour. As Dr Palumbo saw it, everyone accepted that at first the visitors would be reluctant to say much about themselves. But everyone assumed that their reticence would evaporate once they felt secure and appreciated. But it didn't: if anything, it grew stronger. The Africans began to change their names, then their ages, then any details that they had previously let slip about their journeys. Several of the girls turned out to be pregnant, and when one gave her age first as 18, then 25, then 22, Dr Palumbo was at first amused and then mildly irritated; he begged her to find an age and stick to it, if only for the sake of convenience.

By late spring there was very little goodwill left, either in Realmonte or San Biagio. The Sicilians simply could not understand why people on whom they had lavished such genuine affection did not appear to trust them enough to confide their real stories in return. They felt used. Even a few confidences, as Dr Palumbo says, would have made a difference. One morning, San Biagio woke to find three of the visitors had gone, taking the early bus to Palermo. By April there were none left. Even the pregnant girls had gone, and not one of them had said goodbye. In Realmonte, the two couples with their two babies closed their door and their shutters and avoided their hosts who, by now aggrieved and uncomprehending, longed to move them on.

It is not easy for people who have fled violence and persecution, or even poverty and despair, to handle truth. When their story is their only real passport, when they have thrown away their documents and tried to re-invent themselves, it is hard not to embellish the hardships of the past. Refugee life is rife with rumour. Among those who wait to be interviewed for refugee status – be it by the United Nations High Commission for Refugees (UNHCR), which determines refugee status in just over 40 countries, or the immigration authorities of countries who do their own determination – word circulates about how some nationalities are more likely to get asylum than others, about how some stories are more powerful than others, and some more likely to touch the hearts of the interviewers.

The buying and selling of 'good' stories, stories to win asylum, has become common practice in refugee circles among people terrified that their own real story is not powerful enough. How easy then, how natural, to shape the past in such a way that it provides more hope for a better future. Traffickers, transporting clients to the West, are known to recommend identities, to advise nationalities known to be on the list of countries to which people asking asylum cannot be returned without breaching the Refugee Convention clause about 'non-refoulement' – the non-return to places of danger and persecution.

In recent years, as numbers of people arriving in the West and claiming asylum began to grow steeply, and pressure mounted on immigration officers to turn away as many applicants as they reasonably could, so the idea of what is truth and what is a lie has acquired a very particular potency in refugee matters. Credibility has become a benchmark on which everything depends. Asylum seekers found not to be telling the truth are automatically rejected, however genuine their claim may be. 'Lack of credibility' – that is to say, the supposition that the person asking for asylum is lying – has become, in most of the West, the main reason for refusal. For their lawyers, convincing their clients that they must tell only the truth has become of major importance, just as spotting a lie, however unimportant, has become a challenge for immigration officers, who admit that a falsehood, 'something wobbly, however small, like method of travel or date of departure', enables them to throw out a case. The tragedy comes when the real story, the true story, is stronger than the made-up one and would guarantee refugee status while the false one does not. Not easy for the asylum seekers, certainly; but not easy for the interviewers either, to be forced to be so vigilant for lies in the stories of desperate people.

Untruths surround refugees. In recent years, particularly in Europe, a campaign of hostility towards those who arrive in the West without documents – as virtually everyone seeking asylum is obliged to do – has been gaining ground. Dishonest anti-immigration campaigners, manipulating both statistics and government figures and playing on the fears and anxieties of a gullible public, have taken to putting out sensational forecasts about a future under siege from an invasion of desperate and greedy migrants. The website of MigrationWatch UK, a self-styled independent think tank, warns that 'we can expect at least 200,000 and perhaps 250,000 non-EU immigrants a year'. In UNHCR in Geneva, where a battle is currently being waged against the increasingly restrictionist asylum policies of Western countries, the British tabloids and their incessant attacks on refugees are regarded with incredulity and horror.

It was at the turn of the millennium that the *Sun*, the *Daily Mail* and the *Daily Express* sharpened their campaign against immigrants. Headlines have included 'Swan bake: asylum seekers steal Queen's birds for barbecues' (*Sun*), 'Official: asylum tearing UK apart' (*Sun*) and 'Widow, 88, told by GP: make way for asylum seekers' (*Mail on Sunday*). As the feeling grew that reporting in the British media gives undue prominence to scaremongering claims from fringe groups, portraying asylum seekers as threatening young men with contacts in the criminal underworld, so in the spring of 2003, the UK-based free-expression organisation Article 19 carried out a research project on media reporting of refugee matters. It concluded that statistics were 'frequently unsourced, exaggerated or inadequately explained', that the tabloid press was failing to distinguish between economic migrants and asylum seekers, and that the hostility of media coverage was provoking a sense of alienation and shame among refugees. Recent research by the Information Centre about Asylum and Refugees (ICAR) in the UK has found that that this relentless repetition of hostile and inaccurate reporting contributes to increased hostility by the public and in turn to tension and even racial harassment. UNHCR and the National Union of Journalists joined forces to produce a memorandum on good reporting and, in October 2003, the Press Complaints Commission issued guidelines about inaccurate use of language.

Even so, hostile and bigoted reporting continues, with casual disregard for any distinction between asylum seeker, refugee, failed asylum seeker or economic migrant. In most articles, the terms are used randomly, as if synonymous. In the *Daily Mail*, Ross Benson has been running a series of stories about the Roma, warning of an invasion of Gypsies once the European Union is enlarged in May. The Roma, it is widely agreed, remain the most disliked and despised of all European ethnic minorities. In January 2004, the *Sunday Times* took up the theme, suggesting that up to 100,000 Roma were on their way. The next day, the *Sun* added that after three months in the UK these Roma would be 'entitled to health, education, pension and welfare benefits'. The *Daily Express* then inflated the figure to 1.6 million: 'Gypsies prepare to invade Britain'. Though two days later they amended this figure to 40,000, they predicted an 'economic disaster' just the same. Even *The Economist* spoke of the 'coming hordes'. On 22 January,

26 February 2004: front page of the Daily Express: *a typical example of its 'hostile and bigoted reporting'*

the *Mail* front page covered a report by the Organisation for Economic Co-operation and Development, saying that Britain, which was taking one in five of the Western world's asylum seekers, had 'failed to turn the asylum tide'. The article, it later turned out, was based on figures from 2002, and ignored the fact that the UK is currently eighth in the immigration league tables relative to size of population, well behind Austria, Norway, Sweden, Switzerland and Ireland. In any case, under EU agreements, old EU members may keep their labour markets closed to new entrants for a transition period of seven years, and research has already shown that the desire to move to the West from the countries joining in May may not be all that high.

Lies, inaccuracies, exaggerations, untruths: this is the climate in which the current asylum world lives, in which policy is made not so much on evidence as in response to media and public perception, and in which those seeking asylum, buffeted by the chaotic, contradictory and discriminatory asylum procedures now operating across the Western world, scramble for a toehold using any method they can. Not long ago, Kofi Annan, Secretary-General of the United Nations, told the European Parliament that Europe's anti-immigration rhetoric was 'de-humanising' people. 'This silent human rights crisis,' he went on, 'shames our world.' ❏

Caroline Moorehead is a writer and journalist. The above comes from her latest book Human Cargo: Travels among Refugees (Chatto & Windus, forthcoming early 2005)

GREG AND THE BUSINESS
OF METAMORPHOSIS
ROMESH GUNESEKERA

Greg writes for our local paper. He wanted to know the truth about fiction. 'Do you make it all up? Is it all a pack of lies?'

I found it difficult to answer. I was in the Liar's Paradox: everything I say is untrue. True or false?

I stepped as carefully as I could. 'Depends what you mean. If you have a licence to lie, then maybe it isn't really the case . . .'

'What licence? Hey, like, you either tell the truth or you lie, right?'

Since then it has been a slow dawning. The more true something claims to be, particularly in writing, the further it seems from the truth.

Last week I saw Greg on a bench in Priory Park. His collar was loose but he had his tie on, as he did whenever he was working. Most of it, like a spare windpipe, was tucked in halfway down his shirt. He was eating fried chicken out of a carton.

'Light lunch?' I asked.

'I'm doing a story,' he replied.

'No expenses?'

'I needed some air. A new angle. Anyway I'm tired of Julie's sushi.' He crunched a wing bone and dropped the splinters back in the carton. 'Like you, I am finding it difficult to stick to what really happened?' He showed me his notes written in a thin spidery hand.

'Don't they want a straight I-was-there account?'

'I was there, but the story is much more interesting if it has a bit of was-I-there? More is-it-true? Less it-is-true. What do you think?'

I said I didn't know. Recently, the era of the witness has been pushed hard: live TV, frenzied headlines, memoirs, autobiographies and 100 per cent true stories. I find it all a little suspect but I try to toe the line. 'We want to know the truth.'

Greg shrugged. 'We want witnesses and we want their gossip, but the gossip is most interesting if it is tantalising. Unbelievable. Incredible. In the end it is not the witness but the story that we really go for – even I know that. Look, unless you are in a jury, would you want three eyewitness accounts of the same thing? *I was there* – when everybody and their uncle has also been there – is not enough.'

I agreed. 'Maybe I'd prefer three novels.'

'Exactly. Novels are all the same stuff, but each is different, right?'

'But what about your job, Greg? Isn't it information you are meant to give? Not fiction.'

He thought about that for a little, shaking his box of bones. 'You want some chicken? Tangerine-coloured, see?'

'No,' I said.

'They say they've cut a lot of salt out, but it still tastes good.'

'You believe that?'

Greg put down the carton next to him and licked his fingers. 'Look, in fiction you create a world and make it seem real, right? The same as the vision thing that your bog-standard politician does, right? So, me too. I give a picture of the world as I like to see it. Why not?'

'Greg, I am not sure that creating an imaginary world is what a journalist, or even a prime minister, should be doing.' I picked up the ketchup packet he'd dropped. 'When a newspaper or a politician tells us what is going on, shouldn't it be verifiable? Unreliable narrators are charming in novels, but in news – no.'

'Fiction, the subversive art, huh? No authority except the story, right? I know all about that.' Greg pulled out his tie and straightened it. 'I read a real story the other day. Fiction. First time in ages, but I really got into it. Completely forgot my deadline. I started talking in my head. It made me think, you know. Is that the idea? A load of lies you read to find out what is going on in your own head.'

'Inventions for the imagination.'

Greg studied his hand. His fingers moved, awkwardly searching, tapping in the air. 'I can't make sense of this business. You try to tell the truth the best you can and you end up with a lie. Then you get a complete fabrication about a guy turning into an insect or something and hey, that seems so true. How is that possible?' ❑

Romesh Gunesekera*'s most recent novel is* Heaven's Edge *(Bloomsbury, 2002)*

YOU JUST DON'T GET IT!

JAMES VON LEYDEN

ADVERTISING NOWADAYS IS NOT ABOUT
LIES AND TRUTHFULNESS BUT IN-JOKES,
STUNTS AND A SENSE OF BELONGING.
CRITICISM ONLY MAKES IT WORK HARDER

Twenty-five years ago, Fiat ran a poster for the Fiat Palio 127 with the headline: 'If it were a lady, it would get its bottom pinched.' A few days later, an angry graffiti artist added the words: 'If this lady was a car she'd run you down.' The graffito became more famous than the poster. It was hailed as the first salvo in the guerrilla war against advertising, using the advertisers' own weapons to hit back.

Credit: Jill Posener

Today, Fiat would probably co-opt the feisty behaviour in the hope that a bit of it would rub off on the brand: a little 'Spirito di Punto'. Why not? Advertisers have been appropriating the subversiveness of street art for ages. In July 2003, someone plastered graffiti for an underground website called electricmoyo.com all over posters for the Nissan Altima. The culprit turned out to be Nissan itself, attempting to associate the Altima with the coolness of urban music.

Modern consumers are so quick to decode and dismiss messages that ads have to be as edgy as possible to get through. Advertisers have embraced with a vengeance Oscar Wilde's maxim that 'there's only one thing worse than being talked about, and that's not being talked about'. Anything is permissible as long as it generates column inches.

In 2003, the children's charity Barnardo's ran a campaign in the UK that attracted a record number of complaints and ended up being banned by the Advertising Standards Authority. One of the ads showed a baby with a cockroach crawling out of its mouth. In its defence, Barnardo's said the shocking visuals were necessary to overcome indifference and show the continuing impact of poverty on children's lives. The surprising thing is not that advertisers such as Barnardo's get rapped over the knuckles, but that they run 'offensive' advertising in the confident expectation that it will get banned. Twenty-five years ago, having an advertising campaign banned would have led to a charity hanging its head in shame and questions being raised over its status. Now it's just another weapon in the fight for attention.

Brands have always had to differentiate themselves in the marketplace. Contrary to popular perception, the most effective way to do this is not with lies and distortions but through truth – or rather, truths. Once upon a time, it was product truths: 'Rael Brook Toplin, the shirt you don't iron'; 'The milk chocolate that melts in your mouth, not in your hand.' Next came emotional truths: insights, or observations, that resonated with the consumer. 'If only everything in life was as reliable as a Volkswagen'; 'Come home to a real fire.' By their very nature, emotional truths are hard to contradict. Who would argue with British Telecom's observation: 'It's good to talk'?

In the last decade, these emotional truths have taken on a further dimension. Now an entire lifestyle is offered for the consumer's consideration. Thus Nike is not about trainers but self-realisation. Apple isn't about computers but creative thinking. Harley Davidson isn't about riding motorcycles but the fulfilment of dreams. The most successful brands are as far removed from the grubby, day-to-day world of products as possible. They operate in a rarefied and highly allusive atmosphere where product claims are less important than a sense of identity. The choice for the consumer is not so much whether to buy or not to buy based on price and quality, but on whether they identify or don't identify with the brand.

In the 1990s, Benetton ran a campaign with searing images of Aids sufferers and blood-covered newborn babies. Objectors protested that a man dying of Aids had nothing to do with selling jumpers. What they failed to understand was that Benetton wasn't selling jumpers. It was selling an attitude. Another apparel company, French Connection, went even further when it rebranded itself as FCUK in 1997. Millions of 15- to 34-year-olds bought into the FCUK attitude. And if you reject the attitude? Then you weren't in the target market in the first place, so FCUK off.

Where it once made a straightforward pitch in order to sell, advertising now plays a kind of game. It says to the reader or viewer: 'You've a few seconds to spare, why not take a look at this clever, offbeat headline or TV commercial. If you get it, then you're obviously a clever, offbeat kind of person who sees the world the same way we do. Maybe we should get together.' Flattery is an essential part of the game. Any resisters can be disarmed through self-deprecation. If someone hates Marmite enough to attack a poster they'll find the brand has beaten them to it. The manufacturers of Marmite have been running 'I hate Marmite' posters for years (a textbook example, incidentally, of how to leverage a product truth).

In the case of advertising aimed at the elusive 16 to 25 market, self-deprecation alone often isn't enough. The snack Pot Noodle has won a clutch of awards for television commercials which wallow in squalor and self-abasement. Like FCUK, Pot Noodle advertising succeeds through sheer chutzpah. Certainly, it's hard to criticise slogans like 'The slag of all snacks' or 'It's dirty and you love it' without seeming like a party-pooping pedant. None the less, viewers did complain; Pot Noodle got itself banned on TV before the 9 o'clock watershed and the brand moved up a notch in the eyes of its target audience.

Credit: HHCL & Partners, London

Brands like Pot Noodle and FCUK are highly sophisticated in deflecting criticism from their target audiences and attracting a backlash from everyone else, thus cementing their cult status. Only when it attracts criticism from its target audience is a brand in trouble. More often than not, the grounds for criticism will not be that the advertising peddles lies, but that it is – crime of crimes – dull.

All of which isn't to say that advertising doesn't get into murky ethical waters. Daytime TV commercials that persuade people to take out loans they can't afford, advertising aimed at children and cigarette advertising in the developing world are regarded as prime offenders. One could argue that these branches of advertising target vulnerable groups who should be protected by legislation. As for the rest of us, we're adults armed with the sword of irony and the trusty shield of post-modernism. We're fair game. If some of us are hurt or offended in the skirmish, then we're obviously hopelessly out of touch. It's not a case of 'Please accept the company's apologies' but 'Get a life.'

Much of the media operates according to this paradigm. The *Sun* loves it when po-faced *Guardian* readers upbraid it for behaving like a mischievous,

Credit: BBDO, Philippines

fibbing, foul-mouthed scallywag. That's its brand image, stupid! As for *Loaded*, *FHM*, *Maxim*, *GQ* and *Esquire*, the sole difference between them and the now-discredited *Playboy* and *Penthouse* is that the pin-ups are no longer girls plucked from obscurity, attracted by financial reward, but rich celebrities keen to enhance their own 'brand'. It's not quite so easy now to identify who's exploiting whom. In its advertising, *FHM* readily admits that the articles are irrelevant to the primary aim of arousing the reader. The readers are in on the gag, the girls are in on the gag, the publishers are in on the gag. If you criticise the magazine as sexist or exploitative, well, *you just don't get it.*

In this upside-down world, where ads don't look like ads, and self-denigration is self-elevation, is there any way one can make criticism stick? At street level, one solution is simply to become slicker. In the USA and Canada this approach has been elevated into an art form by *Adbusters* magazine. Using a combination of networking, stunts and media sabotage – 'culture jamming' – *Adbusters* has succeeded in harnessing the rage of activists who refuse to play the part of obedient consumers. Of course, the advertisers' response is simply to hijack their techniques and use them in their next ad campaign. As long as the cleverest people go into advertising rather than activism, advertising will remain one step ahead. A more productive approach is to go after the brands themselves, or the environmental or labour policies of the organisations behind them. *Adbusters* is now manufacturing a special Black Spot sneaker aimed at 'kicking Nike CEO Phil Knight's ass'. Somehow one suspects Phil Knight's feathers will not be unduly ruffled.

The most powerful agent of change in advertising is consumer indifference. Like superbugs developing a resistance to antibiotics, consumers in recent years have become increasingly immune to the relentless bombardment of irony. In response, brands have gone back to portraying themselves as straightforward and genuine. Benetton has reverted to simple shots of models in its ads. Coca-Cola's new campaign has British singer Sharlene Hector walking down the street handing out bottles of Coca-Cola while singing the Nina Simone track 'I Wish'. The commercial ends with the strapline 'The real world of Coca-Cola'. Advertising has come full circle. Instead of wrestling with multiple levels of meaning, we can once again take messages at face value. Of course, asking to be taken at face value carries an inherent danger. When Coke claims to represent the real world we can confidently retort, 'No, you don't.' ❏

James von Leyden is a writer and brand consultant

PUSH ON THE FIRST AMENDMENT

After a five-year legal battle, the case of *Nike* v *Kasky* (*Index* 1/03) finally ended in an out-of-court settlement last September. The two parties, one a multinational sporting goods manufacturer with US$10.7 billion in annual sales, the other an environmental activist, agreed that a settlement was preferable to further litigation. Nike paid US$1.5 million to the Washington DC-based Fair Labor Association for 'program operations and worker development programs focused on education and economic opportunity'.

Marc Kasky, a resident of San Francisco, had previously sued other companies, including Perrier and Pilsbury Foods, for false advertising. His action against Nike began in 1997 following a *New York Times* article on the high rate of respiratory illness among Nike employees in Vietnam as a result of exposure to the chemical toluene. The article coincided with a Nike public relations campaign designed to combat criticism of its 'sweatshop' labour operations in China, Thailand, Indonesia, South Korea and Taiwan. Kasky took exception to claims such as:

- 'workers . . . are not subjected to corporal punishment and/or sexual abuse'
- 'Nike products are made in accordance with applicable governmental laws and regulations governing wages and hours'
- 'Nike products are made in accordance with applicable laws and regulations governing health and safety conditions'
- 'Nike pays average line-workers double the minimum wage in Southeast Asia'
- 'workers . . . receive free meals and health care'
- 'Nike guarantees a "living wage" for all workers'.

Nike made no attempt to establish the truth of its claims but based its defence on the First Amendment, claiming the company's right to deceive was covered by the constitutional protection of free expression, a defence that was rejected by the California Appellate Court on the grounds that the First Amendment's protection did not extend to 'commercial speech'.

Nike appealed and the case was referred to the California Supreme Court in 2002, where it was again decided that the company's statements were unprotected commercial speech because Nike was 'engaged in commerce' and its statements 'were likely to influence consumers in their commercial decisions'. California Justice Joyce Kennard wrote: 'When a corporation, to maintain and increase its

Background: Ronaldo's boots auctioned at Christie's, London. Credit: Nils Jorgensen / Rex

sales and profits, makes public statements defending labor practices and working conditions at factories where its products are made, those public statements are commercial speech that may be regulated to prevent consumer deception.' Nike again appealed, and the case was referred to the US Supreme Court.

Over its five-year duration, the case provoked intense media debate over the free-speech rights of corporations. Five of the nation's leading newspapers editorialised in favour of the corporation, pointing out that regulation of corporate speech could stifle the debate over globalisation that gave rise to Nike's statements in the first place. *USA Today* asked: 'Are we all muzzled by California's Supreme Court ruling?' Anti-corporate commentators, under-represented in the mainstream media, objected to the corporate attempt to hijack rights that had been established for the protection of individuals.

The ruling in the Nike case goes against a growing trend to extend to commercial speech the same First Amendment protection provided for other forms of speech. The first instance of this was in 1976 when the Virginia State Board of Pharmacy successfully contended it was unconstitutional to ban the advertising of pharmaceutical prices. In 1980, during the Central Hudson Gas and Electric case, the Supreme Court created a four-part test to determine the constitutionality of regulating commercial speech. It ruled that: commercial speech must concern lawful activity and not be misleading; the court must determine if the government interest advanced by the regulation is substantial; it must also ask whether the commercial speech regulation directly advances the government interest; and it must determine whether the regulation of speech is no more extensive than necessary to serve the government interest.

The Central Hudson test, in particular its fourth clause, is not universally favoured: the tendency of US courts is to cast the protection of the First Amendment over as wide a field as possible, regulating only as a last resort.

The case of *Nike* v *Kasky* was ultimately sent back to California for trial. The US Supreme Court justices upheld the California law prohibiting deception in advertising and expressed a willingness to review the case should it return to them. Nike, meanwhile, fearing the case would not get back to the Supreme Court and anxious to deny anti-corporate activists the chance to inspect its operations, made its out-of-court settlement. While Kasky and his legal team were compensated for their five years' work, they may well have felt less than satisfied by the recipient of the award – an organisation presided over by members of Nike's executive. ❏

Samuel Holden

WHY THEY KEEP ON LYING
PETER PRINGLE

THE TOBACCO COMPANIES ARE THE TRUE
VETERANS OF THE LYING GAME AND IT HAS
COST THEM BILLIONS. BUT IF THEY EVER
STOPPED, THEY WOULD BE OUT OF BUSINESS

In the annals of corporate deceit, few events can compare with the appearance of seven tobacco company chief executives before a committee of the US Congress on 14 April 1994. They raised their right hands, swore to tell the whole truth and, one after the other, said they did not believe nicotine was addictive.

This infamous declaration encouraged a band of US attack-dog lawyers to file a series of lawsuits against the tobacco companies. The litigation forced those companies to release millions of internal documents, including a number showing that the companies had known for years that nicotine was an addictive drug. Tobacco company scientists had even adjusted nicotine levels in their cigarettes to make sure they kept smokers hooked.

The lawsuits went on for several years and ended with a whacking US$206 billion settlement against the companies with the lawyers taking their cut of 25 per cent.

Today, those internal company documents are available on the Web (www.tobaccoscam.ucsf.edu), put there by anti-smoking researchers at the University of California, San Francisco. The documents still make shocking reading about the pattern of deceit. But they also offer a rare glimpse into how the companies toyed with public concern, developing a strategy that kept profits high and public knowledge about the effects of cigarettes to a minimum.

The companies paid scientists to produce junk reports suggesting that smoking was not responsible for the string of diseases associated with their product, especially lung cancers and heart attacks. They went to enormous lengths to suggest that so-called second-hand smoke was not a worry. They funded local groups of restaurateurs and bar owners to fight the rash of legislation limiting smoking in public places.

They erected a protective shield around their executives of the kind usually found in government offices of national security. The documents show that reporters who called asking for information were all suspect – enemies unless proved otherwise. Company rules required elaborate vetting of reporters by the PR department before executives were allowed to speak to them.

When a reporter for the *New York Times* called for an interview with a tobacco executive, he was invited to lunch. The post-lunch internal company memo expressed concern about how the reporter might react to the company's line. 'At the end of the day . . . a tough one to figure out. Seems to want more from us, but I'm not confident that we'll get a fair shake from him. I would suggest we proceed slowly, setting up ground rules and see how he takes and uses our information.'

At the time of the lawsuits – 1994–5 – I was a reporter for the *Independent*, based in New York. I had followed the early skirmishes between the companies and the trial lawyers and decided there was enough material for a book. So, in December 1994, I called the biggest US tobacco company, Philip Morris (which then had its headquarters in New York), and asked for an interview with its chief litigation executive.

The memo about my request to the Philip Morris PR department recorded that I asked for the company's opinion on whether the lawsuits represented a new 'third wave' of litigation against the tobacco companies. (The 'first wave' was in the 1950s following experiments that demonstrated the harmful effects of tobacco tar on mice; the 'second wave' in the 1960s after the US Surgeon General's report declared officially for the first time that smoking was a cause of cancer.) According to the memo, I said: 'The states are now suing you . . . there are class actions . . . how does your company look at all this . . . is it the same, or changed, or what?' Simple questions begging straightforward answers.

The PR person, a rather jolly-sounding woman I recall, made my interview sound like a great idea. Now I know she immediately sent what she described as an 'early warning' memo to the boardroom advising that I had called. She suggested caution. 'He says he is writing a book about the tobacco litigation. But it's difficult from the conversations to find out exactly what he wants. He is a man who speaks rather loosely – trying to pin him down on specifics will take a bit, since he likes to leave himself as much room for maneuvering as possible.'

She said that she would 'pull copies of [his] previous articles re: tobacco . . . I think he is not a supporter, nor necessarily balanced in his views on this subject, but let's take a look at the actual columns and discuss.' Her idea was to 'give [the board] a flavor of where he is coming from.'

The company computer search revealed several tobacco and smoking news stories by me (it was a hot news topic at the time), but one article in particular put the PR department on red alert. The article, entitled 'An inexcusable cloud of death', asked why, given that the US Surgeon General estimated smoking killed 420,000 Americans each year, US tobacco companies were given tax breaks when they donated funds to charities, non-profit groups and artistic endeavours.

The highly profitable tobacco companies were big contributors to the arts and sports. Among the recipients in those days were the Joffrey Ballet, the Jewish Museum, the Guggenheim Museum, the American Museum of Natural History and the National Gallery of Art in Washington DC.

'For an organisation to do this and provide a product that, according to the government, kills people, is more than tasteless, it is preposterous,' I had written. 'The way these companies operate, not just what they produce, turns me into a zealot each time I think of it.'

Understandably, the PR woman advised that I appeared 'to have a distinct slant on our company'. But she strove to be fair: 'Nevertheless,' she continued, 'I think we should take the opportunity next week to give him our message points on class action lawsuits and the current state of tobacco litigation . . . [he] will continue writing; he should at least listen to the industry's side. Even if he doesn't appear to hear.' The replies flew back from the boardroom. One executive suggested that talking to me 'couldn't make things worse and could be better'. A second said: 'I would not recommend talking to him. How can you possibly get a fair hearing when he himself says he is an anti-smoking zealot.'

Even so, an interview was scheduled. But the day before, the PR woman called to cancel. When I asked why, she said it was because of my column and read out the headline. I was amazed that the company had taken so much trouble over me, looking up my articles. If you call up the CIA you expect that kind of vetting – but a tobacco company?

'I don't write the headlines,' I protested. 'And anyway the piece is not about the effects of smoking; it's complaining about the US government giving what would seem to be an unfair tax break.'

'Nice try,' she said. 'This interview will not take place.'

I went on to write my book *Cornered: Tobacco Companies at the Bar of Justice* (Henry Holt & Co, New York / Aurum Press, UK, 1998). It was not a rant against smoking. It was a contemporary account of the tobacco wars in the US and, later, the UK courts. As such, it was certainly not flattering to the tobacco companies. They lost the lawsuits, after all – and paid a big penalty.

When my book was published, the Philip Morris 'early warning' detectors went off again. The PR department warned the boardroom to expect the worst. They said I was 'a bit brash and opinionated. Not necessarily friendly to the issue, nor to us.' The company went on alert. 'Can you check our media files? Might have to go back as far as 96 or 97 . . . do a Lexus/Nexus on Pringle – bio and articles.' There my personal file ends, apparently.

Today, the tobacco battleground has moved on – from addiction to the bans on smoking in public places, especially bars and restaurants. Initially, the tobacco companies always denied the harmful effects of so-called second-hand smoke that are now widely accepted by the scientific community. And the companies maintained the smoking bans would hurt business. They funded studies often using flawed data that said as much.

Now, five US states – New York, California, Delaware, Connecticut and Maine – and about 250 local municipalities have banned smoking in bars and restaurants. But there is mounting evidence that such bans have not been bad for local economies. Once again the tobacco companies are distorting the evidence.

It is odd to find such a big and powerful company taking so much time to vet a reporter. When Philip Morris denied me an interview, I wondered if I might be missing a vital piece of the puzzle: did listening to their side of the story actually matter? Did I miss anything? I guess not. If they had ever told the whole truth about the effects of tobacco and smoking, they might be out of business. ❏

Peter Pringle is a writer and journalist

CAUGHT IN THE MATRIX
DAVID MILLER

POLITICAL DEBATE IN THE US AND UK
INCREASINGLY RESEMBLES THE DYSTOPIAN
VISION ENCAPSULATED IN 'THE MATRIX', WHERE
THE REALITY OF HUMAN BONDAGE IS DISGUISED
BY A SOPHISTICATED VIRTUAL REALITY

In matrix world, Iraq had and may still have Weapons of Mass Destruction; in the real world, it did not. In matrix world, there were links between Iraq and Al Qaida; in the real world, there were not. In matrix world, Lord Hutton is a respected judge who produced an independent report; in the real world, Hutton was a whitewash. In matrix world, Katharine Gun and Clare Short are deeply irresponsible for breaching trust and revealing secret information; in the real world, they blew the whistle on illegal and immoral official behaviour.

To many people who have witnessed the lies and deception of the past couple of years, our leaders seem deranged. Blair and his clique seem to have a tenuous grip on reality. How can it be, people wonder, that they can go on and on and on about Weapons of Mass Destruction when even the head of the Iraq Survey Group has concluded that they probably never existed? How can they appear to take so seriously statements that most of us now know are built on foundations no more secure than the shifting sands of the Iraqi deserts which they no longer even pretend to search?

The attack on Iraq has revealed as never before the yawning gulf between the political elite and the rest of us. It discloses an increasing separation between 'matrix world' – where official pronouncements are treated with some seriousness, even if subject to criticism – and 'real world' where their lies are transparent and their crimes recognised. Matrix world and real world exist in a kind of parallel universe. But the matrix is not entirely hermetically sealed from the real world. Every so often, the distance between the two becomes too great and the matrix has to readjust. In the film *The Matrix*, this is denoted by a glitch where the character played by Keanu Reeves sees the same black cat twice within seconds.

Take the case of the Hutton Report. After Lord Hutton had finished reading his prepared statement, the matrix appeared to be performing its work. The government was cleared of impropriety and the BBC damned. Tony Blair appeared almost immediately in the House of Commons, his face split by a victorious grin. But Hutton's report was just too efficient and the real world started to crash into the edges of the matrix. Within hours, the relief was gone and even key sections of matrix world were able to show their disbelief. The next day's *Independent* cleared the front page, leaving acres of white space and the single word 'Whitewash'. Blair's key ally Peter Mandelson regretfully tried to recuperate the defeat for the matrix: 'It was as if we won a football match 5–0 but the reporters covering it decided it was a draw and a couple of days later decided we had lost.'

When former minister Clare Short made allegations about UK involvement in spying on the UN Secretary-General, the matrix shuddered again. Showing their penchant for football metaphors, an anonymous Blair 'aide' said: 'It was as if we were playing football and someone suddenly pulled out a knife.' For them, this is a game. A game with civilised rules. To point out a breach of the rules is itself a breach of the rules. The 'great game' of power politics necessitates suppressing uncomfortable facts, not least of which is its lethal consequences, especially for people with brown skins. Their game of football towers over the knife-puller in its barbarity, leaving up to 40,000 dead including over 10,000 civilians. Their deaths are so inconsequential that they are airbrushed from the mainstream.

Yet a growing number of people are breaking away from the common sense fostered by our rulers. The phenomenon was visible on the streets of London as thousands protested against the Bush visit in November 2003. As it was the day after the bombings against British interests in Istanbul. TV journalists repeatedly asked demonstrators the former dread question about 'playing into the hands of terrorists'. But protestor after protestor responded by saying that Bush and Blair were to blame for the bombings. Even more dramatically, the Aznar government in Spain was swept from office by similar discontent following the bombings in Madrid, reportedly spread partly by word of mouth, email and text message – but also crucially by a counter-common sense shared instinctively by increasing sections of the population. The conclusion to draw from this is that the ideological strength of our rulers is wavering as their common sense is challenged more and more consistently from below. The more this happens, the more desperate they become and the more extreme the lies. Lies and the propaganda machinery necessary to produce them are, in other words, built in to the very fabric of neo-liberal governance.

What we are seeing in the UK are the birth pains of the neo-liberal political order – the institutionalisation of lying and the destruction of democracy. In order for it to flourish, neo-liberalism needs to foster a fundamentally distorted version of reality: the matrix. This version must be believed or at least signed up to by the political elite in the Conservative and Labour parties (and the Democrats and Republicans), in the military and intelligence agencies and in the transnational corporations.

The mainstream media are also part of the system and dissent is generally kept within manageable bounds. What about the *Mirror* and the *Independent* and the *Guardian*, say the defenders of the status quo? Isn't it in fact the case that the media have 'taken up the role of "critique" of all governments liberal and conservative, that was once the province of the left parties' as the 'eloquent apologist for the invasion of Iraq' and theorist of the 'market state', as Philip Bobbit puts it. Or, as another Blair adviser, Anthony Giddens, has argued: 'I doubt that corruption is more common in democratic countries than it used to be – rather, in an information society, it is more visible than it used to be. The emergence of a global information society is a powerful democratising force.'

Typically, such grand statements mask an almost total lack of evidence on how the media actually perform (never mind how they legitimise or undermine great power) and are but a further indication of the close integration of key sections of academia into the power elite – into the matrix. Just for the record, empirical studies and all the available evidence shows that the mainstream media are systematically if variably biased in favour of official pronouncements. There is dissent at the margins and dissent has been more prominent in the UK media over Iraq than in the Gulf War of 1991. But as the stunning analyses produced by MediaLens show, there are not only limits to the dissent possible in even anti-war papers, but much of the coverage in papers such as the *Guardian* and even the *Independent* conformed pretty well to the official consensus in the run-up to the attack on Iraq. The diplomatic editor of the *Independent*, the self-proclaimed 'arch sceptic' on WMD on the paper, notes that 'no one would have risked having this paper, or probably any other' question the existence of any serious WMD in Iraq because 'the whole government-generated consensus was the other way' and 'you have to remember how strong the consensus was on

Breaking out: Keanu Reeves, hero of The Matrix *(1999). Credit: Rex / Warner Brothers*

Iraq's weapons capability'. This speaks eloquently of the limits of possible dissent in the mainstream media, but also of a constipated and unresponsive political system.

Wholesale lying and misinformation by the political elite has been learned in part from the private sector and the PR industry, which has done so much to advance the interests of mobile global capital. Unsurprisingly, the PR industry is now being welcomed into the heart of government in the UK. Practically unnoticed in the mainstream, the Phillis Report on government communications opened the way for PR agencies to bid for government contracts. Phillis abolished the Government Information and Communication Service, which has acted as a brake on spin. This was unsurprising since the committee was heavily weighted with private-sector PR agencies keen to open up a relatively new market. Within weeks the Scottish executive had led the way by advertising a contract to cover advertising, Web design and PR for itself, 10 agencies, 23 health bodies, 35 quangos and several government bodies. These include the PR activities of the Scottish parliament. The obvious structural conflict of interest if the parliament, to which the executive is supposed to be accountable, has the same PR agency appears not to be a barrier. The contract is unsurprisingly regarded as 'highly attractive' by the advertising and PR industry.

Meanwhile, in Iraq, one of the few British companies to get a contract from the US administration is Bell Pottinger, part of the Chime PR conglomerate. It 'will oversee a massive public relations and advertising drive to begin the transformation of Iraq into a successful democracy', reports the *Guardian*. Actually, what Chime will do is attempt to ensure that neo-liberal 'market democracy' is constructed. This is after all what the company headed by Lord Tim Bell has done in the UK and elsewhere since its creation in 1989.

We live in an age of fakery; spin in government and PR manipulation in business are used to force through unpopular policies or undermine democratic decision-making. All over the world our rulers are attempting to hold the matrix together with ever extending propaganda programmmes. The GM food lobby leads the way. In Johannesburg, the Third World farmers demonstrating at the UN Summit on Sustainable Development in favour of GM foods were 'fake': bussed in, marshalled, press-released and given T-shirts with slogans in English, a language they didn't speak. On the Internet, GM interests have created 'fake persuaders' to manipulate debate on scientific discussion groups and marginalise their critics. In the US, the

Bush administration pays actors to produce fake news reports in favour of its policy on Medicare. In Turkey, BP's consultation on the Baku–Tiblisi–Ceyhan pipeline included a telephone survey of the Turkish village of Hacibayram which 'had been deserted for many years, its houses having fallen into ruins. There were neither telephones nor anyone to answer them.' In the UK, the Blair government 'consultation' on GM simply ignored the overwhelming opposition of the public. It was, in other words, a fake consultation.

At root, the fakery and the misinformation are the necessary by-product of neo-liberal politics. In the post-war period, in conditions approaching social democracy, popular demands had some impact on the governmental apparatus, whether Labour or Tory. The historic compromise between capital and labour, which led to the introduction of the welfare state, the NHS and the nationalisation of key industries, meant there was some link – however tenuous – between popular demands and political and economic decision-making. Under neo-liberalism the main parties are indistinguishable and their policies have no popular basis. They must be imposed by manipulation, fakery and deception.

The accelerating propaganda programmes and the machinery to put them into practice are needed to attempt to keep the matrix functioning. But the decline of trust in governments, and the consequent disengagement from the matrix manifested by millions of people across the globe, are, as Noam Chomsky has put it, 'natural consequences of the specific design of "market democracy" under business rule'. The lies in, other words, will not end when Blair or Bush go; they are the necessary product of the neo-liberal political system. The necessity to lie will only be undermined when governments start to enact the will of the people – in other words, after the current system is fundamentally reformed. ❏

David Miller *is the editor of* Tell me Lies: Propaganda and media distortion in the attack on Iraq *(Pluto, 2004)*
http://staff.stir.ac.uk/david.miller/publications/Tellmelies.html
Thanks to Emma Miller and Jean Shaoul

FREEDOM OF EXPRESSION AWARDS

The Index on Censorship *Freedom of Expression Awards 2004 honouring the outstanding contributions of six men and women to free speech, creativity and freedom of information were presented on 22 March at London's City Hall. The judges also singled out one more individual as 'censor of the year'. The judges were Monica Ali, Geoffrey Hosking, Mark Kermode, Ann Leslie, Caroline Moorehead, Nitin Sawhney, and Ursula Owen and Judith Vidal-Hall of* Index.

INDEX ON CENSORSHIP / GUARDIAN HUGO YOUNG AWARD FOR JOURNALISM

Kaveh Golestan, Iran, an award-winning photographer and cameraman, who worked the sharpest parts of the battle for free expression. In 1997, he was banned in Iran for revealing the horrific plight of children in orphanages and asylums. In 1998 in Iraq, he risked his life to tell the world of gas attacks on Kurdish towns. He was killed by a landmine in northern Iraq last year.

Also nominated British TV journalist James Miller, shot dead by Israeli troops; Inés Peña, Colombian journalist brutalised by paramilitaries; Syrian Web journalist Abdel Rahman Shagouri, held without trial since February 2003.

SPECIAL AWARD

Mordechai Vanunu, Israel, who worked as a nuclear technician at Israel's top-secret Dimona base in the Negev Desert. Concerned by the scale of the project, beyond even the control of the Israeli parliament, he passed details of the programme to the London *Sunday Times* in 1986. Shortly afterwards he was kidnapped, tried in secret and sentenced to 18 years in jail, 11 of which were spent in near total isolation.

WHISTLEBLOWER

Satyendra Kumar Dubey, India, an engineer in Bihar province, who was outraged by the level of corruption on large public construction projects including the major road project in which he was involved. After repeated attempts to draw attention to the situation, he appealed to Prime Minister AB Vajpayee, urging confidentiality. On 27 November 2003, he was shot dead.

Also nominated GCHQ translator Katharine Gun, who leaked US plans to spy on UN delegations; Ukrainian intelligence office Valeri Kravchenko, who exposed illegal surveillance of the Ukrainian opposition; Uzbek rights campaigner Fatima Mukhadirova.

FILM

Lee Hirsch for *Amandla!*, South Africa, which reveals the central role that black South African music played in the long struggle against apartheid. A wonderfully expressive portrait of South African life then and now, it focuses on how music was used to circumvent state censorship.

Also nominated Yuri Khashchavatski, Chechnya, for *Prisoner of the Caucasus*; Siddiq Barmak, Afghanistan, for *Osama*; Jafar Panahi, Iran, for *Crimson Gold*.

BOOK

Mende Nazer and Damien Lewis for *Slave*. When she was 12, Mende Nazer was abducted from her village in the remote Nuba Mountains of Sudan by the mujahidin, sold to an Arab woman in Khartoum and stripped of her name, and her freedom, for seven years. *Slave* is a shocking first-person insight into the modern-day slave trade.

Also nominated Anna Funder for *Stasiland*; Azar Nafisi for *Reading Lolita in Tehran*; Linda Polman for *We Did Nothing*; Yelena Tregubova for *Tales of a Kremlin Digger*.

MUSIC

Daniel Barenboim and Edward Said (d 2003) for the **West–Eastern Divan Orchestra**, Israel–Palestine. Barenboim and Said defied critics from both sides of the Israeli–Palestinian divide to found an orchestra of Israeli and Arab musicians, seeing the 'unity and harmony' it represents as a metaphor for what is possible. It played its first concert in an Arab country in August 2003.

Also nominated Gorki Luís Águila Carrasco, jailed member of one of Cuba's most censored rock bands; Junoon, politically aware Pakistani band; Ferhat Tunc, singer and Kurdish human rights activist.

CENSOR OF THE YEAR

Attorney General John Ashcroft, United States, who took a nationwide tour in 2003 to promote the USA Patriot Act 2001 and to call for its powers to be extended. The act already drastically invades privacy, denies due process, punishes dissent, and gives the US government the power, among other things, to monitor its citizens' reading habits without telling them.

Also nominated UK Home Secretary David Blunkett; Iranian Minister of Culture Ahmad Masjed Jama'i for censoring one of the world's most vibrant cinema industries; Irish Justice Minister Michael McDowell for imposing strict controls on police officers who talk to the media. ❏

A censorship chronicle incorporating information from Agence France-Press (AFP), Alliance of Independent Journalists (AJI), Amnesty International (AI), Arab Press Freedom Watch (APFW), Article 19 (A19), Association of Independent Electronic Media (ANEM), BBC Monitoring Service Summary of World Broadcasts (SWB), Canadian Journalists for Free Expression (CJFE), Cartoonists Rights Network (CRN), Centre for Human Rights and Democratic Studies (CEHURDES), Centre for Journalism in Extreme Situations (CJES), Committee to Protect Journalists (CPJ), Democratic Journalists' League (JuHI), Global Internet Liberty Campaign (GILC), Guatemalan Journalists' Association (APG), Human Rights Watch (HRW), Indymedia, Institute for War & Peace Reporting (IWPR), Instituto de Prensa y Sociedad (IPYS), Inter-American Press Association (IAPA), the International Federation of Journalists (IFJ/FIP), International PEN (PEN), International Press Institute (IPI), Journaliste en danger (JED), the Media Institute of Southern Africa (MISA), Network for the Defence of Independent Media in Africa (NDIMA), Network for Education and Academic Rights (NEAR), Pacific Islands News Association (PINA), Press Freedom Foundation (FLIP), Radio Free Europe/Radio Liberty (RFE/RL), Reporters Sans Frontières (RSF), South African Broadcasting Corporation (SABC), Southeast Media Organisation (SEEMO), Statewatch, Transitions Online (TOL), United Nations Integrated Regional Information Network (IRIN), and other sources including members of the International Freedom of Expression eXchange (IFEX) and World Association of Newspapers (WAN)

ALGERIA

On 23 December 2003, journalist and human rights activist **Hassan Bourras** (*Index* 1/04) had his two-year prison sentence quashed on appeal but was still ordered to pay US$1,440 in damages and an additional US$144 fine for defamation. Bourras had been imprisoned from 6 November to 2 December for two articles that appeared in *el-Djazaïr* about public officials from the city of el-Bayadh. (RSF)

On 23 December 2003, **Ali Dilem** (*Index* 2/02, 3/03), cartoonist for the daily *Liberté*, received a four-month suspended prison sentence and a fine of US$1,430 for defaming the defence ministry. A 3 April 2002 cartoon referred to a dramatic incident the day before, when insurgents used a fake roadblock to capture 21 soldiers. It was captioned: 'The criminal code protects generals but not troops.' **Abrous Outoudert** (*Index* 1/04), former publisher, and **Hacène Ouandjeli**, former managing editor, were also fined $715 each. (RSF)

On 14 January, *L'Expression* editor **Ahmed Fattani** was charged with 'insulting the head of state' by publishing a column by the pseudonymous writer 'Mirou' in late November. Entitled 'Leon the dwarf', it told the story of a 'third world dictator'. However, it did not at any point cite Algerian leader Abdelaziz Bouteflika's name. (AFP)

The 8 February issue of the weekly magazine *Jeune Afrique-l'intelligent* was banned without explanation by the authorities, but the order was

attributed to an article entitled, 'Who the generals vote for', analysing the decisive role of the army in Algeria's recent history. (RSF)

On 20 February, the Algerian media rights group CALP reported a new campaign by imams in state-controlled mosques, targeting the independent press, accusing it of displaying a 'hostile attitude toward Islam', seeking to 'destroy' the president and causing conflict. (CALP)

ARMENIA

The Ministry of Justice is considering amendments to a law on freedom of information drafted by civil liberties groups and parliamentarians and enacted in September 2003. Critics of the amendments suggest they would reverse some of the gains made by the adoption of the existing law. (*A19*)

AUSTRALIA

Spanish dance theatre group **La Fura Dels Baus** has been told that the video films it uses as background to its stage show *XXX*, an explicit exploration of human sexuality, must be cut to meet Australian cinema censorship laws as the show tours across Australia in March and April. The group has presented *XXX* throughout Europe for two years, playing to more than 500,000 people; the scenes, depicting explicit sex acts, were pixellated or obscured by bright lights. (*Sydney Morning Herald*)

The makers of Web file-sharing software **Kazaa** lost an appeal against a court order granting music industry private investigators the right to raid their offices and other premises in search of evidence of copyright abuse. The industry is fighting use of the software to swap music over the Internet. (ACLU)

The censorship laws in place in Australia's conservative state of Queensland serve mainly to encourage the rise of a 'porn mafia', warned Bond University criminologist Professor Paul Wilson on 18 March. He said Queensland operated a separate publications censorship regime to that of the federal government, making material banned in the state freely available elsewhere in Australia and supplying a booming black market in porn. (*The Age*)

AZERBAIJAN

Reporters Sans Frontières accused the Baku authorities of increasing pressure on the independent media and abusing press rights since new head of state Ilham Aliev succeeded his father as president. RSF visited Baku on a fact-finding mission in December 2003. (RSF)

Power supplies to the independent **Chap Evi** press house were cut off for three days on 7 January, stopping publication of opposition papers including *Yeni Musavat, Hurryyet, Baki Khaber* and *Yeni Zaman*. The International Press Institute read it as a fresh bid to bankrupt private printers and force papers to use state-owned presses, where they could be more easily controlled. (IPI, CJES)

Editor **Rauf Arifoglu** of *Yeni Musavat* (*Index* 2/03, 3/03)

went on hunger strike for a week in February while jailed awaiting trial for alleged involvement in October 2003 clashes between police and opposition supporters. He was one of several reporters held for up to three months pending police inquiries into the events, including **Sadiq Ismailov** of the daily *Baki Khaber*, whose editor confirms that he missed the clashes by a day. (JuHI, *Ekho Baku*, RFE/RL)

Reviewing the October clashes, the Azerbaijani Press Council decided in February to invest 20 million manats (US$4,091) and buy 500 special jackets to identify media workers during public protests. The October violence followed an opposition demonstration against alleged election fraud. (RFE/RL)

BAHRAIN

The Arabic version of the reality TV show *Big Brother*, retitled 'The Boss', was taken off air on 1 March after protests by women's groups outside the country's Information Ministry. Producers at MBC said they did not want to be 'the cause of differences of opinion'. Islamist critics said the show was a threat to Islam and was 'entertainment for animals'. (BBC)

BANGLADESH

Salah Uddin Shoaib Choudhury, editor of the weekly *Blitz*, was arrested at Dhaka airport in November 2003 as he tried to travel to a writers' conference in Israel called 'Bridges Through Culture'. Choudhury, who would have been the first Bangladeshi journalist to

speak publicly in Israel, was accused of being a spy and imprisoned. (*New York Times*)

New Age daily reporter **Manik Saha** was killed on 15 January in the south-western town of Khulna when he was decapitated by a home-made bomb thrown at the rickshaw he was travelling in. A letter claiming responsibility was faxed to local papers by Gaffar Tusher, leader of the People's War Maoist faction. On 22 January, Tusher warned nine local correspondents for Dhaka papers to cease coverage of his group and repeated the threat to another 11 at the end of February. (IFJ, RSF, CPJ)

The Wind Bird, a film by first-time Sri Lankan director **Inoka Sathyangani**, won first prize at the Dhaka International film festival on 25 January. The film, which deals with abortion, won the prize even though the country's film censor board had banned it from being shown to the public. Instead, the board allowed a private viewing of the film for only the festival's jury. (AFP)

Correspondent **Iqbal Hasan** of the daily *Janakantha* was beaten up by ruling Bangladesh National Party (BNP) members in the northwestern city of Natore on 9 February. Hasan linked the attack to a report on BNP arson attacks on the homes of opposition Awami League supporters two days earlier. Other journalists were confronted by BNP cadres: photojournalists **Selim Jehangir** (*Index* 1/04) of the daily *Janakantha* and **Azharuddin** of the daily *Prothom Alo* were threatened while taking pictures of the violence, while reporter **Shibli Noman** and photographer **Nazrul Islam Zulu** of the local daily *Ajker Kagoj* were assaulted. (CPJ)

Prabir Shikder (*Index* 3/01), a reporter for *Janakantha* in the western town of Faridpur, was chased on 3 February by a car and three motorcycles, only escaping by mingling with a group of Muslim worshippers. Shikder had a leg amputated in 2001 after an attack prompted by his reports about a local businessman. (Bangladesh Centre for Development, Journalism & Communication)

Abdul Mahbud Mahu, correspondent for the local Cox's Bazar daily *Ajker Desh Bidesh*, was arrested on 14 February under the 2002 Special Powers Act, apparently at the behest of a local BNP leader who objected to Mahu's articles. The act allows police to arrest someone without a warrant and hold them until trial. (RSF, BCDJC)

BELARUS

On 28 November 2003, a district court in Minsk declared missing journalist **Dimitri Zavadski** (*Index* 3/03) dead, after concluding that the ORT cameraman had died after his abduction in July 2000. Two former security police members face charges of kidnapping Zavadski; they have not yet been accused of murder. (CPJ)

On 28 December 2003, the Belarus post office (Belpochta) dropped a contract to deliver leading independent paper, *Beloruskays Delovaya Gazeta* (*Index* 3/03), to its subscribers; the state distributor Belsayusdruk followed suit soon after by refusing to distribute copies in Minsk, Vitsebsk and Brest. RSF described the actions as part of a crackdown on the paper and linked it to death threats received by the paper's Gomel city correspondent **Irina Makovetskaya** on 10 January. (RSF/IFEX)

Although seen as a slight improvement on the current 1995 legislation, a new draft Press Law tabled in December 2003 would still restrict freedom of expression and introduce deliberately onerous licensing and accreditation systems under state-directed agencies. The planned restrictions apply equally to print, broadcast and Internet. (*A19*, IFEX)

Journalist **Natalya Kaliada** was fined €160 on 2 February for publishing articles on a website run by Charter 97, a human rights group not officially recognised by the state. Deputy Attorney General Paval Radzivonaw, frequently cited by rights groups for his crackdowns on the independent media, had earlier ruled Charter 97's activities illegal. (RSF)

Byarozka, the only children's magazine published in Belarusan, faces closure after 80 years. Editor **Uladzimir Yahowdzik** was sacked in December 2003, the publisher lost the rights to the magazine and the last seven staff will be laid off on 1 April. Forty well-known Belarusan writers have protested against the closure in an open letter to Information Minister Uladzimir Rusakevich. (RFE/RL)

Recent publication: *Memorandum on the Draft Law of the Republic of Belarus, On the Introduction of Amendments and Additions to the Law 'On Press and other Mass Media'*, Article 19, November 2003, 22pp

BELGIUM

The Belgian consumer watchdog Test-Achats has brought a suit against several music conglomerates over their use of copy-protected CDs. Test-Achats has sued EMI, Universal Music, BMG and Sony Music, saying it has received over 200 complaints from consumers who seek to make copies for convenience's sake of their purchased music to use on other music-playing technology, (GILC)

BOTSWANA

Communications Minister Boyce Sebetala denied suspending phone-in programmes on Radio Botswana on 13 November 2003 because opposition parties used them to criticise the government. But he added that Botswana TV would stop most political party reports due to 'inadequate human capacity' at the station. This did not affect coverage of the views of President Festus Mogae and his vice-president because, he said, 'they represent the nation in their positions'. (MISA, *Mmegi*)

BURKINA FASO

Examining Judge Wenceslas Ilboudo might reopen his investigation into the 1998 murder of journalist **Norbert Zongo** (*Index* 2/03) following evidence by former Presidential Guard Regimental

Sergeant Naon Babou, who implicated others in Zongo's murder while under separate interrogation for his part in a failed coup. So far only one man, Warrant Officer Marcel Kafando, has been charged with Zongo's killing. (RSF)

BURMA

Burma's Motion Pictures and Video Censor Board has promulgated a new rule that forbids actresses from appearing on screen in Western-style trousers and skirts. Instead, all Burmese actresses must now wear traditional dress. The rule change will affect some movies in production, including several scenes in an upcoming film about Salone, or sea-gypsy, tribes in southern Burma's Mergui archipelago. These must be reshot, as they feature the starlet Nandar Hlaing in jeans, says a movie director in Burma. The film was reportedly commissioned by Burma's military intelligence. (www.irrawaddy.org)

CAMEROON

Twelve independent TV and radio stations face closure on licensing grounds, leaving the field open to state-run Cameroon Radio Television (CRTV). Reporters Sans Frontières say officials claim that 'the media is too sensitive not to be controlled'. President Paul Biya is up for re-election in October 2004. (RSF)

Health Minister Urbain Olangueana Awon has opened a legal and administrative inquiry into a report of 18 February by **Marie Noëlle Guichi** of *Le Messager*, which described how visibly substandard vaccines were being administered to victims of a recent cholera epidemic in the city of Douala in southern Cameroon. (JED)

CANADA

On 20 January, Royal Canadian Mounted Police officers armed with search warrants raided the offices of the *Ottawa Citizen* newspaper and the home of journalist **Juliet O'Neill**, in pursuit of documents O'Neill used for a November 2003 article about the case of **Mahar Avar**, a Canadian telecoms engineer of Syrian descent. He was deported by the US not to Canada but to Syria, and was tortured by Syrian secret police before being released. (CJFE, PEN Canada)

Singer **Alanis Morissette** has decided not to produce a censored version of her new single, 'Everything', to send to Canadian radio stations. The song begins with the line, 'I can be an asshole of the grandest kind'. In the US the A-word is replaced with the word 'nightmare'. 'We've decided here that we're sticking with "ass-hole",' Warner Music Canada's Steve Coady told *Jam!* magazine. (*Jam!*)

CENTRAL AFRICAN REPUBLIC

On 25 February, **Judes Zosse**, director of the daily *L'Hirondelle*, was arrested when he called in to a police station to enquire about the detention of his brother **Didier**. Didier was released without charge and Judes transferred to the country's central jail for questioning about the paper's use of opposition website reports critical of the decision of President François Bozize to take over responsibility for national tax collection. (www.centrafrique-press.com)

CHAD

Vatankhah Tchanguis, director of a rural private radio station, Radio Brakos, was arrested and beaten up on 9 February allegedly on the orders of the local Bahr city police chief after the station broadcast an interview with an opposition spokesman. Released after 48 hours, Tchanguis ended up in hospital in critical condition. (JED)

CHINA

Dissident **Wang Youcai** (*Index* 1/02, 5/98) has been released from jail on medical parole (often used as a way to send individuals into exile) and is headed for the US. Wang, 37, first came to prominence as one of the student leaders involved in the 1989 Tiananmen Square demonstrations. The Dui Hua Foundation said Wang suffered from bronchial disorders and a heart condition. (GILC)

Amnesty International attacked Microsoft and other computer giants in January for selling technology that allows Chinese authorities to control and monitor the Internet. According to Amnesty, 54 people are now detained or imprisoned in China for Internet-related activities, a rise of 60% in just over a year. The criticism of Microsoft came as founder Bill Gates learned on 27 Janu-

THE GOOD DOCTOR'S DIAGNOSIS

Jiang Yanyong, 72, an army doctor who last year blew the whistle on China's cover-up of the Sars epidemic, was also an eyewitness to the consequences of the 4 June 1989 Tiananmen Square massacre. He wrote a 4,700-word letter on 24 February to the National People's Congress, which met in Beijing in March, describing the scenes in his hospital in the hours after the massacre and his efforts and others to agitate for change thereafter. Jiang's letter has since made its way to foreign journalists but some websites that have posted the Chinese version have been blocked.

. . . After 4 June 1989, everything was measured by one's attitude toward the [Tiananmen Square] incident, including the reorganisation of our fraternal unit, the Academy of Military Sciences. Qin Boyi, the academy's president (who had approved the delivery of drinking water to student protesters on a hunger strike), was dismissed. Professor Tang Peixuan, a vice-president, was also dismissed after he told his superiors that when he took part in student movements before Liberation, the Kuomintang (pre-communist) government only used fire hoses on students. He said it was incomprehensible that the people's troops killed countless students and ordinary people with machine guns and tanks . . .

[Playwright Wu Zuguang] later said: 'Everybody has a mouth, which serves two purposes: eat and speak. If this mouth is used to tell lies and if I don't speak my mind, then its only purpose is to eat. What's its usefulness?'

Wu's talks educated me greatly. In 1998, I and some comrades wrote to state leaders proposing that the 4 June incident be reappraised. I called on [former President] Yang Shangkun at his residence. I told him what I saw. Yang indicated that in the 4 June incident, the Communist Party of China committed the most serious mistakes in its history. He said he could do nothing but the mistakes would be corrected in the future.

What I want to say is this: our party must address the mistake it has made. I believe correct assessment of 4 June is what the people want and it will never cause unrest. The claim that stability is of overriding importance can in fact cause even greater instability. Each year before 4 June, some people, like sitting on thorns, are in a state of extreme nervousness. The uneasiness has not gradually diminished. On the contrary, the people have become increasingly disappointed and angry.

I have considered the consequences that I might encounter after writing this letter. But I have decided to tell you all the facts.

Jiang Yanyong
Department of Surgery, Beijing 301 Hospital, 24 February 2004. ❏

Translation by the US Foreign Broadcast Information Service ary that he was to receive an honorary British knighthood for services to enterprise. (AI, RSF)

In February, Chinese Cultural Minister Sun Jiazheng called for tighter controls on the Internet, including 24-hour surveillance, and urged users to join state efforts to police the Web. Censorship of public protest on Internet discussion groups increased on 24 February, when service providers were told to shut down discussion spaces such as www.sohu.com's **Starry Sky** forum and replace them with less contentious material. Email filtering was also ordered to be turned up, resulting in a surge of complaints from users unable to send messages. (RSF)

Five members of the Falun Gong spiritual movement, **Lu Zengqi, Yan Qiuyan, Li Jian, Chen Shumin** and **Yin Yan**, were sentenced to between five and 14 years' imprisonment in Chongqing, western China, on 19 February. The court ruled that their online comments about torture of Falun Gong adherents in jail 'tarnished the image of the government'. (RSF, GILC)

US Internet systems firm VeriSign has agreed a contract with the Beijing authorities to develop a domain name server system that will meet future growth in Chinese Web usage – and give the state even more powers to censor websites by blocking access to them from China. (RSF)

After a crowd crush killed 37 and injured 15 at a lantern festival in Beijing, municipal

government PR officials ordered papers to use specified articles and standard photos of officials at traditional celebrations, to play down news of the disaster. (*South China Morning Post*)

On 6 January, **Cheng Yizhong**, editor-in-chief of tabloid newspaper *Nanfang Dushi Bao*, and six other members of staff were arrested by Guangzhou police. Authorities are thought to be making an example of the newspaper for breaking news of a new Sars case in December, in order to silence other media. (RSF)

On 23 December 2003, a court in Shandong Province rejected an appeal against the two-year jail sentence imposed on photographer **Jae Hyun Seok** (*Index* 2/03, 3/03) for human trafficking. Seok was arrested on 18 January 2003 while filming North Korean nationals attempting to flee China on boats bound for South Korea and Japan, as part of a project documenting the plight of North Koreans in China. (CPJ)

The Chinese Football Association has banned its under-17 team from David Beckham-style haircuts: 'Dyed hair, long hair and weird hairstyles are all strictly prohibited in the training camp and all players must cut hair short.' Feng Jianming, director of the CFA youth department, told the players: 'You must learn how to behave as a true man before becoming a soccer star' (see p10). (BBC, Xinhua)

COLOMBIA

Journalist **William Soto Seng** was murdered on 18

December 2003 when he arrived for work at local Telemar TV in Puerto de Buenaventura in south-eastern Colombia. Soto Seng produced TV opinion, politics and sports programmes. (IAPA)

Journalist and women's rights activist **Inés Peña** was kidnapped and abused by paramilitaries on 28 January in Barrancabermeja, north-eastern Colombia. The local leader of the Organización Femenina Popular (OFP) youth section and the presenter of a youth culture segment for local Enlace 10 TV's news programming, she had criticised the paramilitaries' arrival in the region. Peña is also a member of the Regional Public Prosecutor's Human Rights Youth Network and coordinator of the OFP's María Cano documentation centre. (FLIP)

On 23 October 2003, paramilitaries assassinated OFP member **Esperanza Amaríz** and on 27 January fired shots at an international delegation that was on its way to visit an OFP housing project in San Pablo municipality. In the past three months, three Barrancabermeja journalists have received threats. (AI, FLIP)

On 4 February, journalist **Oscar Alberto Polanco Herrera** was murdered as he was leaving his office at CNC TV station in the city of Cartago in western Colombia. The former director and current host of the station's *Notas de Dirección* show, he had publicly criticised a number of Cartago's officials and institutions. (FLIP)

CONGO

On 31 January and 2 February, the Congolese National Petroleum Company (SNPC) filed six complaints for defamation against the weekly *L'Observateur*, citing three November reports of mismanagement and corruption at the oil firm. It seeks punitive damages of US$33,600, intended to bankrupt the weekly. (RSF)

DEMOCRATIC REPUBLIC OF CONGO

Message de Vie Radiotélévison (RTMV), owned by exiled **Pastor Fernando Kutinos**'s Army of Victory Church, and focal point of the Sauvons le Congo popular opposition movement, resumed broadcasting on 14 December 2003, six months after national police closed the station and seized its equipment. (JED)

Nine workers at Congolese National Radio & Television (RTNC) were sentenced to 12 months' imprisonment on 5 January and other staff ordered to pay compensation over reports covering former government spokesman Kikaya bin Karubi. (JED)

Nicaise KibelBel Oka, publication director of the weekly *Les Coulisses*, received death threats after reports of December violence in the eastern city of Beni accused the rebel Rally for Democracy and Liberation Movement (RCD-ML) of worsening insecurity in the north and east. (RSF)

On 12 February, Congolese security and intelligence services agents arrested Teles-phore **Namukama**, host of a radio show broadcast by the human rights group Heritier de la Justice in Bukavu. He was accused of causing public anxiety by raising reports of the recent discovery of arms caches in Bukavu. (JED)

COSTA RICA

On 23 December 2003, journalist **Ivannia Mora Rodríguez** was murdered while driving her car in downtown San José. Two assailants on a motorcycle shot her at close range and fled. A colleague in the car said there had been no attempt at a robbery. (IAPA)

CÔTE D'IVOIRE

Correspondent **Baba Coulibaly** of the independent daily *l'Inter* and Reuters alleged that he was threatened by Côte d'Ivoire Patriotic Movement (MPCI) opposition group spokesman Sidiki Konaté. Coulibaly linked the alleged threat to his publication of an interview with rival rebel leader Bamba Kassoum. (RSF)

The killer of Radio France Internationale correspondent **Jean Hélène** (*Index* 1/04), Police Sergeant Théodore Séri Dago, was found guilty of murder in 'mitigating circumstances' on 23 January and jailed for 17 years. Dago shot the journalist dead in October 2003 as Hélène waited to interview detained opposition activists. The government was ordered to pay CFA37 million (US$69,300) in compensation to Hélène's family. (RSF, CPJ)

Three journalists, **Charles Sanga** and **Ibrahim Diarra** of *Le Patriote* and **Frank Konaté** of *24 Heures*, were assaulted by members of President Laurent Gbagbo's presidential guard on 31 January. The fight began when one of the guards found a letter on Diarra referring to a meeting of a rebel group he had covered; the guards took Diarra to be a rebel assailant and attacked him. (RSF)

CROATIA

Journalist **Sasa Jadrijevic Tomas** of *Slobodna Dalmacija* was threatened by unknown men on 23 January, just as his paper prepared to print a story about the private life of a high-ranking official in the Ministry of Internal Affairs and his alleged failure to support his son financially. Jadrijevic Tomas is now under police protection. (SEEMO)

CZECH REPUBLIC

Two men assaulted **Tomas Nemecek**, editor of independent weekly *Respect*, spraying tear gas in his face and then kicking him. Nemecek and other media observers have linked the attack to *Respect*'s reports on a criminal gang from north Bohemia. Police have arrested one of the alleged attackers, 25-year-old Frantisek Crnacty. (*Prague Post*)

CUBA

The American Association for the Advancement of Science (AAAS) reported that the US government warned US scientists who were planning to participate in a scientific conference in Cuba that they risked criminal or civil charges if they broke travel bans on US citizens. The

Fourth International Symposium on Coma and Death started on 9 March without the participation of about 70 US medical school professors, doctors and scientists. (NEAR)

Independent journalist **Léster Téllez Castron** has gone on hunger strike as a protest against his imprisonment for nearly two years without trial. He was jailed on 4 March 2002 on charges of disturbing public order, disobeying the law and 'insulting' the Cuban president. (IAPA)

The Cuban government plans to stop unauthorised Internet users, the so-called *informaticos*, by banning the use of the regular telephone network to get online. Cubans can still use cybercafés, but at a rate of US$2.50 for 15 minutes, a price that is beyond all but the most privileged. (RSF)

DOMINICAN REPUBLIC

Cielo FM radio's political show *El Poder de la Tarde* was ordered off air in January by presidential press chief Luís González Fabra. Cielo FM is one of several media outlets that have been seized as assets of businesses charged under the country's anti-money laundering laws. Effectively state-owned, they are unable to resist political influence ahead of President Hipólito Mejía's re-election bid in May. (IAPA)

ECUADOR

Journalist **Miguel Rivadeneira**, head of Radio Quito, received five anonymous telephone death threats on 26 and 27 January after

broadcasting an interview with an army general about the military's role in alleged arms smuggling. (RSF)

On 4 February, a copy of a strategy paper listing suspected 'subversives' among the regional media, allegedly produced by army intelligence officers, was sent to media outlets and political parties. The alleged target list included La Luna and Visión radio stations and the daily paper *El Comercio*. (RSF)

On 9 February, **Carlos Muñoz**, president of Telesistema local TV, was injured and his driver, **Ricardo Mendoza**, was killed in an ambush in Guayas province, Guyaquil. The Revolutionary People's Militias (MRP) claimed responsibility for the attack, accusing Telesistema of not broadcasting its statements. The group threatened other media outlets and journalists. (IPYS, RSF)

EGYPT

Rights activist **Ashraf Ibrahim**, who monitored Egyptian police violence during protests against the US-led war in Iraq (*Index* 4/03), was acquitted of all charges of 'sending false information' abroad and membership of a 'revolutionary socialist group' on 11 March. Ibrahim spent almost a year in jail, noted Human Rights Watch, 'simply because the government didn't like his political views or activities'. He had been arrested in March 2003. (HRW)

Zeinab Sweidan, head of Egypt's state-owned television, announced in February that the TV censorship com-

mittee was banning up to 700 music video clips it deemed inappropriate. Some of the clips in the list — most of which are Lebanese — are deliberately sexy, but the committee also bans videos that show singers or dancers with costumes that reveal their navels. The banned list includes videos by **Haifa, Nancy Agram, Amr Diab** and **Hani Shaker**. The ban applies only to state TV; a bid to ban similar videos from satellite TV stations in August 2003 was universally ignored, and no charges were filed. (*Cairo Times*)

On 29 January, a US journalist on the weekly *Cairo Times*, **Charles Levinson**, was expelled as a 'threat to state security'. No official reason was given but Levinson cited two articles he had written on torture in Egypt, published in US daily papers in November 2003. On 20 February, the Egyptian ambassador to the US reportedly told Levinson he could return to Egypt and resume work. (*Middle East Times*, CPJ)

Egyptian Press Union president **Galal Aref** announced on 24 February that he had been phoned by President Hosni Mubarak and told of 'imminent' plans for a change to the law that would prevent the jailing of journalists on charges solely related to their published words. (*Middle East Times*)

ETHIOPIA

On 2 December, the Ministry of Justice banned the **Ethiopian Free Press Journalists Association** (EFJA) (*Index* 1/04) executive committee from running the group and, assuming responsibility for its management, called its own meeting to elect a new committee of its own choice. The complex dispute divided supporters, but the Committee to Protect Journalists noted the damage caused by the action and the government's poor press freedom record. (CPJ)

The International Press Institute described Ethiopia's draft press law as a 'severe and unnecessary restriction' on the rights of journalists. It argued in a 17 December 2003 report that clauses in the law supposed to help the media were 'heavily outweighed' by legal qualifications that infringe press freedom and the free flow of information in Ethiopia. IPI director Johann P Fritz said that if passed the law 'will become the cornerstone of the government's attempts to suppress and intimidate the media in the country'. (IPI)

FRANCE

On 8 January, the National Assembly passed its digital economy bill, which makes Internet service providers responsible for the legal content of Web pages hosted on their commercial servers. Hosts would become liable under common law if they did not 'act promptly' to block content 'after becoming aware of their unlawful nature'. This could result in heavy fines and imprisonment. (RSF)

French Education Minister Luc Ferry said a ban on religious symbols in French state schools could include headscarves, bandannas and beards if considered a sign of faith.

But he said Sikhs might be able to wear head coverings if these were discreet. (RSF)

On 10 December 2003, French licensing authorities told Reporters Sans Frontières to cease broadcasts of Radio Non Grata, opened on 9 December 2003 to broadcast over the French–Swiss border to Geneva, then hosting the UN World Summit on the Information Society. The station planned to protest against RSF's loss of consultative status at the UN, suspended on 24 July 2003 for a year at Cuba's request after the Paris-based rights group picketed sessions of the UN Commission on Human Rights in protest at the choice of Libya to chair the UN body. (RSF)

GABON

Marco Boukoukou Boussaga, editor-in-chief of the newly launched independent *L'Autre Journal*, died in mysterious circumstances on 15 December 2003, spitting up blood in hospital, the victim of an unknown ailment. Friends suspected foul play. The government had reacted furiously to the first edition of the paper, which detailed IMF criticism of state financial mismanagement. Officials forced printers not to handle the second edition and when Boussaga found alternative printers in neighbouring Cameroon, confiscated the entire run as it arrived in Gabon. The government banned the magazine indefinitely on 19 December. (CPJ)

GAMBIA

Managing editor **Alagi Yoro Jallow** (*Index* 2/03) and editor-in-chief **Abdoulie Sey** (*Index* 1/04) of the biweekly *Independent* were questioned by police over a lead story questioning ownership of the five-star Kairaba Beach Hotel. The pair were later released but the Gambia Press Union has denounced their treatment as arbitrary. (IPI)

GEORGIA

The rulers of the country's autonomous Adjara region did not welcome the popular overthrow of President Eduard Shevardnadze in Georgia, ordering a region-wide ban on public rallies, limiting political activities and banning publications that 'called for destabilisation'. Journalists **Mzia Amaglobeli** and **Eter Turadze** of *Batumelebi* magazine were beaten up by local regime supporters at a rally in support of Shevardnadze's successor Mikhail Saakashvili on 11 January. Imedi TV cameraman **David Gogitauri** was attacked as he filmed a balcony flying the white five-cross flag of Saakashvili's party two days later. (CJES, RSF, Internews)

The family of murdered journalist **Dato Bolkvadze** protested against plans to grant an amnesty to Loti Kobalia, one-time guard commander for ousted president Zviad Gamsakhurdia, who was jailed for 20 years in 1994 for his killing. Kobalia's release is part of a process to reconcile factions from the 1993 civil war. (CJES, Caucasus Press, Itar-Tass)

GREECE

On 28 December 2003, reporter **Antonis Papado-**

'They that can give up
essential liberty to obtain
a little temporary safety
deserve neither liberty
nor safety' Benjamin Franklin

NOAM CHOMSKY ON
ROGUE STATES

EDWARD SAID ON
IRAQI SANCTIONS

LYNNE SEGAL ON
PORNOGRAPHY

... all in INDEX

SUBSCRIBE & SAVE

SUBSCRIBE & SAVE

poulos was sent by TV station Alter to investigate claims of poor conditions in Nikea General Hospital. Hospital security guards arrived and attacked Papadopoulos and his crew. His clothes were torn, his bag taken and he was questioned without authority. Media rights groups have called upon the authorities to carry out a full investigation. (SEEMO)

GUATEMALA

Children's rights advocate **Bruce Harris** was acquitted by a Guatemalan court of criminal defamation charges on 30 January. In September 1999, Harris was sued by a group of Guatemalan lawyers whom he accused of involvement in the illegal adoption of local children. The Guatemalan penal code can jail offenders for up to five years for speech that 'dishonours, discredits, or disparages another person', regardless of whether true or not. (HRW)

Journalist **José Rubén Zamora** says his own investigation into a June 2003 raid on his home has enabled him to identify the lead assailants – Erick Alexander Johnston Barrera, an official close to Attorney General Carlos de León Argueta, former presidential guards Belter Armando Álvarez Castillo and Eduvijes Funes Velásquez, and civil police counter-intelligence officer Iris Edith Soto López. During the 2003 raid the assailants terrorised Zamora and his family, forcing them later to seek exile abroad. (APG)

GUINEA

The 8 February edition of the weekly *Jeune Afrique l'Intelligent* was banned by a court order and confiscated from street vendors. No reason was given but the order was attributed to a report in the issue about arrests of army officials thought to oppose Guinean President General Lansana Conté. Photocopies of the offending issue promptly went on sale in the capital Conakry. (MISA)

Sanou Kerfalla Cissé and **Talibé Diallo**, managing editor and deputy editor-in-chief of *le Diplomate* newspaper, and freelance journalist **Jean Marie Morgan** were interrogated by special branch officers about their reports on alleged electoral fraud during the 31 December 2003 elections. (MISA)

HAITI

Violence in the weeks before the ousting of President Jean-Bertrand Aristide did not spare local journalists. Radio Hispagnola owner **Pierre Elicème** was shot in his car and badly wounded on 21 February. He had received death threats since he agreed to rebroadcast news bulletins from Radio Métropole, shut down after threats from supporters of Aristide's Fanmi Lavalas party. The following day, the Trou du Nord offices of Radio Hispagnola were torched by supporters of former MP Nahum Marcellus. Driven off by anti-government rebels, their supporters then destroyed the offices of Marcellus's own station, Radio Africa, and Radio Télé Kombit (RTK), owned by Aristide loyalist Jose Ulysse.

More than 20 Haitian media outlets, mostly radio stations, have been forced to close, stop broadcasting news or have been threatened this year, mainly by supporters of Aristide, who has accused the National Association of Haitian Media (ANMH) of having links to armed groups. The allegation was denied by Radio Kiskeya director **Sony Bastien** in a broadcast editorial on 5 February, resulting in death threats from other Aristide allies. Several foreign reporters have also been targeted, including a Spanish cameraman attacked with a machete. (RSF)

The family of murdered journalist **Brignol Lindor** were invited to the French Senate in Paris on 3 December 2003 to mark the second anniversary of the reporter's murder in Haiti. Brignol's brother Moréno attended a meeting in the National Assembly to discuss press freedom in Haiti. (RSF)

Spanish television journalist **Ricardo Ortega** of Antena 3 was killed and US photographer **Michael Laughlin** of the *Florida Sun-Sentinel* was injured in Port-au-Prince shootings on 7 March. They had been covering a demonstration by Aristide's opponents, when armed supporters of the ousted leader, known as *chimères*, opened fire on the crowd. Several Haitians were also reported hurt.

HONDURAS

The Honduran Supreme Court handed down a suspended sentence of two years and eight months to journalist **Renato Álvarez** on 18 February for defaming

Eduardo Sarmiento, a leading figure in the ruling National Party, named in a report on drug trafficking. In curious asides to the ruling, Álvarez was required by the court to 'demonstrate good behaviour' and surrender his rights to vote, manage property, stand for public office or exercise parental rights during the suspension period. (Periodistas Frente a la Corrupción)

Journalist **Germán Antonio Rivas** (*Index* 2/03, 1/04), owner of local Corporación Maya Visión TV in Santa Rosa de Copan near the Guatemalan border, was murdered by an unknown assassin on 26 November 2003. Rivas had survived a previous assassination attempt in February 2003 and had been subjected to death threats before. He had exposed coffee and cattle smuggling to Guatemala and a cyanide spill into the Lara River by the Minerales de Occidente mining company, later fined €175,000 for the offence. Though convinced the threats were connected to his work, he would not name possible suspects. (PFC, UNESCO)

HUNGARY

Andras Bencsik, editor-in-chief of the weekly *Magyar Demokrata*, was jailed for 10 months on 21 January for libelling Democrat MP Imre Mecs in articles alleging that he betrayed Hungarian resistance members to the Soviets during the 1956 uprising. The report claimed that four people were executed as a result of Mecs's acts. A second reporter, **Laszlo Attila Bertok**, was given an eight-month suspended sentence. (RSF)

INDIA

The *Indian Express* reported on 16 December 2003 that *dalit* (low-caste) teachers in Gujarat state were being threatened with transfer to other districts if they did not segregate *dalit* children from non-*dalit* children during the serving of midday meals. (*Indian Express*)

RR Gopal (*Index* 3/03), editor of the Tamil-language magazine *Nakkheeran*, was released on bail on 20 December. Gopal had been detained in Chennai's central prison for eight months on charges of 'conspiring to promote the secession of Tamil Nadu state' and illegal 'possession of a firearm'. (RSF)

More than 70 people were arrested in Pune on 6 January during an attack on the Bhandarkar Oriental Research Institute (BORI), organised by the so-called Sambhaji Brigade, a radical Hindu group. The group objects to a book by US academic **James Laine** about a Maratha folk hero, *Shivaji: A Hindu King in an Islamic Kingdom*, which allegedly questions whether Shivaji was a Hindu. Laine had thanked a professor at BORI in the book's credits. The Maharashtra state government later banned the book on public order grounds. (BBC, *Frontline*)

Vaiko (*Index* 4/02, 1/03, 2/03), the general secretary of the MDMK Party in Tamil Nadu, was released from Vellore jail on bail on 7 February after 19 months in detention under the Prevention of Terrorism Act (POTA). Vaiko was arrested with eight other MDMK leaders in July 2002 for making speeches in support of the banned Sri Lankan Tamil LTTE guerrillas. The Supreme Court later upheld Vaiko's appeal argument that merely expressing support for a banned group did not justify arrest under the act. Vaiko's eight co-defendants, including **P Neduraman** (*Index* 4/02), were released on bail on 12 January, Vaiko himself refusing bail until encouraged to do so by colleagues. (Frontline)

Recent publication: *India: Open Letter to the Chief Minister of Jammu and Kashmir on the failed promises of the Common Minimum Progra*, Amnesty International, 2 December 2003, 7pp

INDONESIA

The independent bi-weekly *Beudoh* in Aceh province closed, blaming repeated army harassment. On 5 December, editor **Maarif** went into hiding after being quizzed by the military for 10 hours. He said that officers tried to get him to admit to publishing 'false information' and threatened to kill him if he did not change the newspaper's opposition to the maintenance of martial law in Aceh. (RSF)

On 29 December 2003, kidnapped TV journalist **Ersa Siregar** of Rajawali Citra Televisi was killed, apparently in a bungled rescue attempt by the military in Aceh. Siregar and two colleagues had been abducted on 29 June together with two crew members. Sirigar's cameraman, **Fery Santoro**, is still missing. (RSF)

Millionaire businessman Tomy Winata saw his long-running libel war against the news magazine *Tempo* suffer a setback on 25 February. He had sued *Tempo* and one of its reporters over an article published by an independent website alleging he was linked to a March 2003 attack by thugs on the magazine's offices. The article had quoted **Ahmad Taufik**, the *Tempo* reporter named in Winata's lawsuit, as reporting that the attackers had demanded the paper retract a story linking Winata to a fire that gutted a Jakarta textile market. That story is central to Winata's main charge against *Tempo*. In that case, chief editor **Bambang Harymurti**, **Taufik** and journalist **T Iskandar Ali** could face a maximum of 10 years in prison under Article 14(1) of the Criminal Code on provoking disorder, and a maximum of four years under Articles 310 and 311 of the Criminal Code on defamation. In a separate libel lawsuit, a Jakarta court in January ordered *Tempo*'s editor, publisher and a reporter to pay Winata US$1 million for defaming his reputation with an article that suggested he had tried to open an illegal gambling den. The magazine is appealing. Winata, whose Arta Graha banking and property group holds several lucrative contracts with the military, has denied all the allegations. (PMW, *Jakarta Post*)

The Indonesian government challenged media rights campaigners from the Indonesian Press Council who are seeking to prevent the use of criminal libel laws dating back to the Dutch colonial era to jail journalists who lose defamation cases. The council wants the country's press law to apply; the state Minister of Communications and Information, Syamsul Mu'arif, said that law was 'too lenient'. (PMW, *Jakarta Post*)

IRAN

An 11 January ruling by the Council of Guardians barring 3,500 pro-reform candidates, including 80 sitting MPs, from standing in the February elections immediately prompted 60 MPs to stage a 26-day protest sit-in. Some 1,100 disqualifications were overturned, but 2,500 were left standing. The Reformist Coalition for Iran, an alliance of eight reformist groups, said as a result it could not compete at all in 72 seats. The refusal by the council to review any more cases led to the resignation on 1 February of 120 pro-reform MPs and a boycott call from the main reformist Islamic Participation Front Party. After the full list of candidates was published without change, 550 pro-reformists heeded the call and withdrew from the polls on 14 February. On 15 February, in an open letter from prison, dissident academic **Hashem Aghajari** urged passive resistance in protest at the failure of reform. On the final day of campaigning, 19 February, reformist papers *Yas-e-No* and *Shargh* were closed down for publishing criticism of the elections. The conservatives won an easy victory on the day, with turnout down to its lowest level since the 1979 revolution. (BBC)

Pro-reform journalist **Emadoldin Baghi** (*Index* 2/03) was summonsed by Teheran's revolutionary tribunal on 3 March to answer for an article he wrote for *Yas-e no* in which he called the 20 February legislative elections illegal. Baghi was given a year's suspended jail sentence for other offences in December by the same court. (RSF)

The *Guardian* reported the problems of Iranian heavy metal band **Kahtmayan**, which has to stop audiences dancing during its gigs. Bassist **Ardavan Anzabipour** told the paper: 'If we don't remind them to sit down and stop moving, we won't get permission to play again.' Under Iran's Islamic sharia law, dancing is illegal and audiences must stay seated. The band, founded in 2001, claims to be the first metal band in Iran. 'Other bands arrived late on the scene and many of them just play covers of Metallica songs,' he says. (*Guardian*)

IRAQ

Nine journalists were among 109 killed by bomb attacks on the offices of the Kurdistan Democratic Party and the Patriotic Union of Kurdistan (PUK) in Irbil on 10 February. The nine were photographer **Safer Nader** of *Qulan* magazine, KTV cameraman **Ayoub Mohamed Salih**, photographer **Abdlsatar Abulkarim** of *Altakhy* newspaper, and publisher **Shawkat Shekh Yazden-Aras**, editor-in-chief **Mhdi Khoshnaw**, columnist **Naseh Salim** and editors **Saad Abdulla**, **Salah Saedouk** and **Kamaran Mohamed Omar** of *Rzkari* newspaper. (IFJ)

Journalists from the pan-Arabic TV news station Al

Jazeera were refused access to an Iraqi Governing Council press conference on 31 January in line with a month-long order barring the station from covering the council's activities. The 28 January ban was reportedly a response to phone-in comments made during the station's controversial *Opposite Directions* show, which the council claimed showed 'disrespect to Iraq and its people'. (RSF)

Yanar Mohammed, head of the Organisation of Women's Freedom in Iraq, and publisher of *al-Nisa* magazine and the www.equalityiniraq.com website, was targeted in February by the Jaysh al-Sahaba group, believed to have links to Al Qaida. She has been a leading campaigner through the magazine and website for equality for women and has been warned that if she goes on publishing, she will be killed. (IFJ)

IRELAND

The leader of the opposition Fine Gael party, **Edna Kenny**, has condemned plans to set up a statutory press council, on the grounds that the government will be able to decide its membership, leaving it open to political interference. (*Irish Times*)

The Report of the Irish Legal Advisory Group on Defamation concluded that Ireland's laws on defamation in the Republic of Ireland should be reformed, and proposed the introduction of a defence of reasonable publication, a broadening of the defence of innocent publication and plans to limit damage awards. But Article 19 criticised the group's failure to abolish

criminal defamation fully, and its proposal to create a statutory press council. (A19)

ISRAEL

Newly declassified US State Department documents suggest that Israel once considered attacking nuclear installations in Pakistan. The Israeli plan was discussed on 14 September 1979, by a panel set up by then US president Jimmy Carter. The papers were heavily censored before they were declassified, leaving analysts in doubt as to the seriousness of the threat and the likely targets. The papers were released by the National Security Archive, a Washington NGO that specialises in disclosing unclassified documents under the terms of the US Freedom of Information Act. (*Ha'aretz*)

ITALY

On 23 December 2003, Prime Minister Silvio Berlusconi gave a reprieve to Retequattro, one of his TV stations, which was supposed to move to satellite transmission by the end of the year. The decree follows President Carlo Ciampi's block of the 'Gasparri' law which would have lifted the ban on cross-ownership of media and allowed one person to own more than two national broadcast stations. (BBC)

On 24 February, a court in Trieste sentenced journalist **Massimiliano Melilli** to 18 months in prison and ordered him to pay a €100,000 fine for 'defamation'. The offending articles, published in November 1996 in *Il Meridiano*, reported rumours of 'erotic parties' attended by Trieste

high society. In the articles, Melilli focused on Rosanna Illy, wife of the then mayor and current president of the Friuli–Veneto region, but did not actually name her. Rosanna Illy denied the allegations and sued for libel. (RSF)

KAZAKHSTAN

The upper house of the Kazakh parliament sent a draft media law back to the lower house in February, calling it 'vague and legally flawed' and seeking changes to proposed media licensing and accreditation rules. Rights groups said the December 2003 draft law, added to existing secrecy rules, censorship and privacy rights for politicians, would worsen a system that already failed to meet international standards on free expression. (HRW, IFJ, A19)

Jailed journalist and rights activist **Sergei Duvanov** (*Index* 2/03, 3/03, 1/04) was granted probation and freed on 15 January. Initially detained for 'insulting' the president in reports on alleged corruption, Duvanov was arrested in October 2002 just before leaving for Washington to deliver a report on human rights in Kazakhstan. He was then charged with raping a teenager, allegations that he denies and which have been discredited by international observers. (IFEX, RSF, IWPR, CJES, RFE/RL)

On 30 January, journalist **Svetlana Rychkova** of the *Assandi Times* (*Index* 2/03), a long-time critic of official corruption, was dragged from her car by police, detained and beaten in the town of Talgar, near Almaty. Three days earlier she had refused the police's request to inform on fellow journalists. (IFJ)

A campaign group to defend **Gennadii Benditskiy** of the weekly *Vremya* was set up on 25 January. Benditskiy faces jail for his articles on the disappearance of US$15 million earmarked by the Kazakh Defence Ministry for Russian and Ukrainian arms purchases. The group, including National Library Director **Murat Auezov** and media rights campaigner **Rozlana Taukina**, also seeks the replacement of the country's criminal libel law with a civil one. (RFE/RL)

On 27 January, a long-running intimidation campaign against the independent Arsenal publishing house culminated in a police raid. Officers said they were investigating 'malignant non-execution' of a November 2003 planning order requiring the plant to move its warehouse wall 70cm. The police took a list of staff and their personnel details. (IPI, A19, IFEX, CJES)

On 30 January, an Aktubinsk Court sentenced **Vladimir Mikhailov**, co-founder of the independent daily *Diapason*, to two years in prison for producing TV programmes. Broadcasting requires a licence but, despite the fact that his firm was not actually the broadcaster of the shows, Mikhailov was sentenced for 'fraudulent entrepreneurship'. He is appealing against the judgement. (CJES, RFE/RL)

KENYA

Kenya's Muslim minority have asked their government

to lift a ban on financial assistance from Arab NGOs. Without the funds, development projects in Muslim areas, including health centres and Islamic schools (*madrasas*), would suffer, they said. Millions of dollars in aid was channelled into Kenya annually, mainly from Saudi sources, before it was found that some of the funds also financed the groups responsible for a 1998 truck bombing that killed or injured hundreds of Kenyans. Kenyan Muslim leaders have refused replacement funds from the US Embassy in Nairobi. (CNSNews)

Information Minister Raphael Tuju ordered the seizure of so-called alternative and illegal newspapers on 10 January, among them the *Independent, Kenya Confidential, Citizen* and the *News Post*, whose publisher **Ndirangu Kariuki** was arrested and later released. Five newspaper vendors were also arrested. (NDIMA)

KUWAIT

Writer and journalist **Yasser al-Habib** was released early following a general amnesty to mark Kuwaiti National Day on 25 February. He was jailed for a year in January for comments made on a recorded lecture in which he was alleged to have 'questioned the conduct and integrity of some of the companions of the Prophet Muhammad'. (IPEN)

Valentine's Day cards were nearly banned in Kuwait ahead of 14 February after Kuwaiti Islamist MP Walid al-Tabtabai accused them of breeding illicit relationships

between men and women. (BBC)

In the wake of a Gulf Cooperation Council meeting called to discuss means of tackling 'the roots of Islamic Militancy', the Kuwaiti education minister has suggested that school textbooks could be liberalised to ensure that books 'should not encourage pupils to hate other people and religions'. (BBC)

KYRGYZSTAN

Editors of Russian-language papers *Argumenty i fakty-Kyrgyzstan* (Index 1/04), *Moskovskii komsomolets v Kyrgyzstane, Komsomolskaya pravda v Kyrgyzstane* and *Rossiiskaya gazeta* on 11 December 2003 condemned rules limiting foreign-owned media coverage of elections as discrimination against the country's ethnic Russian community. (RFE/RL)

On 24 December 2003, President Askar Akayev presented parliament with a bill to decriminalise libel. If passed, noted Reporters Sans Frontières, it would end the state's power to jail reporters for up to three years for 'insulting a person's honour' but the use of the law to bankrupt opposition papers with punitive fines would remain a problem. (IRIN)

On 4 February, the Media Resource Centre in the southern city of Osh was attacked by two unidentified masked men who stole hard disk drives from computers, said centre director **Ernis Mamyrkanov**, in an apparent search for information. The internationally funded centre was the location for an

Index on Censorship regional media rights programme in mid-February. (RFE/RL)

LEBANON

On 6 December, **Tahsin Khayat**, owner of the independent news and politics channel NTV, was arrested by military police for 'suspected links with Israel' and held for 24 hours. The station is known for its criticism of the government, and Khayat for his support of President Emile Lahoud's opposition to Prime Minister Rafiq Hariri, but some link the targeting of the station to its coverage of the al-Medina Bank corruption trials, which have implicated several Lebanese political figures. Lebanese Information Minister Michel Samaha later banned NTV for 48 hours on 16 December. He objected to NTV's 'subjective' comments on the state's refusal to grant a work permit to station presenter **Dahlia Ahmed**, a Sudanese national. Station allies have blamed interference from Syria's chief military intelligence officer in Lebanon, General Roustom Ghazalé, and Lebanese state security chief, General Jamil Sayyed. (APFW, RSF)

LIBERIA

Five journalists from the weekly *Telegraph* were charged with 'criminal malevolence' over a report that National Security Minister Losay Kender was an embezzler. Editor-in-chief **Philip Moore Jr**, managing editor **Adolphus Karnuah** and sub-editor **Robert Kpadeh** were charged in court; former business manager **Rennie Moses** and chief reporter **Rudolph Gborkeh** were

charged in absentia. They face a maximum sentence of one year's imprisonment. (CPJ)

Mike Jabeteh of the *Analyst* newspaper was severely beaten and robbed in an attack by a member of the rebel Liberians United for Reconciliation and Democracy (LURD) force. His watch, tape recorder and US$500 also went missing in the attack. His attacker accused him of 'reporting bad things' about LURD chairman, Sekou Damante Comeh. (MISA)

Managing editor **Meeky McKay** and journalist **Hommammed Kanneh** of the *Heritage* paper await trial for 'disseminating obscene material' after reporting on 16 February that Liberian women were appearing in European-made bestial sex videos. The claim was attributed to parliament speaker George Dweh, who later denied seeing such films. But the story and an accompanying cartoon triggered protests by women's groups and a reprimand from the Press Union of Liberia. (MISA)

LIBYA

The state-owned daily *al-Zahf al-Akhdar* (*Index* 1/04) was banned for a week on 27 January for suggesting that Colonel Muammar Gaddafi should no longer be referred to as the 'guide of the revolution' and should behave as a genuine head of state. Libyan authorities said the newspaper had been suspended for 'serious mistakes' and 'publishing articles contrary to the power of the masses'. (RSF)

MALAWI

A study of Malawi's broadcast media law was released by Article 19 tracking the country's failure to found an independent media regulator and turn the Malawi Broadcasting Corporation (MBC) from state to public service broadcaster. The regulator, MACRA, has been criticised for its leniency towards state media and harsh treatment of private broadcasters. Meanwhile, the MBC board is appointed by the president and MACRA has decided that it is not responsible for holding MBC to account in cases of alleged political bias. (A19)

MALDIVES

On 27 January, President Maumoon Abdul Gayoom reported that a commission into the killing of four prisoners at Maafushi jail and anti-government violence in Male in September 2003 (*Index* 1/04) had found that security personnel had illegally fired on prisoners and that they would be prosecuted. **Mohamed Latheef** (*Index* 2/96, 1/04), spokesman for the banned opposition Maldivian Democratic Party (MDP), noted afterwards that the names of the officers responsible had been deleted from the commission report on national security grounds. (BBC, *The Hindu*)

The Maldives Human Rights Commission rejected an application to consider the appeal of **Mohamed Zaki**, one of three 'cyberdissidents' arrested and jailed in 2002 for publishing Sandhannu, an online opposition newsletter (*Index* 2/02, 4/02,

2/03, 4/03). It raised questions about the role of the UN, which had provided US$150,000 to finance the Commission, and the body's mandate. Zaki and fellow prisoners **Ahmed Didi** and **Fatimath Nisreen** had their sentence of 10 years for 'insulting the president' halved to five on 13 November 2003. A fourth prisoner, **Ibrahim Luthfee**, escaped from detention in 2003 while being treated in hospital in Sri Lanka. (www.maldivesculture.com)

In the early hours of 13 February, National Security Service officers arrested up to 70 people associated with the banned MDP, a day before a planned MDP protest against rising crime and just hours after the party elected a new governing council. New council members were among the detainees, including **Ahmed Nazim**, Captain **Abdullah Saeed**, filmmaker **Aminath Najib**, MDP activist **Ahmed Falah**, his wife **Aishath Najib** and their children **Shafeen Ahmed** and **Habhin Ahmed**. (AI, www.maldives culture.com)

MAURITANIA

Distributors, apparently acting under pressure, declined to handle copies of the fortnightly magazine *Afrique Education* on 27 November 2003 after it published an editorial describing the Mauritanian regime as 'pro-slavery' and its president Colonel Maawiya Ould Sid'Ahmed Taya 'a petty racist'. (RSF)

Abdul Salaam Weld Harma, a university teacher, was detained on return to Mauritania after taking part in a debate on the war in Iraq for the Al Jazeera TV chat show *Opposite Direction* on 2 December. (www.arabicnews. com)

Islamic opposition leader **Mohammed Jamil Ould Mansour** was arrested on arrival in the country on 7 January after voluntarily returning from seven months' exile in Belgium. Ould Mansour, who escaped jail after a failed June 2003 coup, was returned to his original prison before being released on 20 January. (IRIN)

MEXICO

Supreme Court Chief Justice **Mariano Azuela Güitrón** told the Inter American Press Association Judicial Conference on Press Freedom on 15 January that he planned to introduce new guidelines to increase transparency in Mexican legal proceedings. The meeting was part of IAPA's 'Declaration of Chapultepec' programme, intended to help judges and journalists learn more about their respective responsibilities. (IAPA)

Eyewitnesses said that riot police killed two and injured 12 in a police raid to clear protestors in the southern town of Tlalnepantla on 14 January. The violence followed protests against changes to the method of electing a town mayor and a disputed election on 1 November. (Indymedia)

On 24 February, Chiapas State Governor Pablo Salazar affirmed his intention to approve Criminal Code reforms that include jail sentences for 'offences against an individual's honour' and said defamation would not be decriminalised or downgraded to a civil offence, as international rights standards require. Local journalists protested against the reforms in the state capital. (PFS)

MOLDOVA

The management of the opposition newspaper *Timpul* had its private bank accounts frozen pending a verdict on a 6 February libel action brought against the paper by car sales company DAAC Hermes SA. The firm has been linked to allegations that it overcharged the government for the supply of 42 Skoda cars for local government officials. DAAC Hermes SA is demanding US$500,000 in damages, plus an injunction preventing *Timpul* from publishing articles about the company in future without prior consent. (*Basapress*)

MOROCCO

Jailed journalist **Ali Lmrabet** (*Index* 3/03, 4/03, 1/04) was freed by a royal reprieve on 7 January after serving eight months of a four-year sentence for insulting the king and offences 'against territorial integrity'. His satirical news weeklies, *Demain* and *Doumane*, remain banned. He has since been recharged with publishing false information despite serving four months for the offence; the public prosecutor has appealed against the sentence as too lenient. (*El País*, RSF)

Lmrabet was among 33 people amnestied to mark the inauguration of a commission to investigate past rights abuses in Morocco. Other journalists released were **Mohammed el-Hourd** (*Index* 4/03), **Mustapha Alaoui** (*Index* 1/04), **Abdelmajid Ben Tahar**, **Mustapha Kechnini** (*Index* 4/03, 1/04), **Abdelaziz Jallouli** (*Index* 1/04) and **Miloud Boutriki**(*Index* 1/04). El-Hourd, editor of *Asharq* weekly, shared a prison wing with Lmrabet and joined him on hunger strike for 38 days. (*El País*, RSF)

NEPAL

On 2 January, **Maheswor Pahari**, a journalist associated with the weekly *Swabhivan* in Pokhara, was arrested. Three days later security forces personnel arrested **Rabindra Shah**, editor of the weekly *Biswo Jagaran* in Janakpur, Dhanusha district. Shah was released the next day. Amnesty International believes that Pahari is being held in the Phulbari barracks, near Pokhara. (CEHURDES, RSF, AI)

A hotline for journalists in distress was set up in December 2003 by the Federation of Nepalese Journalists, to support journalists arrested, harassed or threatened by security forces. OneWorld. net reported that the government had set up a committee to recommend ways to distinguish between professional journalists and political party workers acting as part-time reporters. (www.oneworld. net)

CEHURDES reported on 16 December that **Ram Krishna Adhikari**, a reporter for the weekly *Sanghu* and Times FM radio station, had been missing since 10

December 2003. Adhikari was last seen at a human rights event organised by the Human Rights Organisation of Nepal at the Hotel Orchid in Kathmandu. Adhikari, who has written a number of articles critical of the authorities, is allegedly being held by the security forces. (CEHURDES, RSF)

On 24 December 2003, **Chet Prakash Khatri**, an activist with the Campaign for Peace Programme launched by the Kathmandu-based Informal Sector Service Centre (INSEC), was killed on his way home by an unidentified group. According to INSEC, Khatri had been training students and local people in non-violent methods to remain safe during the conflict. (INSEC)

Padma Raj Devkota, editor-in-chief of the bimonthly *Bhurichula* and local correspondent for *Nepal Today* magazine and *Karnali Sandes*, was killed by the security forces in the western Jumla district on 7 February. The security forces claim that Devkota was killed along with six Maoist rebels. (CEHURDES, RSF)

In an open letter to Prime Minister Surya Bahadur Thapa and army human rights affairs chief Colonel Nilendra Aryal on 16 February, Amnesty International called for 'an immediate inquiry' into the reported extrajudicial killing of 14 suspected Maoist rebels and two civilians during a raid on a village in Bhimad, Makwanpur district, on 5 February. (AI)

On 5 March, the government banned strikes in key eco-

nomic sectors, including transport, tourism, telecommunications and public utilities, in a bid to stem a wave of strikes called by Maoists, opposition parties and students. (BBC)

Recent publications: *Amnesty International's visit to Nepal: Official Statement by Amnesty International*, 4 February 2004, 7pp; *Nepal: Dangerous Plans For Village Militias*, International Crisis Group, 17 February 2004, 7pp

NICARAGUA

Nicaraguan journalist **Carlos José Guadamuz** was killed by an assassin on 10 November 2003 as he arrived for work at Canal 23 TV, where he hosted an afternoon programme. The murderer was seized by studio staff and later identified as a security guard, William Hurtado García. Guadamuz was a former high-ranking member of the opposition FSLN and a former cellmate of FSLN leader Daniel Ortega, with whom he had a highly public falling-out in the late 1990s. His programmes frequently accused Ortega and the FSLN of corruption. (CPJ)

NIGER

A second hearing in the case of **Mamane Abou**, director of the independent weekly *le Républicain*, resulted in a four-month suspended jail sentence and a fine of 2 million CFA francs (US$3,750) for defaming former Finance Minister Ali Badjo Gamatie and Prime Minister Hama Amadou. The paper had accused ministers of using unauthorised Treasury funds to pay for government contracts. Shortly after the ruling he was released from prison, where he had been held for two months. Abou still awaits trial on a second charge of concealing official documents. (CPJ)

NIGERIA

Kayode Fasua (*Index* 1/04), editor of *Contact*, and Tunde Ajayi (*Index* 1/04), editor of *Class*, and Justice Ministry employees Michael Dada and Bola Fatile were charged on 23 November with possessing copies of *Ekiti Razor* newspaper. The paper has effectively been banned by Ekiti state Governor Ayo Fayose, who says it contains material intended to disparage his reputation. Police claimed the arrested men were planning to distribute the banned issue. (MISA)

Three senior editors from *Insider Weekly* were arrested following publication of a story alleging that top government officials were involved in illegal bunkering of crude oil. The three, Osa Director, Chuks Onwudinjo and Janet Mba-Afolabi (*Index* 1/04), were held for two days before being released on bail. (MISA)

Freelance Silvia Sansoni, who has worked for *The Economist* and *Forbes Magazine*, was expelled from Nigeria on charges of breaching immigration laws and 'abusing her accreditation'. The media rights group RSF linked the deportation to the state's growing frustration with Nigeria's consistently poor image in media and business circles abroad. (RSF)

NORWAY

On 2 January, Jon Lech Johansen was acquitted for a second time of charges of computer piracy. He had distributed a program on the Internet that could break the security codes used on DVDs. The court found that Johansen was entitled to access information on a DVD that he had purchased, and was therefore entitled to use his program to break the code. (BBC)

PAKISTAN

On 20 November 2003, military leader General Pervez Musharraf publicly threatened Amir Mir, senior assistant editor of the monthly magazine *Herald,* at a reception for newspaper editors. Musharraf condemned the *Herald* for working against the 'national interest' and allegedly said it was time for the *Herald* and Mir to be 'dealt with'. Two days later unidentified persons set fire to Mir's car and shots were fired outside his home in Lahore. Mir later received a message, purportedly from the Pakistani secret service (ISI), claiming responsibility and warning that it was 'just the beginning'. (HRW, *New York Times*)

On 3 December 2003, Human Rights Watch reported that Rasheed Azam, a journalist and political activist from Khuzdar in Baluchistan Province, had been tortured by the military after his arrest for sedition in August 2002. He had taken a picture of soldiers beating a crowd of Baluchi youths. Azam remains in jail after his bail application was rejected by a local judge. (HRW)

On 16 December 2003, Marc Epstein and Jean-Paul Guilloteau of the French news weekly *l'Express*, investigating Taliban activity on both sides of the Pakistani–Afghan border, were arrested in Karachi for illegally visiting the Quetta region in the south-western province of Baluchistan without permission. A few days later they were also charged with fabricating a news report to bring Pakistan into disrepute. Epstein and Guilloteau were allowed to leave the country in mid-January after apologising and paying a fine, but Khawar Mehdi Rizvi, a local journalist who assisted the two and had been arrested with them, was not produced before a court until 25 January. He was charged with 'sedition' and 'conspiracy' and later with fabricating a report on the activites of the Taliban in Pakistan. Rizvi is in poor physical condition and has reportedly been tortured while in custody. (RSF, BBC, IRIN)

On 29 January, Sajid Tanoli, a reporter for the Urdu-language daily *Shumaal*, was shot dead by Khalid Javed, mayor of Union Council City No 3, Mansehra, in the North-West Frontier Province. Javed was angered by a 26 January report by Tanoli in which he was accused of alcohol trafficking, which is illegal under Islamic law. (RSF, CPJ, *The News*, IFJ)

PALESTINIAN AUTHORITY

On 3 February, the offices of the Gaza daily *al-Daar* were ransacked and its computers damaged, by raiders who did not steal anything, prompting editor-in-chief **Hassan al-Kachef** to suggest that the break-in was 'more likely a warning to the newspaper' for tackling issues such as corruption within the Palestinian Authority. (RSF)

The Ramallah-based TV station al-Quds Educational TV was attacked on 2 February. Masked gunman beat staffers, shot at equipment and demanded tapes from assistant manager **Haroun Abu Arrah**. (CPJ)

On 8 January, al-Arabiya TV correspondent **Saifeddine Chahine**, working on a story about the Palestinian Fatah movement and Palestinian leader Yasser Arafat, was attacked by five hooded armed men on the way to his Gaza City office. (RSF)

PANAMA

New Supreme Court chief justice César Pereira Burgos raised concerns with his calls for stricter controls on the media's coverage of the judiciary. The comments followed media reports of Pereira Burgos's criticisms of Panamanian Comptroller General Alvin Weeden during the trial of former president Ernesto Pérez Balladares. (IAPA)

PARAGUAY

Former Paraguayan president Juan Carlos Wasmosy sued investigative journalists **Nacha Sanchez** and **Mabel Rehnfeld** of *ABC Color* newspaper in February. The two had published a series of reports on a fraud linked to the state-run Petropa oil company, implicating Wasmosy, who is now seeking

US$10 million in damages. (SPP)

PHILIPPINES

On 11 February, DZRC radio commentator **Rowell Endrinal** was gunned down in Legaspi in south-east Luzon on the way to his studios. He had previously received death threats from supporters of business and political interests for his reports on corruption.

Broadcaster **Nelson Nadura** was shot dead by gunmen on a motorcycle as he was leaving the studios of Radio DYME on the central island of Masbate on 2 December 2003. Nadura had just presented his morning programme on local and national politics. (RSF)

POLAND

A Warsaw court issued a gag order on *Poland Monthly* and *Rzeczpospolita* (*Index* 1/04) on 25 November 2003, preventing them from reporting a financial scandal involving the country's largest insurance company PZU. The original suit was brought by businessman Andrezei Perczynski, also linked to the alleged scandal. The International Federation of Journalists described the orders as 'intimidation' to prevent discussion of issues of public importance.

Editor **Andrzej Marek** of *Wiesci Polikie* weekly was ordered to start a three-month prison sentence on 6 February having been found guilty in November 2003 of libelling local official Piotr Mislo by accusing him of misusing public property in print. Marek refused to apologise in

return for a suspended sentence. (RSF)

RUSSIA

Journalist **Yelena Tregubova** described a 2 February bomb attack outside her apartment – just after she phoned a taxi firm to say she was stepping out – as a 'warning' to stay out of the March presidential election debate. Police refused to investigate until the press picked up the story. Tregubova is the author of *Tales of a Kremlin Digger*, her exposé of media manipulation by President Vladimir Putin and his press secretary Alexei Gromov. (*Ekho Moskvy*, BBC, RSF)

New rules on media access to the Russian parliament have significantly reduced journalists' ability to meet and quiz deputies, the daily *Kommersant* noted on 26 January. Access is limited to electronic pass holders, supposedly for security reasons. Even this is not enough for the Unified Russia Party bloc, which has barred its deputies from talking to the press without permission. (RFE/RL)

Moscow correspondent **Vibeke Sperling** of the Danish daily *Politiken* was refused accreditation and permission to work in Russia on 8 January. Based on comments by the Russian ambassador to Copenhagen, the ban was in response to her coverage of human rights violations in Chechnya. She appealed without success. (RSF)

On 29 December 2003, the FSB security police confiscated another 4,400 copies of the book *The FSB Blows Up Russia*, which alleges FSB complicity in the 1999 Moscow apartment bombings later blamed by the Kremlin on Chechen rebels. The chief editor at publishers Prima, **Aleksandr Litvinenko**, was called in by the FSB on 28 January but declined to answer questions. (CPJ, IFEX)

On 12 February, **Rebecca Santana**, a correspondent for the *Atlanta Journal-Constitution* and other US papers, was questioned by FSB agents in Mineralnye Vody and her material on a recent trip to Chechnya confiscated. The same day her fixer and driver **Ruslan Soltkhanov** was taken from his home in north Ossetia. The kidnappers later returned to search his house. Soltkhanov has not been seen since. (CPJ, IFEX)

On 16 February, **Zamid Ayubov**, a journalist with *Vozrozhdeniye Chechni* which backs the pro-Russian Chechen administration, was beaten and detained overnight without charge by Interior Ministry troops in Grozny. Ayubov had been researching an article about the troops' night patrols in the city. (CPJ, IFEX)

RWANDA

On 19 November 2003, editor **Robert Sebufirira** and five other staff from the weekly *Umuseso* (*Index* 2/03) were detained and the paper impounded on its way from Uganda, where it is printed. All were quizzed on articles about the use of state funds to retrain ex-army officers. All were released without charge after two days. (CPJ)

Recent publication: *Burundi: A critical time. Human rights*

briefing on Burundi, AI, January 2004, 25pp

SAUDI ARABIA

Saudi security police officers arrested seven prominent liberal reformers on 16 March, including journalist **Faris Bin Hozam al-Harbi**, who also had his passport confiscated. His past work for *al-Watan* and *al-Sharq al-Awsat* on police and other official corruption led to his detention in April 2002 and constant surveillance on release. He has reportedly been banned from practising journalism by the government. (APFW)

Investigators from the Authority for the Promotion of Virtue and Prevention of Vice arrested 50 people on 1 March and accused them of attending a gay wedding in the city of Medina. The groom, from Chad, had in fact been rehearsing his wedding ceremony before the big event a week later, with a male friend standing in for the bride. His Saudi sponsor cleared up the misunderstanding. (*Arab News*)

A tourist promotion website launched on 27 February specifies that visas will be denied to 'those who don't abide by the Saudi traditions concerning appearance and behaviours', 'those under the influence of alcohol' and 'Jewish people'. (BBC)

Saudi Arabia's religious authorities ordered Muslims in Saudi Arabia to shun Valentine's Day as 'a pagan Christian holiday', explaining that 'Muslims who believe in God and judgement day should not celebrate or acknowledge it'. (*Guardian*)

Saudi Arabia launched a new Arabic-language TV news service on 11 January with a brief to present a less rigid image to the world. Al-Ikhbariya will eventually broadcast 24 hours a day and features the Kingdom's first female news presenter, who reads the news in a black headscarf and Western-style clothes. (BBC)

SERBIA & MONTENEGRO

Hrvatske Rijeci, a magazine for the Croatian minority in the Serbian region of Vojvodina, received anti-Croatian calls and death threats on 13 and 14 January. The threats against the Subotica-based paper have been linked to renewed intimidation of Croats in the region. (SEEMO)

Dominic Hipkins, a journalist with the London *Sunday Mirror*, is wanted by police in Montenegro on charges of 'harming the image of the country'. Four Montenegrins, **Jovo Martinovic**, **Sinisa Nadazdin**, **Dragan Radevic** and **Nenad Zevenic**, who helped him write his article about the smuggling of children for sexual purposes, now face up to three years in jail. Hipkins said he posed as a man seeking to buy children in the city of Podgorica; the police say he fabricated the story and paid local women to make up their accounts. (RSF)

An eyewitness to the assassination of Serbian Prime Minister Zoran Djindjic was shot dead in Belgrade on 1 March. **Kujo Kljestorac** was said to have seen the killers run from the building, and was soon to testify at the trial of the suspected assassins. (Radio B92)

Recent publication: *The Non-Constituents: Rights Deprivation of Roma in Post-Genocide Bosnia and Herzegovina*, European Roma Rights Centre, February 2004, 221pp

SIERRA LEONE

Police raided the offices of independent daily *Awoko* after its staff tried to cover a crash involving a police car. Journalists **Austin Thomas**, **Sylvester Sualley** and **Junior John** were manhandled and some equipment was destroyed. Police returned and threatened to arrest the paper's management after details of the whole incident were published in *Awoko* the next day. (RSF)

SINGAPORE

Singapore is preparing to lift partially its famous ban on chewing gum, in order to comply with a free trade agreement with the US. But only gum aimed at helping smokers to quit will be allowed. Singapore banned chewing gum in 1992 because of a litter problem. (BBC)

SOMALIA

Abshir Ali Gabre, a radio news editor in the south-east town of Jawhar, was seized by local warlord Mohamed Omar Habeeb and held for 14 hours on 24 February after he alleged that Habeeb, also known as Mohamed Dere, had privately signed a January accord between warring Somali factions while publicly opposing it. (CPJ)

Journalists **Ali Bashi Mohammed Haji** of Radio Banadir and **Mohammed Sadak Abdi Guunbe** of Radio Shabelle were arrested in the north-eastern city of Garowe on 21 January and quizzed on their reports to Mogadishu, including coverage of a border dispute between the self-declared autonomous region of Puntland and the self-declared republic of Somaliland. (CPJ)

SOUTH AFRICA

Lawyers for PCUIC, a South African insurance underwriters' body, failed in a bid to win advance sight of newspaper stories critical of their members on 13 November 2003. Judge Essop Patel ruled that such previews would be an unnecessary burden on the press. The case followed an effort to block publication of a *Mail & Guardian* story on 27 October that alleged that US$155,800 had been transferred to a regional public works minister's bank account just days after the ministry paid up on a US$1.02 million contract to PCUIC for insurance services. (MISA)

The ruling did not stop South African 7-Eleven store chain boss George Hadjidakis from trying to use freedom of information laws to force the *Cape Argus* newspaper to release advance details of an article investigating complaints of improper business practices in his stores. Armed with a draft copy, Hadjidakis then won a gagging order in December 2003 that banned publication until the court process was completed. (MISA, *Independent*)

On 5 December 2003, a judicial inquiry into allegations that the country's director of public prosecutions, Bulelani Ngcuka, had been an informer for the apartheid-era security services gave up plans to call former *Sunday Times* newspaper journalist **Ranjeni Munusamy** and other journalists to testify. Munusamy had warned that she would not give evidence, to protect her sources. But investigating justice Joos Hefer said the testimony of Munusamy, who first broke the allegation, would be of 'peripheral value'. (MISA, SABC)

SOUTH KOREA

South Korea banned candlelight protests that drew tens of thousands of people to the streets of Seoul for two nights after the impeachment of President Roh Moo-Hyun in March. Interim leader Goh Kun pledged to guarantee security and oversee the run-up to crucial 15 April general elections. 'Any moves or rallies that cause social disorder will be strictly dealt with in accordance with laws and principle,' a government statement said. (Brunei Online)

The government announced new guidelines requiring mobile phone companies to respect customer privacy rights by deleting bank account data, email addresses, landline phone numbers, job information and birthdays when subscribers change carriers. **Han Jae-Jak** of the People's Solidarity for Participatory Democracy called it a promising development, but wondered whether phone firms would simply transfer copied data to sister companies before deleting it. (GILC)

SRI LANKA

Journalists in the Jaffna Peninsula boycotted a 5 January visit by two senior Buddhist monks as a protest, after an unidentified army officer threatened local correspondent **Veluppillai Thavachelvam**, president of the Jaffna Journalists' Association. (TamilNet, Free Media Movement)

President Chandrika Kumaratunga announced on 13 January that since she had called the last presidential election a year early, by her calculation she was entitled to stay an extra year in power. The next presidential election was scheduled for December 2005. She said she had arranged for this back in 2000, by holding a secret re-investiture ceremony to mark the end of the last year of her first six years as president and the start of the first of the next six, attended only by the chief justice and the then foreign minister. (AFP, BBC)

Christian groups reported an increase in sectarian attacks on churches in the strongly nationalist and fundamentalist Buddhist south of the island. The Evangelical Alliance of Sri Lanka reported in January that some 136 Christian places of worship had been attacked in the preceding year, 56 between Christmas Eve 2003 and 31 January 2004 alone. Nationalists and extremist monks accuse the churches of seeking conversions from the Buddhist majority. On 22 January, the Free Media Movement expressed concern for the

safety of *Lankadeepa* columnist **Upul Joseph Fernando**, a Christian, who has been accused of writing defamatory pamphlets against Buddhists. On 8 February, the Anuradhapura office of the Christian evangelist humanitarian agency World Vision was firebombed. Three Buddhist monks were among the suspects later arrested. (Sri Lanka Project Briefing, Frontline, TamilNet, *Sunday Observer*)

On 16 February, newly appointed Media Minister Lakshman Kadirgamar, a key presidential adviser, cancelled the private ABC radio network's broadcast licence just days before it was about to launch a new TV station. Reporters Sans Frontières said it feared the decision could herald tough measures against the private media, which had tended to back Kumaratunga's United National Party opponents during the December 2001 elections. (*Daily Mirror*, RSF)

With this in mind, the Rule of Law Centre and the international NGO Transparency International wrote to elections commissioner Dayananda Dissanayake, asking him to use his powers under the 17th amendment of the constitution to ensure that state electronic media are not misused for political advantage during the election campaign. (*Daily Mirror*, Free Media Movement, *Sunday Times*)

On 23 February, the Jaffna Library, a cultural icon for the country's Tamil minority community, quietly reopened to students only, more than two decades after it was gutted during anti-Tamil riots in

1981. The library, rebuilt with state funds, had been set to open in a public ceremony last year but pressure by the LTTE forced local authorities to postpone it. (Reuters)

On the official start of the parliamentary election campaign on 26 February, police called on the army to help stem poll-related violence. Thirty-three incidents, including death threats, assault and damage to property, were reported in the 24 hours that followed, the highest daily total of incidents up to that point. Fifteen people were injured and 12 arrested. (AP)

Recent publications: *Inside an Elusive Mind: Prabhakaran* by MR Narayan Swamy, Vijitha Yapa Publications, September 2003, 290pp; *Rituals of Words Without Substance*, Information Bulletin No 33, University Teachers for Human Rights (Jaffna), 14 December 2003; *Anti-Conversion Law Should not be Pursued*, Civil Rights Movement of Sri Lanka, 25 January 2004, 2pp

SUDAN

State prosecutor Mohammad Farid Hassan banned the Arabic daily *al-Ayam* between 16 and 22 November and again on 3 December 2003, charging it with threatening security and stability. On 18 November, editor-in-chief **Mahjoub Mohamed Salih** was jailed for failure to pay an alleged 90 million Sudanese pounds (US$30,000) in unpaid taxes. He was released on 15 January on bail raised by 'friends of the newspaper' who also promised to settle the newspaper's tax arrears. *Al-Ayam* remains suspended. (RSF)

IMPARTIALITY THREATENS FREE SPEECH

A sample survey carried out by independent media experts in relation to the present election shows that there has been no improvement since the [Sri Lankan] General Elections of 2000 when a survey carried out by us exposed the extent to which the state media was manipulated by those in power at the time. The present coverage of the election campaign continues to be totally biased in favour of the party controlling the state media. In this context we have followed the debates regarding the role of the state-owned and state-controlled media in the ongoing election campaign with growing concern. In spite of Mass Communications Minister [Lakshman] Kadirgamer's public declaration that 'The private media belongs to its owners, who may use it as the please. The state media belongs to the people. It cannot be used by the government of the day as it pleases,' all our observations of the media in the election campaign lead us to believe that this is not so.

We in particular note a recent Special Report prepared by the Presidential Task Force appointed to investigate and report on 'Media Practice during the General Election campaign', as published in the *Daily News* of 4 March 2004, which has come up with some statements that conflict with the Minister's declaration.

The Task Force comprising Lucien Rajakarunanayake, Prof Somaratne Balasooriya Sunil Sarath Perera, Prof Tissa Kariyawasam and Dr Ariyarathna Ethugala, states that 'it is a practical impossibility for the State media to represent all sections of the polity'.

We feel that this statement constitutes a derogation of primary responsibility assigned to the state to ensure that principles of equality and equal access of all citizens are respected, especially during an election period. We also refute the argument put forward by the Task Force that any requirement for the State media to remain impartial during the election period would be infringement of its freedom of expression.

We urge the Commissioner of Elections to appoint a team of responsible persons to monitor the implementation of these Guidelines by the electronic media. We also call on him to appoint a Competent Authority to oversee the actions of the state radio and television stations during the forthcoming elections under the power vested in him by the 17th Amendment which addresses the issue of unfair and biased reporting of state-owned electronic media.

Kingsley Rodrigo – People's Action for Free and Fair Elections
P Saravanamuttu – Centre for Monitoring Election Violence
Wimal Fernando – Movement for Free and Fair Elections
JC Weliamuna – Transparency International, Sri Lanka
Programme for Protection of Public Resources
Sunila Abeysekera – INFORM
Sunanda Deshapriya – Free Media Movement. ❑

Recent publication: *Sudan: Towards an Incomplete Peace*, International Crisis Group, December 2003, 37pp

SWEDEN

On 16 January, the Israeli ambassador to Sweden, Zvi Mazel, damaged **Dror Feiler**'s art installation in Stockholm depicting a Palestinian suicide bomber. Mazel disconnected the cables of a mounted spotlight, causing it to crash into the work. He attacked the exhibit as 'obscene' and a 'monstrosity'. Ariel Sharon has praised his stand 'against the growing wave of anti-Semitism'. (CNN)

SYRIA

Syrian Human Rights Association chairman **Haissam Maleh** was prevented from leaving the country and his passport confiscated on 11 February as he tried to board a plane in Damascus. He had spoken out against rights abuses in Syria in the German parliament in December and added his name to a 1,500-name petition calling for reform. (BBC)

TAJIKISTAN

On 4 January, Tajik Prosecutor General Bobozhon Bobokhonov warned independent weekly *Ruz-i Nav* to cease 'groundless criticism of authorities' and insulting President Imomali Rakhmonov, or face closure. The paper, which has grown in popularity since its founding in August, was on occasion prevented from publishing by its state-owned publishers last year without explanation. (RFE/RL)

Tax officials banned sale of the 31 December 2003 issue of the weekly *Nerui Sukhan* after the printer's name and details were removed from the paper's credits at its request following alleged threats from the authorities unless they ceased publishing the popular weekly, founded in February 2003. (RFE/RL)

Tajik media watchdog NANSMIT said on 7 January that it had tracked some 100 possible media rights violations in 2003, ranging from denial of access to information to direct intimidation, indicating that the number of such cases had increased compared with the beginning of 2002. (IRIN, RFE/RL)

The Tajik Prosecutor General's Office is to open a special investigation into the deaths of journalists during the 1992–7 Tajik civil war, it was announced on 7 January. Some 73 journalists, both Tajik and foreign, are believed to have died during the conflict. (RFE/RL, CPJ)

THAILAND

Bangkok Post editor **Veera Pratheepchaikul** was moved to another job in the company that publishes the paper on 20 February. The management committee suggested that he had failed to implement the paper's business plans. However, other media cited the view of anonymous *Post* sources that the dismissal was linked to Prime Minister Thaksin Shinawatra's preparations for forthcoming elections, to muzzle press criticisms of his government's handling of the bird flu outbreak and other issues. **Pichai**

Chuensuksawadi, former editor of the paper and now editor-in-chief of Post Publishing, told the Foreign Correspondents Club of Thailand that although the daily was subjected to government pressure in the past, the heat was greater now. The paper's union members have also issued a statement defending editorial independence. (APMN, *Straits Times*, TJA)

On 21 January, a court in northern Thailand acquitted four soldiers who had been charged with the attempted murder of newspaper publisher **Amnat Khunyosying**. Despite Khunyosying's testimony, the court found that there was insufficient evidence to convict the soldiers. The publisher, who nearly died of wounds inflicted on 18 April 2000, has been subjected to frequent death threats since bringing charges against the soldiers three years ago. (CPJ/IFEX)

TONGA

On 5 December 2003, King Taufaahau Tupou IV signed constitutional amendments and retrospectively validated press laws to circumvent a Supreme Court ruling in May 2003 that had found the original media law's restraints unconstitutional. This will allow the government to keep the ban (*Index* 3/03) on the independent weekly *Taimi'o Tonga*, which is produced in New Zealand. On 18 February, pro-democracy activist **Alani Taione** was arrested after distributing 20 copies of *Taimi'o Tonga* in the airport upon arrival from New Zealand. (RSF)

Ibrahim Hamidi, *head of the Syrian desk of the London Arabic-language daily* al-Haya *recently published a* Lexicon of the Official Syrian Media, *in which top Syrian media officials and journalists explained the obligatory terminology used by the Syrian state press.*

Editor-in-chief of the [Syrian government] daily *Teshreen*, Khalaf al-Jarrad: 'In previous decades, the use of the name "Israel" in the political discourse was considered treason, and the terms "the Zionist entity", "the Zionist gangs" or "the Zionist enemy" were used instead. When the Madrid conference was convened in 1991, terms became more realistic. The official media used the slogan "a just and comprehensive peace", omitting the word "lasting".'

But today the media picture is different. Director of the Syrian [Arab] News Agency, Ghazi Deeb: 'How can we prepare our people for something that is not acceptable at all, because the rulers of Israel are not interested in peace at all?'

. . . The concept 'peace of the brave', [notes Hamidi] which arose [in the Syrian media] in the early 1990s, faded away because it was adopted by Yasser Arafat after signing the Oslo accords – which in the eyes of the Syrians included 'far-reaching concessions'. The official Syrian media called it 'a settlement', not a 'peace accord'. After the rise of Ariel Sharon to the premiership, [the term] 'state terrorism' [came into use]. The word 'Mr' was not appended to Sharon's name or to the names of his ministers. The Israeli 'defence minister' was called the 'war minister', and Israel was called 'the enemy' because it still occupies the Syrian Golan.

In the past decade, the word 'negotiations' has replaced the word 'conflict' and the word 'peace' has replaced the word 'war' . . . The term 'resistance' has replaced the term 'armed struggle'. 'The Islamic Resistance Movement' is presented as 'the Hamas movement' or as 'the national resistance', without the word 'Islamic', and the same goes for the 'Islamic Jihad', because, according to Ghazi Deeb, the 'struggle is between all Arabs and Israel'.

Editor-in-chief of the ruling Baath Party daily *al-Ba'ath*, Mahdi Dakhlallah: 'We use the word "Israel" in the framework of negotiations under international auspices, but we say "the Zionist entity" and "state terrorism" when we speak of Israel's actions.'

The computers in the editorial department of the *Teshreen* daily are programme to put 'Israel' in quotation marks automatically. Editor al-Jarrad: 'I see Israel as a plundering entity existing on the land of the Palestinian people. I do not agree to the free use [of words] that include any normalisation or cooperation with Israel.'

Translated by the Middle East Media Research Institute (MEMRI). Full transcript at www.memri.org

TUNISIA

On 10 December 2003, Tunisian human rights lawyer **Radhia Nasraoui** (*Index* 4/02, 1/04) ended a hunger strike begun on 15 October to protest against alleged harassment by the authorities. She said that doctors and friends had urged her to stop her fast on the 55th anniversary of the Universal Declaration of Human Rights. (RSF)

Editor and journalist **Sihem Bensedrine**'s attempt to register the weekly newspaper *Kalima* (*Index* 2/00) was disallowed on 13 January for a third time. A version of the newspaper is published and unofficially distributed at home but its foreign-hosted website continues to be blocked within Tunisia. On 14 January, a copy of *Kalima* and three CD files of personal data were taken from Bensedrine at Tunis airport. Nine days earlier, she had been attacked outside the Tunisian National Council for Civil Liberties (CNLT) by an unidentified youth. (RSF, IFJ)

Imprisoned journalist **Abdallah Zouari** (*Index* 4/02, 4/03), who began a hunger strike on 27 January in protest at jail conditions, was reported in March to be still fasting and seriously ill. Zouari, of the banned Islamist weekly *al-Fajr*, was jailed in October 2003 for 13 months for defamation and failing to obey administrative orders. (RSF, IFJ)

TURKEY

Paris-based Kurdish satellite **Medya TV** was closed down after five years by an 11 February court order citing its links with the Kurdish mili-

tant PKK group. The court ruled that the channel posed 'risks to public order' and could not obtain a broadcast licence required under a 2001 law, Medya TV chief executive Musa Kaval told AFP. A new channel, Roj TV, was scheduled to have begun broadcasting at the beginning of March. Medya TV directors (*Index* 2/97, 5/97, 2/98, 6/98) alleged that the closure had been organised as part of French–Turkish deals ahead of a state visit to Turkey by French president, Jacques Chirac. (AFP, www.amude.com, www.kurdishmedia.com)

Another bid to free Turkey's four most prominent political prisoners was rejected at the opening of their retrial on 16 January. Kurdish MPs **Leyla Zana** (*Index* 1/97 passim), **Hatip Dicle**, **Orhan Dogan** and **Selim Sadak** were sentenced in 1994 to 15 years in jail for collaboration with the PKK. In 2001, the European Court of Human Rights ruled that their trial had been unfair. Zana was awarded the European Parliament's Sakharov Freedom of Thought Award in 1995. The four are due, in theory, to be released in June 2005 under sentence-reduction provisions in Turkish law. (AFP, www.kurdishmedia.com)

Two local leaders of the People's Democratic Party (DEHAP) were charged and detained on 5 January by the Diyarbakir State Security Court for calling PKK chief Abdullah Ocalan 'Mr' Ocalan in public comments. **Edim Bicer** and **Sadiye Surer** were charged under laws prohibiting 'terrorist propaganda'. (*Cildekt*)

Singer **Ibrahim Tatlises**, who is famous across Turkey and the Middle East, came under fire after singing a song in Kurdish on Turkish TV in December 2003 and publicly welcoming liberalisation of the country's restrictions on Kurdish broadcasts. The ultranationalist Great Unity Party (BBP) asked the singer, who is of Kurdish origin but had never before sung publicly in his own language, to 'apologise to the Turkish nation'. (*Cildekt*)

The embattled *Yeniden Özgür Gündem* newspaper finally ceased publication on 29 February. The paper had been hit by 315 different charges since 2 September 2002. Editor-in-chief **Mehmet Çolak** (*Index* 3/03) was sentenced to 25 months' imprisonment and along with owner **Ali Çelik Kasûmogullarû** (*Index* 3/03) fined 478 billion lire (US$365,000). The court also closed the newspaper for 293 days and fined it another 500 billion lire. On 1 March, the paper was succeeded by a new publication, *Ülkede Özgür Gündem*. (*Özgür Gündem*, TIHV)

Journalist **Ruhat Mengi** faces jail for an article in the daily *Vatan* criticising plans to reduce sentences for rape under proposed Turkish penal code reforms. Mengi wrote that supporters of the plan 'had a sick mentality'. The two MPs who drafted the proposal sued Mengi for damages. Some 44 representatives from women's organisations and lawyers joined Mengi at the first hearing. (BIA)

Culture and Tourism Ministry officials said they would set up a special committee to vet **Mel Gibson**'s film *The Passion of The Christ* before it opens in Turkey on 9 April. Cinema and Copyright General Manager Abdurrahman Celik said they may make further cuts in the distributed version. 'I do not think that there will be so many scenes censored,' said Celik, 'but the council members will examine it very closely.' (*Zaman Daily News*)

TURKMENISTAN

On 24 November, a mosque outside Ashqabat was closed by authorities after the imam refused to display beside the Koran a copy of President Saparmurat Niyazov's testament, *Rukhnama*, a 'spiritual guide' which mixes autobiography, nationalism and folklore. Sunni Islam is, along with the Russian Orthodox Church, allowed to hold services in Turkmenistan, but individual Sunni clerics and congregations have suffered state harassment. (RFE/RL)

On 26 November, Reporters Sans Frontières again protested about the harassment of **Saparmunat Ovezberdiev**, Radio Free Europe's Ashgabat correspondent, who was followed, beaten, drugged and illegally detained on various occasions during 2003. His reports on rights violations have drawn opposition from the security services. RSF commented on 6 January that 'in Turkmenistan, the most repressive country of the former Soviet Union, censorship is total and the media's only job is to sing the praises of President Niyazov'. (RSF, CJES)

Writer **Rakhim Esenov** was detained on 23 February after he privately imported 800 copies of his banned historical novel, *Iventsenosny Skitalets* (*The Crowned Wanderer*), set during the period of the Mogul Empire. Esenov has reportedly suffered a stroke since he was detained and there are fears he may be at risk of torture. In February 1997, President Niyazov publicly denounced the author for making 'historical errors', but Esenov refused to make the 'corrections' Niyazov demanded. (IPEN)

UGANDA

Four more radio stations – Kampala African Radio, Mama FM, Kampala FM and Top Radio – were shut down by the authorities on 8 January after failing to pay deliberately exorbitant fees (about US$1,500) for operating permits, designed, say RSF, to silence private media. (RSF)

On 11 February, the Ugandan Supreme Court ruled that a law criminalising the 'publication of false news' was unconstitutional and incompatible with the right to freedom of expression. Justice Joseph Mulenga said the law was rooted in colonial-era law and was only awaiting reform by parliament. (A19)

UKRAINE

On 14 December 2003, **Volodymyr Karachevtsev**, chairman of the Independent Union of Journalists in Zaporizhzhya region, southern Ukraine, was found hanged in his apartment in Melitopol. Editor **Igor Yenin** said that Karachevtsev had received repeated death threats for his investigations into local corruption. Police

have not ruled out murder. (IPI, *The Times*, RSF)

The country's leading opposition newspaper, *Silski Visti*, was closed on 28 January after being found guilty of inciting ethnic hatred by carrying a paid-for advertisement for an anti-Semitic book by a lecturer at a Kiev business school. The ban followed a writ from a local Jewish anti-fascist group but it has been condemned for silencing a leading independent critic of the state. Opponents of the ban included Ukrainian Jewish MP **Yevhen Chervonenko**, who called the ban 'planned provocation' by the state. He added that the paper should apologise, but not be closed. (RFE/RL, BBC, UNIAN)

Ukraine passed a law on 5 February exempting Ukrainian-language publications from the present 20% sales tax on print media. An open letter criticising the law for discriminating against the two-thirds of publications published in Russian in Ukraine was signed on behalf of 146 newspapers and magazines. (BBC)

The problems of Radio Free Europe/Radio Liberty continued in Ukraine. Privately owned Radio Dovire ceased relaying RFE/RL broadcasts on 16 February, apparently under presidential pressure. It marked the effective end of RFE/RL's FM broadcasts in Ukraine and its all-important independent news bulletins. Another RFE/RL affiliate broadcaster was shut down on 3 March for alleged licence infractions. Its owner, **Sehiy Sholokh**, fled the country, claiming that Presidential

Chief of Staff Viktor Medvedchuk and others had threatened him. The same day, **Yuriy Chechyk**, director of Radio Yuta in Poltava, was killed in a car crash on the way to discuss a possible rebroadcast deal with Radio Liberty's Ukrainian service. Radio Liberty can still be heard in Ukraine on short-wave radio, beamed from Prague. (IFJ, IFEX)

On 6 February, Prosecutor General Vasiliev Gennady refused a request from Ukrainian and international media rights groups to oversee a new examination of the 'Melnichenko tapes' alleged to link President Leonid Kuchma and his staff to the November 2000 murder of journalist **Georgiy Gongadze** (*Index* 3/03, 1/04). (RSF)

Recent publication: *The Press and Power: White Book About Oppression of Mass Media and Journalists in Ukraine*, Trade Union of Journalists of Ukraine, December 2003, 175pp

UNITED KINGDOM

Lawyers representing the British government have abandoned the prosecution of former GCHQ employee **Katharine Gun**, who disclosed information about US intentions to spy on delegations at the UN. The prosecution team at the Central Criminal Court admitted there was no 'realistic prospect' of convicting Gun, who defended her decision to reveal covert US operations on the grounds that she was trying to prevent an illegal invasion of Iraq. (*Guardian*)

Lord Hutton published the report of his judicial inquiry into the death of Dr **David Kelly**, one of the Ministry of Defence's most respected experts on Iraq's chemical and biological weapons, who apparently committed suicide after becoming embroiled in a row between the government and the BBC over an allegedly 'sexed up' weapons dossier used to justify British involvement in the war on Iraq. It cleared Prime Minister Tony Blair and his administration of wrongdoing in connection with the death and criticised 'defective' BBC editorial controls. It also provoked criticism for unfairly singling out the BBC for censure. **Gavyn Davies**, chairman of the BBC's board of governors, resigned hours after Hutton's decision; Director-General **Greg Dyke** followed shortly after. The BBC governors appeared to bow to pressure from Blair's office, issuing an apology after an emergency meeting to discuss the findings of the Hutton inquiry. Lord Ryder, acting chairman of the BBC board of governors, said the network had to confront 'serious defects in the corporation's processes and procedures'. One BBC local radio station, BBC Somerset Sound, went off air for a minute in protest at the resignations and what staff called the 'abject' apology. Former BBC chairman Sir Christopher Bland told BBC radio that the judge had 'white-washed the government . . . but he tarred and feathered the BBC . . . It is legitimate to question whether Hutton was even-handed in the way he treated on the one hand politicians, civil servants and the security services, and

on the other hand the standards of conduct he applied to journalists and broadcasters.' (BBC, AP, *Scotsman*)

The BBC reversed a decision to shelve the satirical radio show *Absolute Power*, starring **Stephen Fry** and **John Bird** as spin doctors, deciding instead to tone down references to the Hutton Report. The BBC had originally said it felt the show was unworthy of broadcast in the current climate. Writer **Mark Tavener** accused his BBC bosses of 'editorial cowardice' and told newspapers the corporation had cut the show over fears it would 'upset Number 10'. (*Guardian*)

The International Federation of Journalists has called for the British government to tone down its attacks on the BBC following the publication of the Hutton Report. IFJ General Secretary **Aidan White** said: 'The BBC has made mistakes, but there is a danger of these attacks sparking a witch-hunt against public service broadcasting at a time when private media are clamouring for deregulation and the break-up of public media institutions.' (IFJ)

Top civil servants altered an official report to disguise the extent to which the Hutton inquiry may have encouraged open government, it was reported on 22 December 2003. The report initially highlighted the importance of Lord Hutton's unprecedented release of confidential documents during his inquiry. The report, *Freedom of Information*, included a foreword from Lord Falconer, secretary of state for constitutional affairs, saying his aim was to build trust and 'make the process of government more transparent and accountable at every level'. (*Guardian*)

The government published the Civil Contingencies Bill after being forced by Parliament to tone down some of its stricter terms. But draft powers to prevent 'assemblies' (protests), travel and 'other specified activities' remain unchanged. The rights advocacy group Statewatch described the bill as 'Britain's Patriot Act . . . at a stroke democracy could be replaced by totalitarianism'. (Statewatch)

Music and media corporation EMI issued a 'cease and desist order' to **Danger Mouse**, aka **Brian Burton**, a Los Angeles DJ who had produced a music collection he called *The Grey Album*. The collection mixed tracks from rap singer Jay-Z's work, *The Black Album*, over melodies and rhythms from the Beatles' record commonly known as *The White Album*. Burton did not seek permission from EMI, which owns the publishing rights to *The White Album*. As a result of the publicity surrounding the case, the small-scale art project, which planned only 3,000 CD pressings, became a global success, with more than 100,000 downloads of the work in the US alone on 24 February, when 300 websites staged a 24-hour protest over what they called EMI's censorship. (*Guardian*)

Photographs by American artist **Betsy Schneider** of her naked daughter were removed from a London gallery after complaints that they were pornographic and could encourage paedophiles. Police visited the Spitz Gallery on 7 March. The exhibition, which showed 63 separate images of the girl as a baby, a toddler and a five-year-old, was later closed and taken down. (*Independent*).

Anti-smoking campaigners, backed by Britain's largest cancer charity, claim that the age classification of films should be as sensitive to smoking as to offensive language and obscenities. 'We are not arguing for a total ban on smoking in films,' said Deborah Arnott, director of the charity Ash. 'But there is strong evidence of a causal link between stars' smoking behaviour and teenage smoking.' Nearly 80% of Hollywood films given a 12 rating feature some form of tobacco use while half of all children's and PG-rated films depict smoking, according to a survey of 775 Hollywood films. (*Guardian*)

Figures detailing the number of telephone tapping and mail interception warrants issued in England and Wales between 1937 and 2002 revealed a dramatic increase since the early 1990s, in spite of the end of the Cold War and the easing of the conflict in Northern Ireland. No figures have ever been released for Northern Ireland. (Statewatch)

Liz Longhurst, mother of a teacher murdered by musician Graham Coutts in March 2003, has launched a campaign to ban Internet sites promoting violent pornography. Coutts was reported to have accessed websites featuring images of necrophilia and dead women before strangling Jane Longhurst. Mrs Longhurst said: 'Just because it may be difficult to block or shut down these extreme pornographic sites is no reason for not trying.' (*Telegraph*)

UNITED STATES

On 22 January, President George W Bush called on Congress to renew USA Patriot Act provisions set to expire in 2005. The 2001 legislation greatly enhanced government surveillance powers. Several conservative Republicans have joined liberal Democrats in opposing the level of intrusion permitted by the law. (AP)

A 2002 Pennsylvanian statute that requires Internet Service Providers (ISPs) to block access to websites and other online areas that local authorities deem to contain child pornography went to the courts in April. ISPs that fail to comply with the law could face fines of up to US$300,000 and seven years in prison. Free-expression groups say orders to block 423 websites around the world from access via Pennsylvania-based ISPs have also struck off a million other sites unconnected to pornography. They cited freedom of information laws in a bid to discover which sites were supposed to be banned, but were told by the state that releasing the list would constitute illegal promotion of child pornography. In a separate court hearing, the Pennsylvanian authorities also sought to prove that First Amendment free-speech rights did not apply, as a website address was 'neither a person, nor a real forum, nor a limited commodity'. (*Wired*, GILC)

Visa requirements for Western European travellers to the United States are normally waived by agreement; but technically this does not apply to journalists visiting the US to work on articles. After the 11 September attacks the rule was again enforced, to the shock of European journalists who were not told of the change or indeed that the rule had ever existed. Austrian journalist **Peter Krobath** was detained at Los Angeles airport, questioned for five hours and jailed overnight with convicted criminals before being forced to leave the country. He had been invited by DreamWorks Pictures to join a press event to promote a new Steven Spielberg film. Under the rules, Europeans visiting the US must apply for a visa if they have 'a criminal record or suffer from a serious transmittable disease or mental disorder; are a drug addict, drug trafficker, or were involved in Nazi persecutions', if they 'were or still are a member of a subversive or terrorist organization' or 'are a professional journalist planning to cover news or informational stories'. (IPI)

Officers at a juvenile detention centre on Rikers' Island, New York, were ordered to cut out an article about a fatal jail beating at the centre from inmates' newspapers. The story detailed the beating of Matthew Velez on New Year's Eve 2000 and described jail staff procedural failings that may have contributed to the youth's death. The officials did not notify the Board of Correction within 24 hours, as required. (Newsday)

ABC TV added a five-second time delay to their coverage of the Oscars ceremony on 29 February, to pre-empt any 'Janet Jackson scenarios'. The singer exposed a breast during her live TV performance at the 2004 Super Bowl US football final. The networks are cautious of plans by Federal Communication Commission regulators to increase fines for such infractions from US$27,500 to US$275,000. Frank Pierson, president of the Academy of Motion Picture Arts and Sciences, warned Academy members that the policy could be a slippery slope to 'a form of censorship'. (*Hollywood Reporter*)

More than 60 top US scientists, including 20 Nobel laureates and several science advisers to past Republican presidents, handed the White House a 46-page report accusing the administration of 'suppressing, distorting or manipulating the work done by scientists at federal agencies'. White House Science Adviser John Marburger III said the charges were 'like a conspiracy theory report'. But he added that 'given the prestige of some of the individuals who have signed on to this, I think they deserve additional response'. (AP)

On 27 January, it was reported that cartoonist **Ann Telnaes**, winner of the 2001 Pulitzer Prize for editorial cartoons, has received a series of threatening emails. The threats are linked to her cartoon depicting Iraqi Shia cleric Ayatollah Sayyid Ali Sistani, which appeared on *The Iranian: Satire, Cartoon* website. (CRN)

In January, the Recording Industry Association of America (RIAA) launched a fourth wave of lawsuits about online file-sharing activities. The association sued 532 Internet users who have supposedly engaged in copyright infringement by sharing music files online. Altogether, the RIAA has filed lawsuits against nearly 1,000 alleged file-sharers over the last 12 months. (GILC, RSF)

The US House of Representatives is considering a proposal to extend copyright-style restrictions to facts. The Database and Collections of Information Misappropriation Act would essentially bar people from knowingly making available 'a quantitatively substantial part of the information in a database' created or maintained by another person without that other person's permission. The proposal would apply to databases stored in digital form, including such information as Internet search engine results. (GILC)

In January and February, the Pentagon refused to allow three leading human rights groups – Amnesty International, Human Rights First and Human Rights Watch – to attend and observe military commission trials of detainees at Guantánamo Bay, despite the Bush administration's promise that the commissions would be open to the public. The Department of Defense made the refusal on the basis of 'limited courtroom seating and other logistical issues'. (HRW)

UZBEKISTAN

On 22 December 2003, jailed journalist and human rights activist **Ruslan Sharipov** (*Index* 3/03, 1/04) was excluded from a national presidential amnesty because his crime was said to be 'too serious'. Sharipov was sentenced to five and a half years in jail in August 2003 for homosexuality, and for sexual relations with a minor – a charge that media rights groups have dismissed as faked. (CJES, WAN, RFE/RL)

On 12 February, **Fatima Mukhadirova**, 63, who had led a public campaign for justice for her son **Muzafhar**, alleged to have been boiled alive by security service torturers, was sentenced to six years' hard labour for alleged membership of the banned Hizbut-Tahrir Party, propagating an Islamic state and undermining constitutional order. After an international outcry she was released on 24 February and fined US$280 instead. (IRIN, IHF, HRW, OSCE)

Recent publication: *Uzbekistan: Unfair trials and secret executions*, Amnesty International, November 2003, 14pp

VIETNAM

On 31 December, former journalist **Nguyen Vu Binh** was sentenced to seven years' imprisonment with three years of house arrest to follow after a three-hour hearing before a 'people's court' in Hanoi. He had been held in solitary confinement since September 2002. One month before his arrest, Binh criti-

cised a controversial border treaty with China in an article entitled 'Some Thoughts on the China–Vietnam Border Agreement', which was distributed on the Internet. He had also been in contact with the Human Rights Commission of the US Congress to criticise the human rights situation in Vietnam. Binh, who received the prestigious Hellman/Hammett Writers' Award in 2002, was a journalist at the official Communist Party of Vietnam journal, *Tap Chi Cong San,* for almost 10 years. In December 2000, he resigned from his post to attempt to form the independent Liberal Democratic Party. (HRW)

YEMEN

Armed men burst into the home of **Sadeq Nasher**, managing editor of the daily *al-Khaleej*, on 19 February, destroying his possessions and terrorising his children. They were told that their father's paper should stop its investigations into the murder in December 2003 of prominent Yemeni left-wing politician **Jarallah Omar al-Kuhali**, 'or he will come to the same end as him'. (APFW)

On 10 March, Journalist **Saeed Thabit Saeed** was charged with 'publishing false news damaging to national interests and security'. Saeed, a member of the board of the Yemeni Journalists' Syndicate, was detained for three days following a report on an alleged assassination attempt on the son of the Yemeni president. His trial continues. (APFW)

ZAMBIA

On 1 January, Zambian Information Ministry (MIBS) officials ordered commercial radio station Breeze FM to stop relaying BBC programmes. Managing director **Mike Daka** said MIBS official Juliana Mwila had said the station could carry foreign news only from the Zambia News Agency, the Southern African Broadcasting Association (SABA) and the Pan-African News Agency. (MISA/IFEX)

Photojournalist **Mackson Wasamunu** of the state-owned *Zambian Daily Mail* was beaten and detained by police as they cleared street vendors from Lusaka's city centre on 28 January. Lusaka police commander Chendela Musonda intervened to free the photojournalist and vowed to investigate the incident. (MISA)

The media and public were barred from attending hearings on 3 February of a tribunal investigating charges of misconduct made against the director of public prosecutions, Mukelebai Mukelebai, by President Levy Mwanawasa. Judge Esau Chulu ordered proceedings to be held in camera, despite Mukelebai's lawyer's request that they be held in public. (MISA)

British-born journalist **Roy Clarke**, a satirical columnist for the *Post* newspaper, pleaded not guilty on 16 February to charges of assaulting a police officer. The alleged assault occurred when Clarke tried to report the abduction of his daughter. Clarke still faces trial and possible deportation on charges of insulting President Levy Mwanawasa, who he compared to a 'foolish elephant' in one of his columns. (MISA)

ZIMBABWE

Harare police seized *Standard* photographer **Shadreck Pongo** at a demonstration on 18 November 2003 organised by the Zimbabwe Congress of Trade Unions, beat him with batons, destroyed his camera and dumped him, severely injured, in the street. Assistant Police Commissioner Wayne Bvudzijena warned media workers to 'distinctly separate themselves from demonstrators' in the future. (MISA)

Bright Chibvuri, an editor for the *Worker* newspaper, alleged that ruling ZANU-PF youths and state security agents were responsible for assaulting him as he covered a parliamentary by-election in Kadoma on 30 November 2003. Chibvuri said that his injuries were suffered in front of uniformed police officers.

The state Media and Information Commission (MIC) has confirmed that it will not accredit journalists from Associated Newspapers of Zimbabwe, publishers of the opposition *Daily News* (*Index* 2/03). The commission said the reporters would only be accredited if they worked for other papers. *Daily News* staff will not publish the paper until they are accredited; the commission will not accredit them because the *Daily News* is not registered with the state. (MISA, IFEX)

Sports editor **Robson Sharuko** and sports journalists

Tendai Ndemera and **Rex Mphisa** were fired by the state-run *Herald* newspaper in February, after it emerged that they had worked for Voice of America (VOA) radio. On 25 February, the MIC said this ran contrary to 'national interests and security', accusing VOA of 'lies' that contributed to a deterioration in Zimbabwe's image. (RSF)

Herald managing editor **Pikirayi Deketeke**, news editor **Innocent Gore** and reporter **Tsitsi Matope** face criminal defamation charges over an article that accused a senior ZANU-PF official of fraud. Under the Access to Information and Protection of Privacy Act, they face several years in jail. (RSF)

Compiled by: James Badcock (North Africa); Ioli Delivani (Eastern Africa and the Horn); Veronique Dupont (South America); Billie Felix Jeyes (Southern Africa); Monica Gonzalez Correa (Central Asia and Caucusus); Samuel Holden (East Asia); Patrick Holland (Britain and Ireland); Andrew Kendle (South Asia); Gill Newsham (Turkey and Kurdish areas); Beatrice Pembroke (Western Europe, North America); Sara Pfaffenhöfer (Russia, Poland, Ukraine, Baltic States; South East Asia); Jason Pollard (Gulf States and Middle East); Melanie Rawlingson (West Africa); Jugo Stojanov (Eastern Europe); Mike Yeoman (Central America and Caribbean)

Edited by Rohan Jayasekera and co-ordinated by Natasha Schmidt

THREATENED SPECIES:
BOOKS IN THE ARAB WORLD

القارئ العربي

حتى

إنسان العصر

'BELEAGUERED, FRAGILE, UNDERNOURISHED AND UNDERVALUED' IT MAY BE, BUT THE ARAB BOOK IS BY NO MEANS EXTINCT. INDEED, THE RENEWED INTEREST IN ISLAM MAY HAVE GIVEN IT A NEW LEASE OF LIFE

ARAB BOOKS & HUMAN DEVELOPMENT
EUGENE ROGAN

THE CHALLENGES FACED BY ARABIC BOOK
PUBLISHING ARE CONSIDERABLE BUT IS
IT REALLY RESPONSIBLE FOR ALL THE
PROBLEMS OF THE ARAB WORLD?

The 2002 *Arab Human Development Report* (*AHDR*) was a landmark document. Written by Arab social scientists, it was the first auto-critique to address the challenges faced by the Arab world at the start of a new century. The *AHDR* set out an agenda of reform based on three perceived 'deficits': the freedom deficit, a deficit of empowerment of women and the 'human capabilities/knowledge deficit relative to income'. To support their bold assertions, the *AHDR*'s authors assembled data from a wide range of sources and, drawing on the model of the United Nations Development Programme's Human Development Reports, sought to view the social and economic challenges from new and innovative angles. Consequently, the *AHDR* 2002 provided a wealth of new ideas to stimulate discussion and debate on the contemporary Arab world.

Given the weight of data and arguments, the general reader might be forgiven for having overlooked a brief paragraph, in a chapter otherwise dedicated to research and information technology, on the state of books in the Arab world. 'There are no reliable figures on the production of books,' the report contends, 'but many indicators suggest a severe shortage of writing; a large share of the market consists of religious books and educational publications that are limited in their creative content.' Drawing on the 1999 study of S Galal, *Translation in the Arab Homeland: Reality and Challenge*, published by Cairo's higher council for culture, the report continues:

> The figures for translated books are also discouraging. The Arab world translates about 330 books annually, one-fifth of the number that Greece translates. The cumulative total of translated books since the Caliph Maa'moun's [*sic*] time is about 100,000, almost the average that Spain translates in one year.

It is no coincidence that the authors chose the Caliph Ma'mun as a starting point. The caliph is credited with initiating one of the most important translation projects in human history. A convinced rationalist, al-Ma'mun (r 813–33) established in Baghdad the famous 'House of Wisdom' (Dar al-Hikma) dedicated to the translation of Greek philosophical works, preserving in Arabic the wisdom of ancient Greece for all posterity. There is an irony in the thought that the Arab world today, representing 270 million people spread over 22 countries, can manage only one-fifth of the translations of modern Greece, a country of just 11 million.

Such round figures are hard to substantiate: the National Book Centre of Greece, founded by the Ministry of Culture, does not keep records on translations into Greek. However, they reported a total of 6,826 books published in Greece in 2002. While it is possible that one-quarter of the publications were translations, it is not clear that this would be a sign of publishing vitality. The figure for Spain is spurious; its total figure for book publishing, of which translations would be a minor part, does not exceed the tens of thousands each year. Yet these shortcomings in the statistics have not hindered the international reception of the *AHDR*'s data on Arab book publishing. Its figures were seized upon by *New York Times* columnist Thomas Friedman to illustrate the isolation of the Arabs in an increasingly globalised world.

On education, the report reveals that investment in research and development is less than one-seventh the world average; and Internet connectivity is worse than in sub-Saharan Africa ('Arabs at the crossroads', *NYT*, 2 July 2002).

Friedman derived the title of his column from a quote in the *AHDR*: 'The Arab world is at a crossroads. The fundamental choice is whether its trajectory will remain marked by inertia . . . or whether prospects for an Arab renaissance, anchored in human development, will be actively pursued.'

The authority of the *AHDR* and the *New York Times* combined to give these data great weight in public debate. Respected analysts noted for their sympathy with the Arab world, such as Vartan Gregorian, quoted the book figures to demonstrate the need for an opening of the Arab mind to outside influences as a strategy for countering the power of Islam in Arab politics. US Secretary of State Colin Powell, too, explicitly cited the 'crossroads' quotation to validate a new US policy to invest in social change in the Arab world.

Books in the Arab world had come to be associated with the forces inhibiting an Arab renaissance. And so the authors of the *AHDR* 2003 returned to the subject in some detail. While cautioning readers about the lack of reliable statistics 'on the actual amount of literary production in the Arab world', they draw on Unesco figures to assert that, in 1991, 'Arab countries produced 6,500 books compared to 102,000 books in North America and 42,000 in Latin America and the Caribbean'. Still drawing on Unesco figures, the 2003 report claims:

Book production in Arab countries was just 1.1 per cent of world production, although Arabs constitute 5 per cent of the world's population. The publication of literary works was lower than the average level of book production. In 1996, Arab countries produced no more than 1,945 literary and artistic books, which represents 0.8 per cent of international production. This is less than a country such as Turkey produces, with a population about one-quarter that of the Arab countries. In general, Arab book production centres mainly on religious topics and less on other fields such as literature, art and the social sciences.

This preoccupation with religious books, first raised in the 2002 report, recurs throughout the 2003 text. 'There are no accurate statistics on the types of books preferred by Arab readers,' it notes, 'but according to many publishers and observers, the bestsellers at the Cairo International Book Fair are religious books, followed by books categorised as educational.' The report then directs the reader to a table that purports to support these generalisations. Comparing the relative distribution of published books, by field, in 10 Arab countries and the rest of the world in 1996, the table shows that the Arab world did produce more than three times the world relative distribution of books on religion – some 17.5 per cent compared with just over 5 per cent of the rest of the world. However, religious books represented a distinct minority – and the smallest category overall – of the relative distribution of books in Arabic, with the social sciences representing closer to 20 per cent, the sciences exceeding 20 per cent and the arts and literature tallying the highest figure of some 22.5 per cent.

The Arab book, the 2003 report concludes, is a 'threatened species' and the challenges faced by Arab book publishing are very real. Print runs of books are low, ranging from 1,000 to 3,000 copies for the average novel. 'A book that sells 5,000 copies is considered a bestseller,' it states. With fewer books being published and small runs, publishing runs the risk of becoming 'economically infeasible'.

According to Fathi Khalil al-Biss, vice-president of the Arab Publishers' Union, who is quoted in the report, Arab book publishing has been threatened by three factors: censorship and the practice of banning books among the 22 Arab states; low readership, blamed on economic stagnation and competition from the mass media; and lack of adequate distribution of books across the Arab world. Al-Biss adds that a lack of respect for intellectual property rights is also a deterrent.

Just as Colin Powell drew on the first *AHDR* to justify the 'US–Middle East Partnership Initiative' of 2002, so the US administration drew on the two reports in drafting its 2004 working paper for the G8 summit in which it set out the parameters of a 'Greater Middle East Partnership'. On the basis of the now familiar numbers – however unreliable – it blames the dearth of Arab publishing for the underlying problems in education and literacy and is, yet again, preoccupied with the relative share of Islamic books. The 'US Working Paper for G8 Sherpas' quoted in *al-Hayat*, concludes:

> The region's growing knowledge gap and continuing brain drain challenge its development prospects. Arab countries' output of books represents just 1.1 per cent of the world total (with religious books constituting over 15 per cent of this) . . .

Given the concerns for 'building a knowledge society' set out in the 2003 report, the state of the Arab book deserves further examination. After all, books are one of the most important vehicles for the dissemination of knowledge in a society. While the issues raised by the two reports are very real, the paucity of hard statistics, the normative value assigned to certain types of books and the unspoken assumption that the Arab world lags behind the rest of the world in intellectual terms for want of a sufficient number of translated works, are matters that need further discussion.

A series of lectures and debates at the Middle East Centre of St Antony's College, Oxford, on which this file is based, reflects both the dynamics and challenges faced by books and those who write them in the Arab world. ❏

Eugene Rogan *is director of the Middle East Centre at St Antony's College and lectures on the modern history of the Middle East at the University of Oxford*

VARIETIES OF CENSORSHIP
NASSER AL-HAZIMI

The Political Factor One of the oldest political reasons to destroy books that we have come across during our collection of the material for *The Burning of Books* is an incident that occurred in Medina in the year 82 AH, when a book that contained the virtuous deeds of al-Ansar [those who helped the Prophet Mohammed in Medina] and the people of Medina was burned, as 'Abd al-Malik ibn Marwan feared that it might fall into the hands of the people of the Levant, who would then know the virtues of the Medinese, in contrast to the Umayyad propaganda about them'.

The Tribal and Social Factor In a book entitled *The Insights of the Storytellers and Philologists*, the minister Jamal al-Din al-Qafati says in his translation of Ibn al-Ha'ik al-Hasan bin Ahmad al-Hamadani: 'And his book about Yemen and the wonders of its people, who are known as "The Wreath", which is in ten volumes . . . is a great, beautiful and rare book of which I have only seen disparate parts . . . in spite of the fact that it is scattered here and there it is almost half a classificatory work. I found it in a collection of books that my father left which he obtained during his stay here. It is said that this book is almost impossible to find due to the disgraceful things it mentions about the tribes of Yemen . . . The people of each tribe destroyed every copy of this book that they found and traced all copies of it to destroy them too. This is why it has become rare. Such a course was often taken so that the works of the authors and poets who spoke pejoratively about a people of a given place or tribe would be traced and destroyed until they were forgotten.'

The Psychological Factor The best example of this is the incident in which Abu Hayyan al-Tawhidi burned his books, with which we dealt with some amusement. There is another incident that happened to a poet when he erased one of his poems in a fit of pique, an incident we mentioned in this book in the translation of Ahmad bin Muhammad al-Nami al-Drami.

The Fanatical Factor Ignorance and fanaticism have often affected our Arab heritage, wiping out everything in different ways, amongst which there are the social, the religious, the sectarian, the racial and the political, in addition to other fanatical persuasions which played a role in destroying the books of our heritage. This is what happened with the book *The Victory of the Imam Dar al-Hijra's Sect*, written by the imam and judge 'Abd al-Wahhab bin Nasr al-Baghdadi, who was a Maliki, when it fell into the hands of some Shafi'i judges in Egypt, who threw it into the Nile due to sectarian fanaticism. ❏

From The Burning of Books in Arab Heritage *by* **Nasser al-Hazimi** *(Al-Jamal Publications, 2003)*

MAJED

LEILA ABOULELA

'What are you doing?' Hamid couldn't see her properly because he didn't have his glasses on. She was blurred over the kitchen sink, holding the bottle in her hand. She was not supposed to be holding that bottle. How did she get hold of it? He had hidden it behind the videos late last night, behind *Enter the Dragon*. He had washed his glass carefully over the kitchen sink, gargled with Asda Protect then crept into bed beside her, careful, very careful, not to wake up the youngest ones. Majed slept in the cot in the corner of the room, the newborn baby slept with them in the double bed so that Ruqiyyah could feed her during the night. During the night when Hamid had to go to the toilet he tried to be careful not to wake them up. Though sometimes he did, bumping into Majed's cot, stumbling on a toy. One night he had found himself, almost too late, not in the toilet but surrounded by the shoes that littered the entrance to the flat. He was startled into full consciousness by the baby crying.

'Ruqiyyah, what are you doing?' He should make a lunge at her, stop her before it was too late. It was precious stuff she was threatening to pour down the drain. But the whole household was in his way. A pile of washing waiting to go into the washing machine, the baby, sunk down and small, in her seat on the floor. She was creamy and delicate, wearing tiny gloves so that she would not scratch herself. The kitchen table was in his way. Majed sat on his high chair covered in porridge, singing, banging the table with his spoon; Sarah talked to him and chewed toast. Robin scooped Rice Krispies into his mouth while staring at the box; Snap, Crackle and Pop flying and things you could send for if your parents gave you the money.

Ruqiyyah put the bottle down. But only because there were plates and baby bottles in the sink. She started to wash them up, water splashing everywhere.

She looked at Hamid and shook her head.

Hamid groaned. He was relieved he couldn't see her eyes, her blue eyes filled with tears maybe. She had not always been Ruqiyyah, she once was someone else with an ordinary name, a name a girl behind the counter in the Bank of Scotland might have. When she became Muslim she changed her name, then left her husband. Robin and Sarah were not Hamid's children. Ruqiyyah had told Hamid horror stories about her previous marriage. She had left little out. When she went on about her ex-husband, Hamid felt shattered. He had never met Gavin (who wanted nothing to do with Ruqiyyah, Robin and Sarah, and had never so much as sent them a bean), but that man stalked Hamid's nightmares. Among Hamid's many fears was the fear of Gavin storming the flat, shaking him until his glasses fell off, 'You filthy nigger, *stay way* from my family.'

'Ruqiyyah, wait, I'll get my glasses.' He looked at the children. He looked back at her, made a face. When the children finished their breakfast and headed towards children's TV, they could talk. They couldn't talk in front of Robin. He was old enough to understand, pick up things. He was sensitive. Hamid ruffled Robin's hair, said something jolly about Snap, Crackle and Pop. Robin smiled and this encouraged Hamid to be more jocular. Whenever Hamid was stressed, he changed into a clown. The hahaha of laughter covered problems. Hahaha had wheels, it was a skateboard to slide and escape on.

'I'll get my glasses.' He stumbled away. He needed the glasses. The glasses would give him confidence. He would be able to talk, explain. She was so good, so strong, because she was a convert. But he, he had been Muslim all his life and was, it had to be said, relaxed about the whole thing. Wrong, yes it was wrong. He wasn't going to argue about that. Not with Ruqiyyah. Instead he would say . . . he would explain that on the scale . . . yes on the scale (he was a scientist after all and understood scales), on the scale of all the forbidden things, it was not really so wrong, so bad. There were worse, much worse, the Heavies, the Big Ones: black magic, adultery, abusing your parents (something the dreadful Gavin had done – *pushed the old dear round her living room* – may he rot in Hell on account of this for all eternity and more). Hamid would explain . . . Once he put his glasses on and the world cleared up he would explain. Human weakness etc, and Allah is all-forgiving. That's right. Then a sad, comic face. A gentle hahaha. But she could counter that argument about forgiveness, though. He must be careful. She would say that one has to repent first before one could be forgiven. And she would be right. Of course. Absolutely. He had every intention to repent. *Every* intention. But not now, not this minute, not today. A few more days, when he got himself sorted out, when this bottle was finished, when he finished his PhD, when he got a proper job and did not need to work evenings in Asda.

He found his glasses near the bed between the baby lotion and the zinc and castor oil. He put them on and felt better, more focused, more in control. Ruqiyyah hadn't yet dealt with the room. There were nappies on the floor, folded up and heavy. She had, though, stripped the sheets off Majed's cot. There were soft cartoon characters on the plastic mattress. Hamid rescued the prayer mat off the nappy-covered floor and dropped it on the unmade bed. He opened the window for the smells in the room to go out and fresh air to come in. Outside was another grey day, brown leaves all over the pavements. A gush of rainy air, a moment of contemplation. *Subhan Allah*, who would have ever thought that he, Hamid, born and bred on the banks of the Blue Nile, would end up here with a Scottish wife, who was a better Muslim than he was. Why had he married her? Because of the residence visa, to solve his problem with the Home Office once and for all. A friend had approached him once after Friday prayers (he did sometimes go to the mosque for Friday prayers, he was not *so* useless), and told him about Ruqiyyah, how she was a new convert with two little ones, how she needed a husband to take care of her. And you, Hamid, need a visa . . . Why not? Why not? Ha ha. Is she pretty? Ha ha. There had been a time in Hamid's life when the only white people he saw were on the cinema screen, now they would be under one roof. Why not? He brushed his teeth with enthusiasm, sprayed himself with Old Spice, armed himself with the jolly laugh and set out to meet the three of them. Robin's shy face, the gaze of a child once bitten twice shy. A woman of average height, with bright anxious blue eyes, her hair covered with a black scarf, very conservatively dressed, no make-up. He breathed a sigh of relief that she was not lean like European women tended to be. Instead she was soft like his own faraway mother, like a girl he had once longed for in the University of Khartoum, a girl who had been unattainable. And if, on that first meeting, Ruqiyyah's charms were deliberately hidden, they were obvious in her one-year-old daughter. Sarah was all smiles and wavy yellow hair, stretching out her arms, wanting to be carried, wanting to be noticed. After the awkwardness of the first meeting, a lot of hahaha, tantrums from Robin, desperate jokes, Hamid stopped laughing. He entered that steady place under laughter. He fell in love with the three of them, their pale needy faces, the fires that were repressed in them. His need for a visa, her need for security, no longer seemed grasping or callous. They were swept along by the children, his own children coming along, tumbling out soon, easily. Two years ago Majed, three weeks ago the baby. At school when

Ruqiyyah and Majed went to pick up Robin, no one believed that they were brothers. Ruqiyyah with her children: two Europeans, two Africans. The other mothers outside the school looked at her oddly, smiled too politely. But Ruqiyyah could handle the other mothers, she had been through much worse. She had once escaped Gavin to a women's refuge, lived with rats and Robin having a child's equivalent of a nervous breakdown.

He must make it to the kitchen before she poured the Johnnie Walker down the sink. He was angry. His secret was out and now that it was out it could not go back in again. It wasn't fair. If she was suspicious why hadn't she turned a blind eye, why had she searched for the proof? It wasn't fair. These were his private moments, late at night, all by himself, the children asleep, Ruqiyyah asleep. The whole soft sofa to himself, a glass of whisky in his hand, the television purring sights that held his attention, kung fu, football, sumo wrestling, Prince Naseem thrashing someone. Anything that blocked out the thesis, the humiliating hours spent mopping up Asda's floor, the demanding, roving kids. Anything cheerful, not the news, definitely not the news. The last thing he wanted at that time of night were his brothers and sisters suffering in the West Bank. His own warm, private moments, the little man on the bottle of Johnnie Walker. That little man was Johnnie, an average sort of guy and because he was walking, striding along with his top hat, he was a Walker, Johnnie Walker. Or perhaps because he *was* Johnnie Walker, he was represented as walking, striding along happily. It was interesting, but in the end it didn't matter and that was what Hamid wanted at that time of night. Things that didn't matter. At times he took his glasses off, let the television become a blur, and he would become a blur too, a hazy, warm, lovable blur. Nothing sharp, nothing definite. The exact number of years he had been a PhD student. Don't count, man, don't count. Laughter blurred things too. Hahaha. His thesis was not going to make it. He must, his supervisor said, *stretch himself.* His thesis now, as it stood, was *not meaty enough.* There was a lot of meat on Asda shelves. When he cleaned underneath them, he shivered from the cold. Not meaty enough. Johnnie Walker was slight and not at all meaty and he was all right, successful, striding along, brimming with confidence. Why shouldn't a man with an unfinished thesis and an ego-bashing job at Asda sit up late at night, once in a while, settle down in front of the television and sink in. Sink into the warmth of the whisky and the froth of the TV. Once in a while?

Majed lunged into the room. He squealed when he saw Hamid sitting on the bed. 'Majed, say *salaam*, shake hands.' Hamid held his hand out. Majed took his fist out of his mouth and placed it, covered in saliva, in his father's hand. Then he pointed to his cot, transformed because the sheet wasn't on it. It wasn't often Ruqiyyah changed the sheets. Majed walked over to his cot, mumbling exclamations of surprise. He put his hands through the bars and patted the cartoon characters on the plastic mattress. 'Mummy's washing your sheet. You'll be getting a nice clean sheet,' Hamid said. It was rare that the two of them were alone together. Hamid held him up and hugged him, put him on his lap. He loved him so much. He loved his smell and roundness, his tight little curls and wide forehead. Majed was a piece of him, a purer piece of him. And that love was a secret because it was not the same love he felt for Sarah and Robin which was calm and sensible. He dreamt about Majed. Majed crushed under a bus and Hamid roaring from the pain, which came from deep inside, which surfaced into sobs, then Ruqiyyah's voice, her hand on his cheeks, what's wrong, what's the matter, and the wave of shame with the silent coolness of waking up. I'm sorry, I'm sorry, it's nothing, go back to sleep. The more he loved Majed and the newborn baby, the kinder Hamid was to Robin and Sarah. He must not be unjust. Ruqiyyah must never feel that he favoured their children over Robin and Sarah. It was a rare, precious moment when he was alone with Majed, no one watching them. He threw him up in the air and Majed squealed and laughed. He stood Majed on the bed and let him run, jump, fly from the bed into his outstretched arms. Then he remembered Ruqiyyah in the kitchen. The memory dampened the fun. He sent Majed off to join Sarah and Robin in front of the television (already the blocked-nose voice of *Rugrats* filled the flat), and walked back to the kitchen.

Ruqiyyah was clearing the things off the kitchen table; the baby was asleep in her chair on the floor. With his glasses on now, Hamid could clearly see the whisky bottle. Two-thirds empty, two-thirds . . . His heart sank, that much . . . or had she already poured some out? No. No, she hadn't. He knew what she was going to do. She was going to clear the kitchen, wash everything and put it away, then ceremoniously tip the bottle into the empty sink.

She started cleaning up Majed's high chair. Her hair fell over her eyes. She wore an apron with Bugs Bunny on it. She was beautiful, not like women on TV, but with looks that would have been appreciated in another part of the world, in another century. Her lips were naturally red. He had thought, before they got married, that she was wearing lipstick. She wore *hijab* when she went out, she got up at dawn and prayed. This seriousness that he didn't have baffled him. Something Scottish she brought with her when she stepped into Islam. The story of her conversion amazed him as much as her stories about Gavin shocked and sickened him. She had read books about Islam. Books Gavin had snatched and torn up. Not because they were about Islam, but because she was sitting on her fat arse reading instead of doing what he wanted her to do.

She wanted to learn Arabic. Hamid would doze in bed and next to him she would hold *Simple Words in Arabic*, over the head of the baby she was feeding. 'How do you say this?' she would ask from time to time, nudging him awake. When Hamid read the Quran out loud (he went through religious spells in Ramadan and whenever one of the children fell ill), she said, 'I wish I could read like you.'

He started to help her tidy up. He closed the flaps on the box of Rice Krispies, put it away in the cupboard. When she finished wiping the table and started on the floor, he lifted up the baby's seat and put it on the table. If she would talk to him, shout at him, it would be better. Instead he was getting this silent treatment. He began to feel impatient. What had made her search for the bottle? A smell . . . ?

Attack is the best form of defence. Laughter blurs things, smoothes them over. Hahaha. He began to talk, he put on his most endearing voice, tried a joke. Hahaha. She didn't answer him, didn't smile. She pushed her hair away from her face, poured powder into the drawer of the washing machine. She bent down and began to load the washing into the machine. It was linen. The sheets that had been on Majed's cot. Hamid said, 'But how did you know? Tell me.'

She sat on her heels, closed the door of the washing machine. She said, 'You pissed in Majed's cot. You thought you were in the toilet.' She twisted the dial that started the wash cycle. 'I pretended to be asleep. He didn't wake up.'

There is a place under laughter, under the hahaha.

Hamid saw her stand up, pick up the Johnnie Walker and pour what was left of it down the drain. She poured it carefully so that not a single drop splashed on the sink where later the children's bowls and bottles would wait to be washed. ❏

From Coloured Lights *by* **Leila Aboulela** *(Polygon, Edinburgh, 2001)*

LOST IN TRANSLATION
FADIA FAQIR

THE DIFFICULTY OF PUBLISHING IN THEIR
OWN COUNTRIES AND THE PROBLEMS OF
TRANSLATION ARE DRIVING MORE ARAB
WRITERS LIVING IN THE WEST TO ADOPT
THE 'LANGUAGE OF THE OTHER'

The Arab book is a beleaguered creature, undernourished, undervalued
and deprived of the very oxygen that makes it grow and prosper: freedom
of expression. In the 22 countries of the Arab world, with a combined
population of 284 million, a 'bestseller' may have a print run of just 5,000
copies, the result of censorship, high illiteracy rates – about 60 million
adults in the Arab world today cannot read or write – and other constraints.

There are 22 departments of censorship in the 22 countries of the
Arab world. Security services ban, burn or confiscate publications if they
consider they violate political, moral and/or religious sensitivities. They
also prevent the sale of certain books and promote the sale of others.
Further, it is difficult for books to move easily across Arab borders to
their natural markets; this, too, increases the cost of production and
hinders publishing and circulation. Creativity, innovation and knowledge
are curtailed.

As a result of the economic sanctions against Libya, for example, you
cannot buy any book that resembles anything scholarly. Colonel Gaddafi's
The Green Book is on sale everywhere, together with the published
proceedings of a conference on *The Green Book*. Libyan writers have
no option but to add their manuscripts to the long queue at Al-Dar al-
Jamahiriyya li al-Nashr wa al-Tawzi, a government-sponsored publishing
house. They may wait up to 10 years or more to get published. Most
hapless authors do not dare take their manuscripts out of the queue for
lack of other options and for fear of being put back at the end of the
queue if they later change their minds.

Jordanian authors submit their manuscripts to the erratic and whimsical
censor, who sometimes sends them back covered in red marks and with
nuggets of advice such as 'kill the main character'. Many authors save up to

Beirut 1999: schoolgirls so long at the fair. Credit: Joseph Barrak – STF / APP

pay publishers the printing costs of their novels, the reverse of the normal practice in the West.

There is also the matter of self-appointed censors who initiate witch-hunts against authors, as in the recent case against Nawal el-Sadaawi. Samia Mehrez, Professor of Modern Arabic Literature at the American University in Cairo, came under attack for assigning to her class the fictional autobiography of the Moroccan writer Mohamed Choukri, *al-Khubz al-Hafi (For Bread Alone),* because some students and parents judged it 'pornographic' (see p171).

Without any valid travel documents or a visa the Arab book travels west. But the picture is equally grim on the other side. There is growing suspicion of those who can speak other languages, particularly Arabic.

A few years ago, Francis Fukuyama said: 'The US State Department was well rid of its Arabists and Arabic speakers because by learning that language they also learned the "delusions" of the Arabs.' Primo Levi argued that some people perceive a person who can speak another language as 'an outsider, a foreigner; strange and, therefore, a potential enemy'.

Since the mid-nineteenth century, some have argued that the Arabic language and the Arabs are afflicted with a mentality and a language that has no use for reality. In 1988, Edward Said tried to interest a New York publisher in the works of Naguib Mahfouz: 'But after a little reflection the idea was turned down. When I enquired why, I was told (with no detectable irony) that Arabic was a controversial language.' Even after Mahfouz won the Nobel Prize, his publishers felt it necessary to flag that he had been influenced by Flaubert, Balzac and Proust to make him palatable to a Western audience.

Although Arabic ranks sixth in the world league table of languages, fewer and fewer people have an acceptable knowledge of it. 'Written, literary Arabic with its grammatical complexities is notoriously difficult to learn. Arabic readers need to master an ancient and intricate blueprint of foreign grammar, syntax and vocabulary,' says Daniel del Caastillo. This might partly explain the uphill struggle to find qualified and properly trained translators to work with. On the Arab Women Writers Series (Garnet Publishing), for instance, the quality of the translations, with few exceptions, was poor indeed. Not only does the quality of their education leave much to be desired, some Arabic departments are now under threat of closure.

Many Arabs living in the West have decided to cut out the middleman and create an 'Arab book' in the language of the other. The reasons behind this decision vary, but it is a by-product of the colonial encounter and, as Salah Trabelsi says, of a rising awareness of 'multiculturalism that provisionally disowns one's self to listen to and to perceive, beyond differences, a kinship of gestures and of desire'. The writing of some Arabs in the West treads the divide between two cultures and suffers as well as benefits from occupying such a dangerous site. 'Displacement urges transcultural writers to revisit their culture of origin by the essential questioning of their relationships with their body, faiths, rites, languages,' Trabelsi adds.

The large body of writing in English by Arabs or authors of Arab origin has not yet been subjected to serious study and analysis. Geoffery Nash's book *The Arab Writer in English: Arab Themes in a Metropolitan Language, 1908–1958* is the first serious study of what he describes as the 'internationalisation of literature' and its impact on Arab writers. Let me fill this gap and coin a new term, 'Arabs writing in English' (AWE). This covers the body of work by Arab writers who write in the English language and whose mother tongue is usually Arabic. It is also associated with the works of members of the Arab diaspora, people such as Ahdaf Soueif, who was born in Egypt. As a category, it comes under the broader realm of post-colonial literature, produced in previously colonised countries such as Egypt, Lebanon, Sudan and Jordan.

AWE is transcultural writing that problematises social issues, sense of identity and terms of reference. It is 'neither soft-edged amalgamation nor slavish mimicry', but proposes 'creative new identities for the individual and the collective subject'. (Trabelsi, 2003)

As an Arab writer, writing about the Arab culture in English, I find myself preoccupied with themes of exile and representation that reflect the condition of an 'expatriarch', a writer who has crossed from one culture into another because of her father. This transcultural position is reflected in the intricate process through which my writing is composed and through my endless attempts to carve a small territory within the English language for myself. Behind the all-embracing problems of creative duplicity, from a post-colonial position emerges one writer's struggle to comprehend an alien world and cope with the profound consequences of living a bicultural identity.

Leila Aboulela's *halal* fiction, which propagates an Islamic world view, is also a good example of transcultural and transnational literature. She was born in Cairo of an Egyptian mother and a Sudanese father, brought up and educated in the Sudan and graduated from the University of Khartoum with a degree in economics. She then enrolled at the London School of Economics to study statistics, followed by a decade living in Scotland with her husband and children. She won the Caine Prize for African Writing in 2000 for her short story 'The

Museum'. Her novel *The Translator*, hailed by the *Muslim News* as the 'first *halal* novel written in English', was nominated for a number of prizes. *Coloured Lights*, a collection of short stories, is her most recent work (Polygon, 2001).

Aboulela's commitment to an Islamic world view does not take away from her lyrical style and her attention to detail. Like the West Indian-born writer Jean Rhys, on whom she models her work, Aboulela's writing deals with the theme of a helpless female, an outsider, victimised by her dependence on others for support and protection. And although the ending of the novel is unconvincing, the reader understands totally the inner struggle the two main characters must endure to suppress their emotions. Whether the inter-faith and cross-cultural dialogues succeed or fail becomes irrelevant, for what remains is a sense of irretrievable loss and a lingering sadness.

This sense of loss and sadness can also be found in Rabih Alameddine's writing. Alameddine was born in Jordan to Lebanese parents and has lived in Kuwait, Lebanon, England and the United States. He began his career as an engineer, and then moved to writing and painting. He is the author of two novels, *Koolaids*, Lebanon's 'Philadelphia', and *I, the Divine*, as well as *The Perv*, a collection of short stories.

Koolaids: The Art of War focuses on the HIV/Aids epidemic in the US and the Lebanese civil war. Through a series of non-linear, multi-narrator stories, diary entries, plays, newspaper clippings, excerpts of email correspondence and poetry, he creates what has been described as 'uniquely multinational, multisexual fiction'. *Koolaids* is an attempt to weave a narrative that make sense in this post-modernist labyrinth, and to construct a self out of the shreds of representation by the other and one's own self-presentation. Alameddine's experimental fiction might set the tone for what is to come, a possible model for writers with fragmented selves, languages and loyalties. ❏

© ***Fadia Faqir*** *is a Jordanian/British writer and academic. She is the author of* Nisanit *(Penguin, 1990) and* Pillars of Salt *(Quartet Books, 1996), editor and co-translator of* In the House of Silence: Autobiographical essays by Arab women writers *(Garnet, 1998), and senior editor of the Arab Women Writers Series (Garnet Publishing)*

KOOLAIDS

RABIH ALEMEDDINE

Cervantes told me that history is the mother of truth. Borges told me
historical truth is not what took place; it is what we think took place.

So Billy Shakespeare was queer.
Ronnie was the greatest president in history, right up there on Mt Rushmore.
Aids is mankind's greatest plague.
Israel only kills terrorists.
America never bombed Lebanon.
Jesus was straight. Judas and he were just friends.
Roseanne's parents molested her as an infant.
Menachem Begin and Yasser Arafat deserved their Nobels.
And Gaetan Dugas started the Aids epidemic.

I met Scott in 1980. We were both twenty. I saw him across the dance floor
at the Stud. I knew who I was going home with that night. Scott was my type
to a tee. Pug-nosed, baby-faced, blond with a cute butt was my kind of boy.
I walked all the way across the space and cornered him. Convincing him to
come back home with me was a piece of cake. All I had to do was mention
I was a painter. He had a thing for artists, he said. I had a thing for cute blond
things. He said he loved my accent. I said I loved his butt. Off to my studio
in North Beach we went.
    We never consummated our desires. We arrived at my studio. I turned
the light on. He walked over to the painting I had finished that day. He stood
in front of it entranced. At first I was flattered. After the first five minutes
I started getting horny. I stood behind him contemplating my painting and
started rubbing my crotch on his behind. The scene was turning me on.
Fucking the cute butt of a boy admiring a painting of mine was my idea of
heaven. Scott started to speak and I lost my erection. He started telling me
about my life, my dreams, my fears. He started telling me about my mother,
about my father. He told me about the war which tore my life apart. He
related what he saw in the painting. It was the first 60 by 80.

We spent that night in bed talking. We never fucked, ever. He meant everything to me. That first night he started calling me Habibi, which means 'my lover' in my native tongue, a cognomen which nobody ever questioned, not even his future lover. He never used my real name, or any of the numerous Americanised nicknames I picked up along the way. I had always assumed he found it difficult to pronounce. I was wrong. His last words before he took his last breath were, 'I love you, Mohammed.' An impeccable pronunciation.

~

We live in a neighbourhood called Galerie Semaan. It is named after the furniture store which designates the edge, the edge of the neighbourhood. The area will become famous years later because of the fierce battles that occurred there, but for now it is simply my neighbourhood. It is on the south-eastern side of Beirut, about a mile from the beach. It is right on the edge of Beirut, after which you have the mountains and the various suburbs. The neighbourhood proper consists of about ten buildings, most of which have the six floors allowed by zoning the area. It is bounded by the road to Chouifat and the south on one side, and an orange grove on another. On the west side there is something called the New Road, which is neither new nor a road, but a wide gravel path beyond which are slums where Palestinians and some Shiites live. The northern side is dominated by the Beirut to Damascus road. Although we live in a flat section of Beirut, the Beirut to Damascus road starts a steep incline right at the edge of our neighbourhood.

For us kids, the boundaries are very important. We really cannot leave our neighbourhood. We cannot cross into the orange grove because that guardian shoots trespassers, particularly if they are kids. I see him sometimes with his shotgun. He hunts birds that come into the grove. Hunting is everyone's favourite pastime. My dad tells me that the guardian is harmless. None of us kids wants the risk. We also do not go past the New Road. We don't mix with the people who live there. One day our neighbourhood boys crossed over to play soccer on an empty lot there. Once we started playing, all the slum boys beat us up. We never crossed that line again. ❏

© **Rabih Alemeddine**, *from* Koolaids *(Abacus/Time Warner, 1998)*

FOR BREAD ALONE

MOHAMED CHOUKRI

He stopped the car in a dark section of the road. The lights of the city sparkled in the distance. He turned on the overhead light. So the short ride ends here. With a caressing movement he runs his hand over my fly. And the other ride begins. Button by button, very slowly, he unfastened the trousers, and my sex felt the warmth of his breath. I did not dare look at his face or even at his hand, whose warm pressure had made my sex rise up.

¡Bravo! he was saying. *¡Macho Bravo!*

He began to lick it and touch it with his lips, and at the same time he tickled my crotch with his fingers. When he pulled half of it down his throat, I felt his teeth. And if he bites it? I thought. The idea cooled my enthusiasm. To bring it back, I began to imagine that I was deflowering Asiya in Tetuan. When I finished, he still had me in his mouth. He took out his handkerchief and wiped his lips. His face was congested, his eyes very wide, and his mouth stayed open. I buttoned my fly and folded my arms over my chest as if nothing had happened. Taking out a pack of cigarettes, he offered me one and lit it for me. Then he lit a cigarette and turned on the radio. A beautiful calm music came over the air. I sat enjoying it, and was reminded of Oran and my work with the lovely Monique. Monique! Today it's only a name to be remembered and forgotten.

We did not say a word to one another as we drove back to the city. He gave me fifty pesetas and let me out near the place were he had called to me. He shook my hand and said: *Hasta la vista.* His hand was warm and smooth. I waved to him. *¡Hasta la vista!*

The air was full of smoke from the car.

They suck it for five minutes and they give you fifty pesetas. Do they all suck, the ones who are like that old man? Are all the *maricones* as nice as he was? Do all the ones who suck have cars, and do they all give fifty pesetas? A new profession, to add to begging and stealing. I must pick one of the three until a further choice appears. ❏

From al-Khubz al-Hafi *by* **Mohamed Choukri** *(Saqi Books, London, 1993)*

COVER UP
MAI GHOUSSOUB

CAN YOU READ AN ARABIC
BOOK BY ITS COVER?

When my colleague André Gaspard and I came to London in the late
1970s, fleeing the civil war in Lebanon, we were total strangers in this city.
We were such newcomers that when we started al-Saqi Books and wanted
to mail our first catalogue, we looked for addresses in the telephone
directory. We spent whole nights looking for likely names and potential
readers for our books. With the catalogues sent, we waited – and panicked.
Imagine our great joy when a librarian from the Oriental Department of
Cambridge University Library showed up in our bookshop, holding the
catalogue in one hand and, with the other, selecting all the novels of
Naguib Mahfouz. The novels were in Arabic, for in 1979 Mahfouz had
not been widely translated into English.

A few weeks later, the same librarian called us and in a hesitant voice,
interrupted by many embarrassed English coughs, asked: 'Is there a chance
you can provide me with some different editions of Mahfouz's novels?
Nobody in the acquisition department reads Arabic and they all think
I'm ordering pornographic books or erotica!'

We rushed back to our shelves and looked at the only editions available
of Mahfouz's novels. We looked at the covers and smiled. These covers
have been with us since the 1950s and it had never crossed our minds that
their images could be considered sexy by anyone. These were the popular
images exhibited all over Cairo, Beirut or Damascus as posters for the films
based on Mahfouz's or Abdelqudous's novels. As far as I am concerned,
they are more playful and artistic then titillating. But since the day the
gentle librarian called, I have become enamoured with the subject of
book covers.

Can you read an Arabic book by its cover? 'You can't judge a book
by its cover,' say the English; '*L'habit ne fait pas le moine,*' say the French.
Different languages, same sentiment. But the Arabs, who have always set
great store by The Word, say '*Yuqra' al Maktub min Inwanihi*': you can tell
a book from its title.

If we look at the covers of popular Arab novels, we are tempted to believe the French. But this is too easy. A cover is a façade and a façade reveals as much as it hides. The covers of Mahfouz and Abdelqudous, for instance, speak much about our and our society's image of itself; fashion, like façades or covers, is the bearer of our traditions as well as our transgression of these traditions; it is also the bearer of our impulses and imagined selves.

If we study these covers, they will tell us about the image of the ideal or attractive woman in popular iconography: white, blonde. These images speak of the subconsciously accepted equation that Western-equals-fairer-equals-more beautiful. Most men in these pictures look oriental: darker, moustachioed, dressed in a traditional Egyptian peasant hat. The women, on the contrary, are all inspired by Anita Ekberg, Gina Lollobrigida or some other Hollywood sex symbol.

As far as I am aware, these images represent neither the themes nor any dimension of Naguib Mahfouz's socially oriented literature. On the other hand, the constant tension between modernity and tradition is revealed by the sophisticated blonde lady vs the covered peasant, both desirable in their own way, both competing for the minds and hearts of Arabs and their vision of their society's future.

So we cannot read an Arabic book by its cover? Consider today's Cairo, a place where most advertising posters are for Islamic fashion shops and feature veiled models advertising the latest headscarf or the latest in Islamic sportswear. They speak of the continuous cohabitation of opposites and the dreams or visions of Egyptian society – indeed, of many Arab societies.

In an area where censorship is still the norm, the cover or the façade can be a good way to trick the censor. Many people used to send books by mail only after having replaced the original cover with a respectable one borrowed from elsewhere. Many dissident books or religiously incorrect ones travelled successfully across borders thanks to a new binding carrying a title such as *Studies in Medical Surgery* or some similar innocuous rubric. No one can really ban ideas. Censors can only make life more miserable for people or narrow and impoverish momentarily the intellectual life or the freedom of choice of people. They can deprive the poorest, those who are most isolated, less travelled and with no access to private satellite dishes. That impoverishment is summarised by the question many visitors to London ask as soon as they visit our bookshop: 'Where is the banned books section?'

Palace of Desire *and* Deceitful Dawn *by Naguib Mahfouz. Credit: Mai Ghoussoub*

When I was in high school our French teacher ridiculed a fellow student because she had catalogued Baudelaire's *Les Fleurs du mal* under 'botanic' in the school library. Clearly she had no way of guessing the content of the book from the title on its cover.

I once had precisely the opposite experience. I had been asked many times about the original Arabic edition of Sheikh Nefzawi's *The Perfumed Garden*, a book that is widely exhibited and sold on the streets of Morocco but banned, in principle, throughout the Middle East. I was told about the bookseller who had printed it in the early 1970s in Beirut, so sought him out and found his son in charge of the business. When I asked the son about Nefzawi's book, he asked me to be discreet and admitted having many copies in stock. But, he insisted, 'a lady like you' should not read this book. He was quite satisfied with my answer: 'Don't worry. I sell books, I don't read them!' When I saw the book, I felt my answer should

New Cairo *and* The Journey of Ibn Fattouma *by Naguib Mahfouz.*
Credit: Mai Ghoussoub

have been, 'I sell books, I don't look at their covers.' In this case, the cover consisted of a rough copy of a US ad from the 1960s showing a model carrying a tray on which the publisher had replaced the original commodity advertised by a penis!

He was jailed for a few days as a result of his entrepreneurial spirit. He would have done better to have continued the old Arabic tradition of book covers in leather with abstract Islamic patterns and calligraphy embossed in gold. These served the classical Arab writers well for many centuries, covering a multitude of works from Quranic exegesis to sex manuals. Sometimes it can be better not to be able to tell a book by its cover.

Can we change the identity, the content, of a book through its cover? Are identities inherited or are they constantly shifting? Fascination with book covers as cultural vitrines led me, with another artist, Shaheen Merali, to explore the issue of identity, of globalisation, our reality as New

Europeans through the art of book covers. Our installation 'Dressing–Readdressing' manipulated book covers, tarbooshing (putting on a fez) and veiling figures on classical English books, Westernising the covers of Arabic books.

Covers, façades, dress are important. Some believe they do influence attitudes and behaviour. National leaders often believed in the symbolic power of dress. Atatürk banned the fez from men's heads in the conviction that modernity and the red head-covering were incompatible. Hoda Shaarawi, the founder of the Egyptian women's movement, took off her veil only after her husband's death. Today in France, many young female Muslims are challenging the authorities as well as their parents and claiming their '*droit à la différence*' by choosing to cover their heads with the Islamic hijab.

When we went through the opposite process of dressing Arab covers in Western style, we realised that identity and authenticity are even more constructed then the discourse about them reveals. Dressing an Arab or Indian man in a tie, putting a 'cool' T-shirt on a Bedouin woman, triggered no visual surprise: globalisation is largely Westernisation. Arab tribesmen can easily exchange their tribal solidarity for that of a football team. The uniformity imposed by the veil on women is not far from the uniformity of famished models selling the latest designer clothes. In our world of exchanged identities and fast-travelling images, it is more and more difficult to read a book by its cover. ❑

Mai Ghoussoub is a founder of Saqi Books, now celebrating its 21st birthday. It publishes a wide range of fiction and non-fiction from award-winning novelists to seldom-heard minority voices

VOICES OF THE EXILED

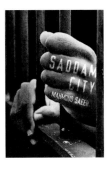

TALKING BOOKS
KHALED AL-HROUB

WHAT ARE THE LIMITS OF DEBATE IN ARAB TV'S ONLY BOOK PROGRAMME?

Al Jazeera is a 24-hour TV news channel broadcasting from Qatar and with a reputation for controversy that, like its audience, has grown considerably since the invasion of Iraq. There are, it is true, fashion shows, sports, 'hot topics', but a laid-back book programme, 45 minutes of talking heads mainly of interest to intellectuals, is difficult to square with the channel's overall image.

But that's what I do: run a weekly book programme, *Al Kitab*, devoted to pretty heavyweight discussion with authors. From time to time, the producers speak about spicing it up with visuals and so on, but as an academic I want academic argument, discussion where questions remain open. I don't feel the need to find black-and-white answers to any of the questions that come up in my programme. On the contrary, when it comes to contentious issues I believe in grey areas. The lack of a conclusion doesn't bother me. Open-ended debate allows for more probing, research and living with uncertainty. Surprisingly perhaps, the programme is becoming an integral part of the network; not a mass attraction maybe, but increasingly popular with its target group.

Rather than focusing on books published in the Arab world that are available through local bookshops and widely reviewed in the Arab media, I look at books on the Middle East – Arabs, Islam, social phenomena, political subjects, cultural controversies – published in the West. The aim of this is to give the audience some idea of what is published in the West, mainly on Arab and Middle Eastern issues. If the book under review is 'straightforward', uncontroversial, I do not worry much about bringing in guests with differing views. But if it touches on controversy or sensitive issues, the channel itself will insist on having opposing views in the interest of 'objectivity'.

There's little we shy away from. I would say we've discussed a number of the most sensitive issues in the area. I've hosted programmes dealing with the political situation of the Shia in the Gulf, in Bahrain, Saudi Arabia, Iraq and Oman – one of the hottest issues in the region; the pros and cons of secularism and Islam in the Middle East; the future of Arab societies; the role of women, of masculinity and of feminism. Last month we took a look at a book on patriarchy and sex in Arab societies; a bit of a disappointment for many viewers as there was no sex in the entire discussion, but the patriarchal relationship between men and women in those societies as seen by the author.

Can you give us an idea of roughly what percentage of the books on your programme are written in Arabic and what in English or other Western languages?

I would say 20 per cent in Arabic and the rest in Western languages.

So in one sense, you're using television to introduce Arab viewers to Western books that they probably wouldn't know about otherwise. Almost a process of translation?

This is the main idea: to show people that there are so many books published in the West engaged in debates and discussions on the Middle East about which we know nothing – and about which we write so little. Maybe this is the first step to encouraging people from the audience, academics and intellectuals, to engage with these subjects; to open up some closed areas.

Another purpose is to try, indirectly, to influence Western writers by demonstrating that we are monitoring what they are publishing. In other words to say to them: if you made some mistakes, next time be careful because we're watching; and not only watching, we are exposing your writings throughout the Arab world. Interestingly, some of the Western authors we interview on the programme don't feel comfortable repeating on TV what they said in their books.

I can think of one programme where we discussed secularism in the Middle East and the author of *Secularism in the Arab World* was trying to track down all the most radical secular voices in the Arab world between roughly the mid-nineteenth century and mid-twentieth century – the 'formative' period, as Albert Hourani described it. It's not an easy subject on Arab TV with an audience for whom religion is a central element in society. I was trying to persuade her to open up on these sacred boundaries: to bring them down to earth and explore their sacred nature. But I could feel her willing me to move on; to move to the next chapter . . .

You had Ahmad al-Shahi on the show. Did he go into any of the scandals that came out of the sheikhdoms of eastern Arabia?

Of course he talked about the sheikhs in these areas, mainly in the United Arab Emirates. But there's a fine line between trying to extract information and creating problems for an author writing about a given country, maybe his own country to which he might, for instance, be denied access next time he or she wanted to visit. We talked about these things before the show and, as far as I remember, al-Shahi said something like, 'These are the red lines, I can't talk about them.' When we discuss any books that deal with contemporary politics and leaders, we have the same problem.

What we want to do is raise the ceiling: to minimise the sacred areas and open up these things. But we try to keep a balance. On the one hand, I don't want my guests to feel I'm trying to spice up the show and raise the ratings by going into these things; on the other, we're trying to push the boundaries. Having said that, there are some total no-go areas for us. For example, we can't talk about a book discussing sexual relationships outside marriage; religious freedom or any other freedom – the freedom to be an atheist, for instance. I can't discuss the books of Ibn Waraq – he writes under a pseudonym and casts doubt on the authenticity of the Quran.

What do you do about the Palestinian problem? If you have a book, for example, that's pro-Arab and written in the West, how do you get the other view, the Israeli view, across?

To be honest, I usually avoid such books. What is the point in simply demonstrating that the Palestine issue is a just cause for an audience who vehemently believe in this? Further, the format of the programme is to have Arab reviewers/critics reviewing non-Arab books, so it is really difficult, next to impossible, to have somebody on the show to defend Israel.

You say you hold Western writers to account for what they write, but when I am writing a book the last thing on my mind would be what they might say about it on Al Jazeera. If you are a serious writer, then you are responsible for what you write and you have to be prepared to defend it against serious critical scrutiny by other colleagues, not against the media. As a writer, I don't have any 'red lines'. And anything that I write I'd be happy to discuss in front of any audience and my views would be exactly the same, whatever the audience. What is your 'red line'? Are you worried about offending Arab regimes?

No, this is my least worry. The ceiling of criticism on Arab regimes is high. My worry is about discussion on social and cultural issues. We have had critical discussions on political structures from Algeria to the Gulf States, Saudi Arabia, Jordan, Palestine. However, approaching social issues is like walking through a minefield. My own observation is that we enjoy, relatively speaking, a higher degree of freedom in talking politics than in cultural and social matters, particularly where religion is concerned. We can't touch these things. This is the true red line.

In the USA the pressures of corporate sponsorship have got worse in terms of what can and can't be said on TV. Does Al Jazeera exert pressure on what can and can't be touched? Does it dictate the priorities – impose the red line? You give the impression that external sources of power or money do not impose pressures.

I work as a freelance so there is a distance between myself and the Al Jazeera project as a whole. I really cannot deal with the power politics, pressures, money and other things relating to Al Jazeera. But they deal fairly with my programme. I suggested the idea and they said yes, even though commercially it's not great: nobody advertises on the programme, unlike fashion shows where every company wants to advertise their stuff. They're happy with the idea intellectually and the feedback from different quarters of the Arab world is good. Maybe they think its unique character helps the channel's image. As to the red lines, it's entirely up to me. Sometimes I avoid books I know won't go on air.

Given that Al Jazeera is a popular channel that covers fashion and sport as well as news, do you have any statistics or any idea who is watching Al-Kitab? *Do we know who else, other than intellectuals, is tuning in?*

We don't have good feedback or ratings assessments in the Arab world. But I remember a Sudanese taxi driver in Abu Dhabi who said, 'Oh, you're Khaled al-Hroub, I like your programme.' And a man who was working in a hotel in Morocco said the same thing, I was amazed. On the other hand, sometimes I go to intellectual forums or conferences and find that very few people know about my show. Sometimes people can really surprise us. ❑

Khaled al-Hroub *is the presenter of* Al-Kitab *and is currently working in Cambridge*

TIPS FROM A MOTHER TO HER SON

AHMAD BIN YOUSSEF SHARF
AL-DIN AL-TIFASHI

It was narrated that Ka'b bin Sur was handsome and well intentioned. His mother wanted to marry him off, as a natural part of his graduation into a man.

She said: 'Listen to my advice, my boy, and accept my will.'

He said: 'I'm listening, and will obey your order.'

She said: 'When I have married you off and let you go in to be with your wife, put your hand out to her, embrace her on the lips and kiss her between the eyes. Then take her in your hands and sit her on your knees. Kiss her more, and touch her on her chest, her stomach, her navel and her back. For this eliminates misgivings, and makes a flaccid penis stand erect. Then take off the clothes so that you may get to that which is right, and put your fingers between her buttocks, and rub the head of your penis between the edges [labia]. If she gets aroused and gives herself to you, then go for it and don't hold back. If she starts acting coquettishly and sighing, then do exactly the same for her. Don't forget this advice; with it you can obtain any girl.'

He said: 'Mother, I know a lot about such things, and as you can see I have a large penis. I am an expert at sex, so I ask your word that whoever you marry me to, you will tell her not to forbid it from me, even if we carry on through until morning.'

She got up straightaway to satisfy her tyrannical son, and on her way she met a woman who wanted a suitable husband for her beautiful daughter. This resulted in the meeting of the sun and the moon. ❑

From The Descriptions of Women *by Ahmad bin Youssef Sharf al-Din al-Tifashi (died 651AH [13th century]) (The Bookhouse; all details on cover blacked over)*
Translated by James Howarth

MEETINGS OF THE SPIRIT
ALIYA SHUAYB

She meets layers of mist
When the first
Moment of ecstasy trembles
And the sharp darkness of the night
Enters her.

She meets bushes
That sleep secretly
On the arms of the dewy grass. ❏

From Anakib *by **Aliya Shuayb** (Dar al-'Aliya, 2003), banned by the Kuwaiti authorities*
Translated by James Howarth

BOOKS IN BEIRUT
GHASSAN TUÉNI

FICTION, FACTION, SCANDAL, HISTORY
AND ISLAM SCRABBLE FOR SPACE
AT BEIRUT'S ANNUAL BOOK FAIR

The top sellers at the 2003 Beirut Arab Book Fair were all books on Islam, the topic that currently dominates international relations and gives new relevance to what we all thought was a defunct concept: the clash of civilisations – the confrontation between pure power or hyperpower and the 'power of despair', an invisible force of the poor and the weak.

Three books dominated the fair: an Arabic version of Tarif Khalidy's masterpiece *The Muslim Jesus*; a translation of a weighty tome *Un réformisme chiite. Ulémas et lettres de Gabal Amil de la fin de l'Empire ottoman à l'indépendance du Liban* by Sabrina Mervin, first published in Paris by Karthala, Cermoc and IFEAD in 2000; and a collection of articles on 'confessionalism' by former Lebanese prime minister Salim el Hoss.

On the fiction front, it was not love stories, novels or thrillers that dominated the bestseller lists, but two books of a more curious kind. One was a collection of scandalous stories or rumours about the governments of the present Lebanese Prime Minister Rafic Hariri, which I call 'fiction' given that the author, former MP Najah Wakim, was forced to retract his most 'important' stories in the face of a writ. The other, not dissimilar, was devoted to 'scandals' surrounding the life of the assassinated militia leader Elias Hobeika, a phenomenon of Lebanon's 'dirty wars' that are now over but that continue to haunt the nightmares of many. The book was not on display at recent fairs, having been withdrawn from circulation under legal duress after breaking all sales records. Its 'anonymous' author was never pursued in court, having fled to the USA.

In complete contrast to all the above, and it being Beirut, there were, naturally, a number of important scholarly works on Lebanon.

How has Beirut become the publishing centre of the Arab world? Throughout the nineteenth century, Cairo, with a much larger population base and of greater international importance, was its only rival. But the twentieth century and the creeping onset of censorship in Egypt saw a reversal of fortunes. Soon after World War I, Cairo's academic freedom was

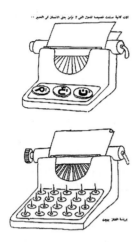

Egyptian caricaturist Bahgat is part of a generation of radical artists and writers formed by Nasser's July revolution. In his cartoons, Bahgat attacks political and socially sensitive issues such as polygamy and black stereotypes in the Arab world. Banned from drawing for a decade under President Anwar Sadat, Bahgat created the memorable cartoon dictator, Bahgatos, once he was allowed to publish again. The customised typewriters, from a 1985 Arab Human Rights Organisation report, were created for 'governments opposed to freedom of expression'. The three-key machine types out one word – 'Yes'.

curtailed by religious opinion and censorship reared its head. The classic case was the banning of Taha Hussein's book on *Jahilya* poetry, which was considered offensive to the Quran. The trend continued under Gamal Abdul Nasser in the 1950s when writing and publishing became dependent on the state and lost any real semblance of liberty. Third-generation Lebanese started to return to Beirut or emigrated to Europe and the Gulf. Soon after Anwar Sadat's accession, even those like Mohammed Heykal, who had been largely spared the rigours of censorship, turned to publishing in Beirut and writing for the Lebanese press.

Beirut progressed from 'provincial' to Arab national to near international stature: the more the Arab world, and particularly Egypt, sank into despotism under their militocracies, the more Lebanon became the *agora* and *forum* where everything Arab was debated, secrets unravelled and modernity discovered, experimented with, explored and exported.

Since the 1950s, the Lebanese University Press has been active; and even before then there was the Université Saint-Joseph and its publishing house dating from the nineteenth century. Its *Éditions Orientales* played a vital role in discovering, editing and publishing major Arab authors, teachers, philosophers and poets, as well as reissuing original medieval Arab translations of Greek philosophers such as Aristotle.

University presses are now enriched by the growing number of institutions of higher learning and research that have publishing programmes. With a single exception, however, none of their lists is strong on criticism or dissent: the 'defence of the Arab Cause' is largely equated with the defence of the dictatorial regimes in power; intellectuals have, by and large, according to the author of this rare criticism Professor Constantine Zurayk, remained subservient to the said regimes and assisted them in 'crushing the people and taming public opinion'.

Needless to say, such a critique could have been mounted in no other Arab capital. Nor is it the first time Beirut has played host to dangerous and unpopular views – Nasr Hamed Abou-Zeid and his *Critique of Religious Discourse* (*Index* 4/96); Sadek Jalal el-Azm and his *Critique of Religious Thinking*, and many more who have chosen the sanctuary of Beirut for publication. Choice extends to the city's newspapers and magazines, which have done much to highlight the cases of Arab writers in trouble with their governments and have opened their columns to them. *Al-Mulhaq, an-Nahar*'s literary supplement, has done a great deal to support Syrian writers such as the philosopher Mohammed Chahrour and the poet Riad el-Turk, and to ensure that the censor in Damascus was cheated of his victory by publishing their work.

The most striking recent example is the case of Islamic Jamaa militant Khaled el Berry who upon repenting in 2001 published a sensational memoir and analysis of Jamaa's doctrine and indoctrination. The title defies the current wave of suicide bombers and martyrs: *Life is More Beautiful than Heaven* (published by Dar an-Nahar).

No study of the book world in Lebanon would be complete without including the important role played by the Institute for Palestine Studies in Beirut. The Edward Said phenomenon is the best illustration of the creative force of the Palestinian diaspora that not only reoriented Arab thought and literature, but transformed Arab culture into a formidable political force, not only where its own, Palestinian, affairs were concerned, but in every other Arabic field. It was even able to force a dialogue on Israeli intellectuals and non-Israeli Jews.

Is not Edward Said's choice to be buried in Lebanon – rather than in the more 'naturally beloved' Jerusalem, or even Ramallah – a form of posthumous credo in Beirut's commitment to the liberty of the word, recognition that it has earned the right to host even the most perilous debates of our time? ❏

Ghassan Tuéni is president of Dar an-Nahar publishers in Beirut and former editor-in-chief of the Beirut daily an-Nahar

ANA YUSIF

MAHMOUD DARWISH

Father! I am Yusif
O father!
My brothers neither love me
nor want me in their midst.
O father, they assault me,
they stone me and
with insults they shower me.
My brothers wish me dead
so they give their false eulogies.
They shut your door before me,
and from your field
I was expelled.
They poisoned my grapevines,
O father!
When the passing breeze
jested with my hair,
They all became envious,
outraged at you and me.
What have I done to them, father,
And what loss have I caused?
Butterflies rest on my shoulder,
wheat bows towards me
and birds hover above my hands.
What then did I do wrong, father,
and why me?
You're the one who named me Yusif!
They pushed me down the well
And then they blamed the wolf.
O father! The wolf is more merciful
than my brothers.
Did I wrong anyone
when I told about my dream?
Of eleven planets, I dreamt,
and of the sun and the moon
all kneeling before me. ❏

*Mahmoud Darwish is
the foremost Palestinian
poet writing today.*
Reproduced in Creating
Spaces of Freedom
*(Prince Claus Fund /
Saqi Books, 2002)*

SPREADING THE WORD

BERNARD HAYKEL

CULTURAL AND SECTARIAN
DIFFERENCES FRAGMENT
THE ARAB BOOK MARKET

There are a good many myths and shibboleths circulating about the state of the Arab publishing market, chief among them that it is currently disproportionately weighted in favour of Islamic book production. Critics call the Arab publishing world 'a desert', describing it as 'book-starved in a storied land'. Let me cite just one comment that sums up Western views:

> In the modern era, an unholy alliance between repressive Arab regimes and certain conservative Muslim scholars has led to the domination of certain interpretations of Islam that serve the governments but are hostile to human development – particularly freedom of thought, women's empowerment and the accountability of governments to their people . . . Although the Arab region represents 5 per cent of world population, it produces only 1.1 per cent of the books in the world. There is an abundance of religious books published in the Arab region – more than triple the world average – but a paucity of literary and artistic works. (Thomas Friedman, *New York Times*, 19 October 2003)

Although it is true that we have seen a relative increase in the volume of Islamic publications over the past 20 years, the figures are nothing like those implied by Friedman; and it is a gross oversimplification to conflate the influence of Saudi Arabia and its Wahhabite clerics with that of Iran and the Gulf and use it to explain the state of publishing. *Publishing in Lebanon: Reality and Politics* (published by al-Merkaz al-Lubnani lildirasat) is a study of the 26 major publishing houses in Beirut and gives a very different picture: only 52 per cent of Lebanese publishers produce anything remotely resembling religious or Islamic books; and these constitute no more than 15 per cent of their total production. Beirut publishes only 30 new Islamic titles per month. These are not large numbers.

The maximum print run of such books is 3,000 and more often between 1,000 and 2,000. The few publications that exceed this are exceptions. They include:

- Books subsidised by a government. This is most often the Quran, which is published in millions, plus specific religious works commissioned by, say, Saudi Arabia, to be sold or gifted within the country. Print runs of the latter may run to 10,000–20,000.
- Islamic 'bestsellers' typified most recently by *Laa Tahsan (Don't Be Sad)*, an Islamic take on the 'feel good/self-help' books of the West. Written by Ael Qamni, a Wahhabi scholar, it is a compilation of Quranic quotations and *hadith* (sayings of the Prophet) enjoining Muslims not to feel sad and suggesting what they can do to cheer their spirits. There are others, all offering answers to predicaments that currently preoccupy Muslims: what attitude to take to the events of 11 September, or what the Quran has to say about Jews.
- The classics of Islam, among which are *40 Hadith, Interpretation of Dreams*, Ibn Qasir's *Tahsir an-'Azim* and Sayyid Sabeh's *Fiqh al-Sunna*. The latter is the most widely sold work on *fiqh* (Islamic law) in the Arab world and has been quietly pushed by the Muslim Brotherhood and the Saudis for some time.
- 'Fashionable' books, similar to the bestsellers but dependent on whatever the trend of the moment happens to be. For instance, certain Sufi books are currently enjoying a renaissance. The books of Ibn al-Arabi are in fashion at the moment, so much so that even booksellers who do not approve of his work are forced to sell him for the good of their business – but with the health warning: 'This book may send you to hell!' And these may well be 'under the counter' sales.

It is the 50 or so titles of this last group that broadly constitute what we might term an 'Islamic' book, though even here I have included books on the interpretation of dreams, on ethics and etiquette. A comprehensive definition of what exactly we mean by an 'Islamic' book is a complex matter. Put simply, it must have something to do with Islam as a religion or legal system and, for most people, will be pre-modern. Then there are those books written more recently by Islamists or Islamic scholars that deal exclusively with religious topics. Generally, such books are distinguished by their handsome binding, rich gilded tooling and calligraphy. None of these books is under copyright and will be produced by many publishing houses in lavish editions in competition with one another. They sell in the hundreds of thousands.

There is a further category of books that may break the mould: banned and censored books. Sales figures are not enormous, and they will be sold discreetly to a niche market. A typical example of this would be a book published in London by a Saudi opposition group exposing the sexual debauchery of the Saudi royal family. For this the reader can expect to pay in the region of US$100.

So much for the 3,000 rule. What of the structural features of the market? There is no doubt that the kingdom of Saudi Arabia and its petro-dollars have played a dominant role in the kinds of Islamic books that are produced, how they're marketed and where they're sold. On the Shia side, the Iranian revolution has played a similar role. Saudi influence shapes the sensibilities of readers by promoting particular writers and thus determining what is available. They have succeeded in supplanting many of the classics by modern writers more to their liking.

Apart from the pervasive influence of Saudi Arabia and Iran, the Arab book market is fragmented both geographically and along sectarian lines. Distribution is localised: a book published in the Maghreb is hard to find in the Mashreq; one published in the Mashreq, if it's in Lebanon, is more likely to be found in the Maghreb, but a book published in Jordan is unlikely to be found in Morocco. This is repeated across the Arab world. The huge print runs funded by a particular state will never circulate outside its borders, even though thousands of copies may be rotting in a government warehouse somewhere.

A Shia bookshop in Beirut's southern suburbs will not sell Sunni books and vice versa in west Beirut. The pattern is repeated wherever the sectarian divide is found. Each of these is a highly specialised niche market, much of it catered to by specialist sectarian publishers whose products are distributed only to booksellers of like sympathies. Publishers who will cater to any persuasion are likely to be leftist Greek Orthodox Christians in Beirut.

The market is further fragmented by its highly personal nature. Even when it may cost more, a publisher would rather go to the man he knows, who speaks his language and will meet his terms, than look further afield. The Lebanese publisher has the comparative advantage in that he can provide this personalised service and doesn't have to compete on cost with, say, Singapore. Apart from the fact that there is little to no censorship in Lebanon, Lebanese publishers also have the comparative advantage of greater experience in export and marketing than others.

Cairo Book Fair 2001: among the believers. Credit: Marwan Naamani – STF / AFP

But political agendas apart, there are genuine reasons for the growth in Islamic books relative to other books in the market since the late 1980s. One reason is the rediscovery of our heritage, our tradition, after the disruption of colonialism. The new Islamic sensibility that emerged as a result of the Iranian revolution and the influx of petro-dollars coincided with the more literate population that had emerged from the mass education of the 1940s–1960s. They went back to discover, edit and publish manuscript sources from the past. When people talk about the Islamic book market, they talk not so much about *kutub al-din*, religious books, as about *turath*, books of our heritage.

And there's the zeitgeist effect: we live in the spirit of the times. If you speak to a Beirut publisher now, he'll tell you that all he sold in the 1950s and 1960s were Arab nationalist, socialist books, books on Palestine and the resistance. Now he has to sell expositions on whether one should pluck one's eyebrows, proper Islamic bathroom etiquette, and Islamic legal stuff, the laws of jihad and the like. As a result of Saudi funding, the political mood in the Muslim world and in the Arab world specifically has veered towards Islam and Islamism. It's noticeable that when you go to a book fair in Amman or Sa'na or Cairo, the Islamic books are cheaper to buy because they tend to have some Saudi or Qatari subsidy. The rise of an Islamist world view that has been subsidised by the Saudis and others has undoubtedly affected this market.

The personal computer, particularly since the introduction of Arabic software in the late 1980s, has made an enormous difference to the production and editing of Arabic books; they are cheaper than ever before. It is an amazing sight to go to some remote village in Yemen or India and see young *madrasa* scholars at 10 terminals, with open manuscripts next to them, simply editing non-stop.

However, the miracles of technology have made little difference to distribution in the Arab world. Online bookshops tend to be related to outlets based in the West (there is a thriving publishing industry in London, for instance, producing a good deal of oppositional literature that is then smuggled into the countries concerned and sold under the counter) and serve Muslims living in the West; and even here, the pattern of sales reflects the same divisions and fragmentations that plague the Muslim world at large. Generally speaking, Arabs are not great readers and don't buy a lot of books. Poverty and high illiteracy rates clearly are one factor. Islamic books, unless you're a specialist, are not that easy to get to grips with, except the classics that are read more in a ritual fashion than for comprehension. ❑

Bernard Haykel is a scholar of Islamic studies and associate professor at New York University. He is author of Revival and Reform in Islam *(Cambridge, 2003)*

DRUNKENNESS AFTER DRUNKENNESS
ABU NUWAS

Abu Nuwas (747/762– 813/815) was among the best writers of the Abbasid school of poetry in Baghdad. He lived a life of open debauchery and his poems reflect this in their emphasis on drinking songs, love poems (usually about young men) and obscenity. He even attacks Islam. He also wrote satires, didactic verse, panegyrics and ascetic verse. He became a folk hero and stories about his exploits at the court of Caliph Harun al-Rashid appear in The Thousand and One Nights.

So pour wine for me and say it is wine;
Don't pour in secret what can be public.

No good life without drunkenness after drunkenness;
If its duration is long then time will be short.

There is no crime but your seeing me sober, no advantage
But in my drunken shakes and stammers.
Reveal the name of whom you love without allusion;
There is no good in veiled pleasures,

Nor good in depravity without scandal,
Nor in scandal not followed by unbelief.

With all my brothers in depravity,
Their brows are crescent moons surrounded by stars,

I woke a taverness from her nap,
Once Gemini had set and Aquila had risen.

She said, 'Who knocks?' We answered, 'A gang
Lightened of medicine, wine entices them,

They must fornicate.' She said, 'In exchange
Take one bright as a dinar, languor in his glance.'

'Hand him over. The likes of us are impatient
To ransom our families for the likes of him.'

She brought him out like a moon at full term;
Enchanting, he was no mere enchantment.

So we went to him one by one,
Breaking the fast of our exile.

So we passed the night, God watching a gang
Let trail the robes of depravity – and this no boast. ❏

From Literatures of the Middle East: From Antiquity to the Present
edited and with introductions by Willis Barnstone and Tony Barnstone
(Prentice Hall, USA)
Translated by Richard Serrano

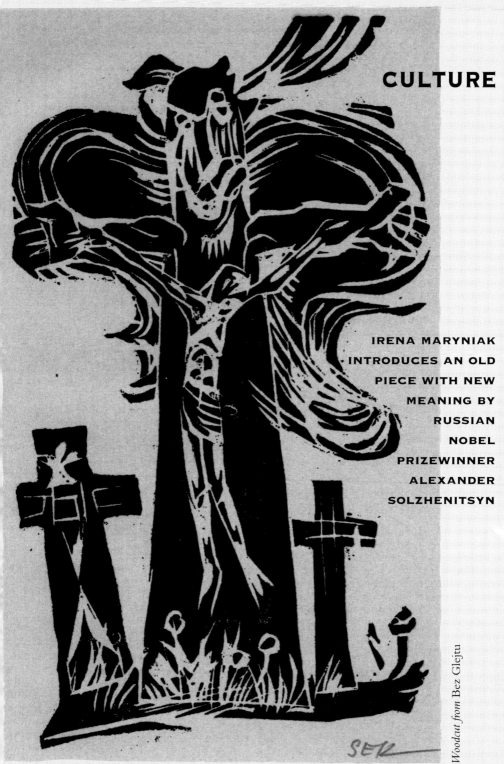

CULTURE

**IRENA MARYNIAK
INTRODUCES AN OLD
PIECE WITH NEW
MEANING BY
RUSSIAN
NOBEL
PRIZEWINNER
ALEXANDER
SOLZHENITSYN**

Woodcut from Bez Glejtu

SPEAK TRUTH TO LIES

IRENA MARYNIAK

Alexander Solzhenitsyn is too often recalled as that latter-day Tolstoy
turned 'one-man Armageddon' who materialised from the Soviet melting
pot in the mid-1970s to embarrass and denounce the Western liberal
establishment. His style was arrogant, his language inflammatory and,
though he was the Soviet Union's most prominent dissident, outside Russia
his posture seemed ungrateful, inflexible, nationalistic and authoritarian.
But his attacks on the West's 'moral crisis', the legacy of the Enlightenment
and material progress also provoked reluctant admiration, mostly at his
determination to leave nothing unsaid. He was, after all, doing no more
than he had done at home: thinking his own thoughts, uttering them,
opening everybody's eyes to dangers as he perceived them, and offering
unwelcome solutions.

Solzhenitsyn's personal experience, as a once-loyal Marxist betrayed
by his own beliefs, in many ways determined his absolutist position and
his challenge to the view that values – 'justice' or 'good' for example – can
have a changeable aspect. He had spent 11 years in prison camps and exile
after being arrested in 1945 for writing letters containing remarks critical
of Stalin. There, in the camps, he first met people able to talk openly and
grapple with real issues in ways that were impossible in conditions of
freedom where family, career and the future were considerations. This
brought him to the conclusion that to abdicate 'truth' in favour of temporal
advantage was to impair and damage individual psychological integrity and
freedom. Truth was a thing perceived through personal conscience and
the heart. It was about clear vision and the disinterested communication
of experience and information; lying was about the betrayal and failure of
memory, record, language and consciousness, individual as well as social.

'Live not by Lies' was released on 14 February 1974, one day after
Solzhenitsyn's arrest and deportation to West Germany. Written about
four years earlier, it pointed to the double standards of an ideology that
had come to serve the ends of power, to public fear and inertia. It called for
a campaign of non-cooperation with a harsh and often brutal communist
regime that survived largely by suppressing information and creating
fantasies about itself. It urged the Soviet people to be true to their own

perceptions and understanding, and not subscribe to any form of words that belied or misrepresented these. 'In our country the lie has become not just a moral category but a pillar of the state,' Solzhenitsyn said in an interview published in *The Times* three weeks before his expulsion. 'In breaking with the lie, we are performing . . . an act that would immediately have an effect on our way of life.' Once the bond with the web of distortion and propaganda had been broken, the way would be open for the restoration of a severed link with previous generations, and for psychological recovery.

Alexander Solzhenitsyn on his return to Russia in 1994

Solzhenitsyn's banishment followed the KGB's confiscation of the manuscript of *The Gulag Archipelago* and his subsequent decision to publish it in the West. The 2,000-page exposure of the secret Soviet prison camp network in which millions had died affirmed in a furious and anarchic form that literature could and must reclaim the past and restore voices to the silent and the dead. It also reflected a view that any falsification or misrepresentation of memory is a mutilation of minds and relationships, as well as of information and historical record. In the Soviet Union this had taken on the dimensions of a social catastrophe, Solzhenitsyn wrote, after decades of 'dictated opinion, dinned into us from the electrified gullets of radio . . . [which] have made mental cripples of us'.

Solzhenitsyn's authority was unquestionably corroborated by the emotional response his writings generated in the Soviet Union at a time when the veil over Stalinist atrocities was just beginning to be lifted. 'One day in the life of Ivan Denisovich', published in the journal *Novyi mir* in 1962, sold out in a matter of hours. A story evoking the experience of a Stalinist prison camp, it touched on things intensely remembered but never discussed and unleashed a torrent of public feeling and, soon afterwards, an official campaign of defamation and abuse against its author. Within weeks a clampdown from the authorities ensured that no other 'unsanitised' manuscript about the camps saw the light of day for another two decades.

By 1974, the Soviet press was regularly labelling Solzhenitsyn renegade, traitor, counter-revolutionary and accusing him of 'cynical falsifications'. There were anonymous phone calls, threats to his life, official suggestions that he might be criminally charged. His manuscripts were seized. All this led him to pursue a defensive strategy that included a troubled alliance with the Western media, which he frequently viewed with suspicion and distaste. Sensationalism, trash and trivia made him uncomfortable. But foreign reporters also gave him the global prominence he needed to go on writing while calling for more free speech in the Soviet Union, denouncing arrests and repression and, most controversially, any move towards détente in Cold War relations.

This uncompromising posture was also shaped by his sense of a writer's accountability in a literary tradition cut short by the intrusion of ideology, censorship and the 'socialist realist' model that Soviet authors and artists were required to emulate. 'This is . . . the sealing up of a nation's heart, the excision of its memory,' Solzhenitsyn wrote in his Nobel Prize acceptance speech. 'Mute generations live out their lives and die, without giving an account of their experiences either to themselves or their descendants.' It takes the artist to transcend the bounds of personal experience and communicate the experience of those without a voice. Further, the call to speak makes a writer integrally part of the state and its accomplice in the most organic, brutal way. 'If the tanks of his fatherland have bloodied the pavement of a foreign capital, then rust-coloured stains have forever bespattered the writer's face.'

The intensity of a writer's bond with his nation and state, and his moral responsibility before his fellow citizens, are awe-inducing. 'Trust your eye; tell it like it is; report, inform, remind; stand up and be counted; don't mince your words; heal. "One word of truth shall outweigh the whole world," the Russian proverb has it. It is on such a seemingly fantastic violation of the law of conservation of mass energy that my own activity is based,' the Nobel lecture concludes, 'and my appeal to the writers of the world.'

Calls like these are the stuff of action, not democratic discourse. Can this language and its message have any resonance 30 years on, in a Russia with tanks in Chechnya; reporting, information and debate well curtailed; and only positions and postures flowing freely and cheaply in the public domain? ❏

Irena Maryniak

LIVE NOT BY LIES

ALEXANDER SOLZHENITSYN

At one time we dared not even whisper. Now we write and read samizdat and sometimes when we gather in the smoking room of the Science Institute we complain frankly to one another. What kind of tricks are they playing on us, and where are they dragging us? There is gratuitous boasting of cosmic achievements while poverty and destruction exist at home. Propping up remote uncivilised regimes. Fanning up civil war. And we recklessly fostered Mao Tse-tung (at our expense) – and we shall be the ones sent to war against him and we will have to go. Is there any way out? They put anybody they want on trial and put sane people in asylums – always they; we are powerless.

Things have almost reached rock-bottom. A universal spiritual death has already touched us all and physical death will soon flare up and consume us and our children. But, as before, we still smile in a cowardly fashion and mumble with our tongues tied. What can we do to stop it? We haven't the strength. We have been so hopelessly dehumanised that for today's ration of food we are willing to abandon all our principles, our souls and the efforts of our predecessors, as well as all the opportunities for our descendants, Just don't disturb our fragile existence!

We lack resolution, pride and enthusiasm. We don't even fear universal nuclear death, nor do we fear a third world war – perhaps we can hide in crevices. We just fear acts of civil courage. We are afraid to lag behind the herd and to take one step alone – and suddenly to find ourselves without white bread, heating gas and a Moscow registration. What was drummed in our ears at political courses we have now internalised: live comfortably and all will be well ever after. You cannot escape your environment and social conditions. Existence determines consciousness. What does it have to do with us? We cannot do anything about it.

But we can! We lie to ourselves to preserve our peace of mind. It is not they who should be blamed but ourselves. One can object, but cannot imagine what to do. Gags have been stuffed into our mouths. Nobody wants to listen to us and nobody asks our opinion. How can we force them to listen to us? It is impossible to change their minds. It would be logical to vote them out of office, but there are no elections in our country. In the

West people resort to strikes and protest demonstrations, but we are too downtrodden and it is too horrifying for us. How can one suddenly renounce a job and take to the streets? Other fatal paths tested during the last century by our bitter Russian history are even less suitable for us, and truly we do not need them.

Now that the axes have done their work and everything that was sown has sprouted, we can see that the young and presumptuous people who thought they would make our country just and happy through terror, bloody rebellion and civil war were themselves misled. No thanks, fathers of enlightenment! Now we know that infamous methods breed infamous results . . . Let our hands be clean!

Is the circle closed? Is there really no way out? Is there only one thing left to do – to wait without taking any action? Maybe something will happen by itself. But it will never happen as long as we daily acknowledge, extol and strengthen – and do not sever ourselves from – the most perceptible of its aspects: lies. When violence intrudes into peaceful life, its face glows with self-confidence, as if it were carrying a banner and shouting: 'I am violence. Run away, make way for me – I will crush you.' But violence quickly grows old. After only a few years it loses confidence in itself, and in order to maintain a respectable face it summons falsehood as its ally – since violence can conceal itself with nothing except lies, and the lies can be maintained only by violence. Violence does not lay its paw on every shoulder every day: it demands from us only obedience to lies and daily participation in lies. And this submissiveness is the crux of the matter. The simplest and most accessible key to our self-neglected liberation is this: personal non-participation in lies. Though lies may conceal everything, though lies may control everything, we should be obstinate about this one small point: let them be in control but without any help from any of us. This opens a breach in the imaginary encirclement caused by our inaction. It is the easiest thing for us to do and the most destructive for the lies. Because when people renounce lies it cuts short their existence. Like a virus, they can survive only in a living organism.

Let us admit it: we have not matured enough to march into the squares and shout the truth out loud or to express aloud what we think. It is not necessary. It's dangerous. But let us refuse to say what we do not think. This is our path, the easiest and the most accessible one, which allows for our inherent, well-rooted cowardice. And it is much easier (it's shocking even to say this) than the sort of civil disobedience that Gandhi advocated.

Our path is not that of giving conscious support to lies about anything at all. And once we realise where the perimeters of falsehood are (everyone sees them in his own way), our path is to walk away from this gangrenous boundary. If we did not paste together the dead bones and scales of ideology, if we did not sew together rotting rags, we would be astonished how quickly the lies would be rendered helpless and would subside. That which should be naked would then really appear naked before the whole world.

So in our timidity, let us each make a choice: whether to remain consciously a servant of falsehood (of course, it is not out of inclination but to feed one's family that one raises one's children in the spirit of lies), or to shrug off the lies and become an honest man worthy of respect from one's children and contemporaries.

And from that day onward he:

- will not sign, write or print in any way a single phrase which in his opinion distorts the truth
- will utter such a phrase neither in private conversation nor in public, neither on his own behalf nor at the prompting of someone else, neither in the role of agitator, teacher, educator, nor as an actor
- will not depict, foster or broadcast a single idea in which he can see a distortion of the truth, whether it be in painting, sculpture, photography, technical science or music
- will not cite out of context, either orally or in writing, a single quotation to please someone, to feather his own nest, to achieve success in his work, if he does not completely share the idea which is quoted, or if it does not accurately reflect the matter at issue
- will not allow himself to be compelled to attend demonstrations and meetings if they are contrary to his desire
- will immediately walk out of a meeting, session, lecture, performance or film if he hears a speaker tell lies, or purvey ideological nonsense or shameless propaganda
- will not subscribe to or buy a newspaper or magazine in which information is distorted and primary facts are concealed.

I have not enumerated, of course, all possible and necessary ways of avoiding lies, but whoever begins to cleanse himself will easily apply the cleansing pattern to other cases. It will not be the same for everybody at first. Some will lose their jobs. But there are no loopholes for anybody who

JAKO LILIE

Hlína se na noc zavírá
laténské meče počaté ohněm
vstoupily do ní
a mlčí

Má země poseta
krvácejícími šperky

Na dně veškeré tmy
pluje dívčí spona
jako lilie
na keltském pohřebišti

15. VIII.1972

From Bez Glejtu (No letter of
safe conduct: poems 1969–1979)
by Jiří Hynek, with woodcuts by
SEK, published as samizdat by
the author in Prague in 1979

Like a Lily

The soil is closing for the night / LaTene swords
conceived by fire / entered it / and are silent
My country covered in / bleeding jewels
On the bottom of all the darkness / floats a girl's
hair slide / like a lily / at a Celtic burial ground

15 August 1972

wants to be honest. On any given day, any one of us, even those securely working in technical sciences, will be confronted with at least one of the above choices. Either truth or falsehood: towards spiritual independence or towards spiritual servitude.

And he who is not sufficiently courageous to defend his soul – don't let him be proud of his 'progressive' views, and don't let him boast that he is an academician or a people's artist, a distinguished figure or a general. Let him say to himself: I am a part of the herd and a coward. It's all the same to me as long as I'm fed and kept warm.

Even this path – the most moderate of all paths of resistance – would not be easy for those of us who have become too set in our ways. But it would be far easier than a hunger strike or a self-immolation. The flames would not touch your body, your eye would not burst from the heat and your family should always be able to get black bread and fresh water.

Has not the great European nation Czechoslovakia – betrayed and deceived by us – demonstrated how even an armourless breast, if it holds a worthy heart, can stand up to the onslaught of tanks?

This would not be an easy path, but the easiest of all possible ones. Not an easy path – but there are people among us, dozens of them, who have been observing all these conditions for years and who live by the truth.

Therefore you will not be the first to take this path, you will join others! It will be easier and shorter if we embark on it in great and friendly numbers. If we are in thousands it will not be possible for them to do anything to anyone. If we are in tens of thousands we will not recognise our own country!

If we are too frightened, then we should stop complaining that we are being suffocated. We are doing this to ourselves. If we bow down even further and wait longer, our brothers the biologists may then help to bring nearer the day when our thoughts can be read and our genes restructured.

If we are too frightened to do anything, then we are hopeless and worthless people and the lines of Pushkin fit us well:

> What use to the herds the gifts of freedom?
> The scourge, and a yoke with tinkling bells
> – this is their heritage, bequeathed to every generation.

Moscow, 12 February 1974 ❏

CHINESE ART: SHANGHAI GOES PLOP
EDWARD LUCIE-SMITH

Tuesday 24 February

Arrive mid-morning on the overnight Virgin flight from London. It's four years since I was here last, and the airport is new since then. Immigration is extremely quick; my bag appears on the carousel after only ten minutes and there is, thank God, someone waiting to meet me at the exit from the customs hall.

We drive to the city in thickening smog. Immense featureless towers loom up around the elevated highway as we get closer to the centre. I am told, later, that Shanghai now has more than 1,000 buildings that officially count as skyscrapers. We pass through a brightly lit shopping street – the windows and billboards advertise every imaginable US, French and Italian luxury brand. Turning a corner, we arrive at our destination – a courtyard surrounded by three tall apartment blocks. A bilingual sign tells me that this is the Ambassy [*sic*] Club. My quarters are in a smaller building that shares space with a health complex and a swimming pool. This is reserved for guests of the lessees of the apartments. The manager of the complex says that the tenants are '40 per cent Caucasian, 40 per cent Japanese and 20 per cent Chinese'.

Before going to bed I look for an English-language news programme on the television set in my room. I can find only one and that is entirely devoted to news about business, the economy and stocks and shares. As far as I can make out, the Chinese news programme on offer provides exactly the same content. No mention of Iraq. No images of President Bush. No disasters, natural or otherwise.

Wednesday 25 February

Johnson Chang flew in late last night from Hong Kong. He has a gallery there called HanArt. More important, he is a hugely influential curator, largely responsible for the international success of the new Chinese avant-garde. He is the only person I know who travels more than I do. He

The Wright Brothers: top flight through 'Wisdom Avenue'.
Credit: Edward Lucie-Smith

was previously in Shanghai a little over a week ago, acting as cicerone to Thomas Krens, the formidable director of the Guggenheim Museum in New York, who is negotiating with the Chinese authorities to open a branch of his institution here, in succession to Bilbao and Las Vegas. The negotiations turn not simply on finance but on the proportion of US as opposed to other kinds of art that the Shanghai Guggenheim will contain. Krens is a master of cultural imperialism.

Johnson and I have been friends for the best part of 10 years and our role is to advise the city government of Shanghai on the commissioning and placement of new sculptures before the Shanghai international Expo scheduled for 2010. We go off to collect the third member of our party, the Japanese curator Toshio Shimizu, who is staying in a vast, gloomy art deco hotel near the Bund.

After this, we have our first encounter with some of the contemporary sculpture that already exists in Shanghai. First a tour to see some existing abstract sculptures – shiny examples of abstract 'plop art', purely ornamental, careful to avoid any specific meaning. Then we go to Longhua in the western suburbs. This has a pagoda that is reputed to be the oldest building in the city and, next to it, a park called the Martyrs' Memorial, created in a single year at the beginning of the 1990s. Here there is meaning aplenty.

The 'martyrs' were the leftist workers and intellectuals killed by the Kuomintang in 1927 – a story best known in Europe through André Malraux's novel *L'Espoir*. One wonders what the great French aesthete would have made of these noisily rhetorical works. Some, in stone, look like commercial Chinese soapstone carvings of the nineteenth century blown up very big. A colossal figure in bronze has evidently been inspired by the famous Robert Capa photograph of a combatant being shot dead in the Spanish Civil War. There are other borrowings as well. One part of the garden has inscribed walls of polished black granite, echoing Maya Lin's Vietnam memorial in Washington DC. And there are also little pyramidal structures that show the influence of the Chinese-American architect IM Pei. Scattered around, to add authentic flavouring, are a number of the ornamental 'scholar's rocks' without which no Chinese garden is complete.

The park is conspicuously clean and well kept, but the Chinese wandering around in it – there are no tourists – seem to treat it without much reverence. A family is using the plinth of one of the stone groups as a place to play cards.

210   INDEX ON CENSORSHIP 2 2004

After lunch we adjourn for our first formal consultation. Our hosts are young technocrats, very proud of their city. They tell us that there are 1,000 sculptures now in Shanghai and that they intend to raise this number to 10,000 by 2010.

Thursday 26 February
We go off to another and even more remote suburb to look at the race track that the Shanghai municipality is building for Formula One. Roaring down flat, dusty roads, dodging alarmingly aggressive trucks, we eventually find the site. The whole project, scheduled to be ready by September 2004, seems even more conspicuously unfinished than the Olympic buildings now being prepared in Athens. It is, however, swarming with workmen, quick-moving in yellow safety helmets and checked shirts. The team in charge is another group of enthusiastic young technocrats. In the courtyard of the prefab site office there is one very local touch – beautifully kept dwarf trees of various kinds in large ceramic pots. I can't imagine any British site office bothering with this, however large and prestigious the project.

After lunch a second consultation, this time with a team who will be responsible for building a new railway station in the southern part of the city. Here there is only a model for us to look at as construction has not yet begun. It will be a handsome circular building with a shallow domed roof rather like a huge lotus leaf. There is a place for one major piece by a sculptor and Shimizu already has a candidate, a German living in Tokyo. The trouble is that the grounds surrounding the station have already been elaborately designed – over-designed would be a better description – by a group of young architects ('just students really,' mutters Johnson in English as he sits beside me at the conference table). The designs, rather like the park at Longhua, are an uneasy combination of the traditional and the glitzy: areas designated as zones of Air, Water and Earth, in conformity with the principles of ancient Chinese geomancy, plus an avenue lined with upright neon lights. The sculpture Shimizu recommends is an abstract metal shell with a light inside it. A complicated argument ensues in rapid Shanghai dialect. Most of this, obviously, I can't follow, though it's clear that the 'students' are desperately clinging to their concept. Whoever wins, the result is clearly going to be extremely bright and shiny, which seems a pity, given the elegant restraint of the main structure.

Jesus – and an intruder – in the School of Athens. *Credit: Edward Lucie-Smith*

Friday 27 February

Downtown to the Bund to look at the sculptures proposed as alternative solutions for an important waterfront site. The sculptors are all protégés of the slick realist painter Chen Yi Fei, first brought to prominence in the West by the late Armand Hammer. The disconcerting thing is that the whole lot are so unimaginative. One is a huge enlargement in shiny metal of a feather. Another is simply a giant sundial. A third is a blown-up version of a traditional Chinese compass. The local press accost me – I try to be as non-committal as possible. In any case I suspect there is no Chinese translation for the term 'plop' in this context.

We drive off to inspect yet another sculpture park, on the distant outskirts of the city, on the shores of a lake. This one, however, is a surprise. Called 'The Oriental Green Boat' it is a very recent creation, next to a big campground used by young people. A party of these arrives soon after we do. They wear camouflage uniforms, and sit on the ground in neat rows, waiting to be instructed. Later, another party appears; slightly older schoolgirls in crisp red jackets.

One feature of the park is a full-scale mock-up of an aircraft carrier – an inexplicable object, since China has no such warship in its own fleet. The mock-up seems to have been copied from a US vessel: a choice with complex political undertones.

The main feature of the park, however, is a huge collection of figurative sculptures in academic style, under the collective title 'Wisdom Avenue'. It celebrates a wide variety of both Western and Eastern worthies, with a choice that spans religion, art and science. The sequence begins with two ambitious sculptural groups, placed facing one another. On the right-hand side are Chinese sages, rather mannered and etiolated. On the left there is a collection of figures adapted from Raphael's *School of Athens* in the Vatican – Plato and Aristotle in the centre, but now with the figure of Jesus seated humbly at their feet. Off to one side, the Emperor Augustus extends an imperious hand.

HERE IS ST THOMAS AQUINAS, AND HERE, LOOKING FULL OF SWAGGERING CONFIDENCE ABOUT HIS RIGHT TO BE PRESENT, IS LUTHER

The display grows ever more surreal as one progresses. Here is St Thomas Aquinas, and here, looking full of swaggering confidence about his right to be present, is Luther. Newton, placed in an especially prominent position, is depicted as a boy contemplating a gigantic apple. Leonardo da Vinci is accompanied by a huge cut-out of the Mona Lisa, in sheet steel painted bright yellow. It looks like a reinterpretation of Leonardo's painting made by the American Pop artist Roy Lichtenstein. Further along are Mendel the geneticist, Sigmund Freud and Mei Lanfang, famous for his interpretation of women's roles in Chinese opera. The display finishes with a large model of the DNA molecule, which in this form looks exactly like one of the shiny plop sculptures I have already seen.

Johnson is shocked by my enthusiasm for 'Green Boat', and uses his mobile to cancel a visit from a rich French collector of contemporary Chinese art. I point out to him that all this is in fact no worse in terms of kitsch than Jeff Koons's giant *Puppy* made of flowers that was shown in the Rockefeller Center, New York, in the summer of 2000, just when the Chinese complex was being created. At that time, Susan K Freedman, president of the New York Public Art Fund, described *Puppy* as 'one of the most significant sculptures of the twentieth century'. The difference, it seems, is that sophisticates can read *Puppy* as ironic, while that is not possible here.

Sometimes, not knowing the language of the people who surround one can actually offer an advantage. Being for all practical purposes both deaf and aphasic makes one look more closely. It gradually dawns on me that the 'Green Boat' images are an even stranger assemblage than they at first seem. There are no representatives from Islam, from India or from other countries of the Far East: no Avicenna, no Sinan, no Hafiz, no Akbar, no Gandhi, no Lady Murasaki, no Hokusai. This is purely a dialogue between the history of the West and that of China. There is also one major Chinese absentee. Marx and Engels are pictured in sunken low relief on a large granite slab, but there is no portrait of Chairman Mao. Representations of women are also almost entirely absent. The message is that China is remaking itself in terms of old-fashioned Western rationality – the very rationality that the West, locked in combat with fundamentalist Islam, now seems intent on abandoning.

27 February, evening (my birthday)

We spend the night at Zhu Zhuan, a 'canal village' on the outskirts of Shanghai. I have been here before; it is the most popular tourist attraction in the region, a miniature oriental Venice which is also an exquisitely preserved fragment of pre-modern China. Newly prosperous citizens of Shanghai love to bring their children here, to learn something of their country's past. In the open-fronted shops that line its narrow lanes a range of craftspeople are at work: a blacksmith, a weaver, a basket-maker, a maker of combs – a kind of human petting zoo. There is a young maker of miniature portrait sculptures in coloured dough. With great speed and deftness he produces a birthday portrait of me, while a small group of fascinated children look over his shoulder.

My birthday celebration is held at the house of Hu Xiancheng, the artist who is the leader of our group. He is also largely responsible for the preservation of the village, at a time when everything in old China was

Leonardo in 'Green Boat': how gold is my Mona. Credit: Edward Lucie-Smith

being pulled down. By preserving it, he made its fortune, as its inhabitants now recognise. Here he is deservedly a hero figure.

I am the only Caucasian present at the party, which is held on traditional lines, with a small band of live musicians – two men who play the *erhu*, a two-stringed fiddle known in China since the time of the Sung Dynasty, and two rosy-cheeked peasant girls equipped with the Chinese equivalent of castenets. One musician tells me proudly that he is 70, a pretty good age in China. I can't resist retorting that I am one year older.

Saturday 28 February
My last day in China on this trip. For the first time it is raining – a steady drizzle. We go to another, somewhat larger community called Zhu-jia-jiao in the orbit of greater Shanghai. Here we visit an abandoned cement factory that the community administrators plan to turn into a craft centre and a residential facility for visiting foreign artists. It is a relic of Mao's original attempt to make China into a major industrial power – an aim that has since been accomplished more slowly and with better planning. The construction is of appalling quality and the buildings have fallen into ruin in the strangest way, often with upper storeys still intact while the lower ones are falling apart. The general effect is sinister: Piranesi without the classicism.

Finally another lunch in a private room in an elegant restaurant, situated in a part of the town that has already been restored. Maps are passed around. 'Here is where we are going to build another sculpture park. And here, perhaps, the special sculpture park for children that you suggested . . . Do try this, a speciality of our region.' 'What is it?' I ask incautiously, breaking a firm personal rule, which is never to enquire about any dish that hits the table at a Chinese mealtime. 'Oh, it's delicious – fried baby toad.' ❏

Edward Lucie-Smith is a writer and art critic

UNCLE BOB AND THE BURIAL NOTES
ESTHER MOIR

So here I am at last – after all the plans, with no less than 19 people wanting to send out messages, money, medical supplies to family and friends here. At breakfast, looking out over the lush vegetation of Ruth's garden that is so African, I cannot help but notice that while I have milk Ruth is eating her oats with water, and while she makes her tea with herbs from her garden I am able to start the morning with a Lyons Quick Brew tea bag. Milk is a huge luxury, coffee is virtually unobtainable. It gives me a jolt, and reminds me that however much I thought I was prepared for my three weeks here, nothing I had read or heard had prepared me for the reality.

As I gaze out on to her garden it seems like Paradise – but like the Garden of Eden there are hidden fault-lines below the surface. Martha has been with her for 20 years and is Ndebele, while Begonia is Shona and married to Winston who comes from Malawi, which means he is looked down upon here. These three have their own houses and the fourth, Paul, who is Shona, is here during the week but returns to his family at the weekend. There is considerable tension between the two women, although the men appear more equitable. There is of course nothing new here. Without taking into account the history of relations between Shona and Ndebele, the story of present-day Zimbabwe lacks a vital dimension. As the days go on, I find time to hear their stories, told to me with that African fortitude that often seems to verge on acceptance to the point of fatalism. All four, whatever their background, are equally dependent on Ruth for their livelihood. This responsibility for their black staff is one of the complicated factors to the question never far from every white person's mind: to stay or to leave?

So already the familiar and unfamiliar jostle in my mind and this will be one of the fascinations of my time here. I have come to see friends and because I love the country: its colours, its light, its people. For 'occupation' when applying for my visa, I had written 'grandmother', thinking that sounded sufficiently innocent to disarm suspicion. During my holiday, I wanted the opportunity to see for myself something of what it feels like to be living in Robert Mugabe's Zimbabwe today.

Tratabeland: street power in Zimbabwe. Credit: Trygve Bolstad / Panos

At first, when I arrived on a half-full plane (I was certainly the only holidaymaker; all the others were either on business or here to see family members), it had all seemed quite prosperous and reassuring: an excellent road from the airport as one would expect, the heart of the city busy and evidence of new expensive houses. But I know that I have to interpret what I see.

Our first stop is the bank, and there I am greeted by posters of cheerful young African faces with the messages 'be wise, build your ark now' and 'be prepared for any misfortune'. And here also is my first lesson in survival. I arrived with sterling hoping to be less of a burden to my hosts, but I learned that to change it officially in a bank would be sheer folly.

While the official bank rate is Zim$824 for US$1 the 'parallel market' offers over Zim$6,000 – worth waiting for! [July 2002 rates: US1$: Zim$57 Ed] So I find a friend who knows the black market and must be prepared to wait about a week. I also learn to get petrol vouchers and at which petrol stations they can be redeemed. I wait for the news that petrol is available and then we rush at top speed while supplies last.

Rather dazed by all this, I hope our next trip, to the supermarket to buy milk, might be rather simpler. If we have to wait until power returns and it reopens, this is not unusual – after all, the traffic lights have also been out. But then came the shock of prices – all those zeros are totally bewildering. I read, in what was to be the first of my many Alice in Wonderland experiences, that a loaf cost Zim$2,800, a can of baked beans Zim$4,000, cooking oil Zim$7,500, margarine Zim$10,000, powdered milk Zim$18,000. I was not to know then that these were only this week's prices. Inflation is escalating at such a rate that prices can and do rise weekly, if not daily. Officially it is 500 per cent; in fact it is certainly more, and set to rise.

We go to the local supermarket, set in an arcade of small shops, quite a number of them closed. Ruth has given me a 'bearer note' so that I can have a little spending money until my undercover financial negotiations materialise. I go into a small pharmacy which is almost empty and when I come to pay I stand behind a woman who is holding a pot of face cream. When she is told the price she says philosophically, 'Then I shall put it back.' I buy my odds and ends, handing over the note that has become a joke – mispronounced by the Africans as 'burial note'. The name has stuck: 'We're burying this country.'

It has bought me virtually nothing. I walk a few yards down and stand beside a newsstand, debating as I look at the price of a daily paper. A young black man joins me. 'Is this worth Zim$1,500?' I ask, and so we fall into easy conversation. He is envious of my living in England, for to get there is his greatest dream, as I am to find of so many others. He asks me what differences I find since my last visit three years ago. I pause, searching for words, and he suggests that people have become more mute, more docile. He is a man with a good education and what should be a good business in cables, but he is sad. I then ask about Mugabe, and he tells me that he is cunning, not clever but cunning; he is *afraid* – afraid because of the many people he has murdered, political rivals, members of his own family. 'He is afraid of his own footsteps, they are marked in blood.'

As we are going back I ask Ruth about the prices, for passing hardware and clothing stores I am baffled: an iron costs Zim$100,000; a blouse Zim$60,000; men's shoes Zim$150,000. If you are paid in foreign currency you can survive; if not, life becomes an unrelenting struggle. As a freelance teacher, Ruth earns Zim$8,000 for a lesson at school, and Zim$12,000 at home. The school fees do not include transport which she has to find herself. A full tank of petrol costs about Zim$225,000. Meanwhile, she has been told that her email charges are to rise by one-third. At the moment she is surviving because she has sold her car, unable to pay the insurance. Instead, she is looking after two cars belonging to friends who have left the country.

I have been here no time at all and already it's getting to me – the uncertainty, the struggle of daily living. Today the water is off and, as there seems to be no reason, the joke is that Uncle Bob is filling the reservoir for his latest house. If the power were to fail as well this would become serious. Ruth has a borehole, but without electricity she cannot use her pump. She is more fortunate than many and we load up large canisters to take to her less fortunate neighbours. It is quite a relief when her pupil rings to say she cannot come for her lesson that morning, though I find the reason deeply shocking. Their house is to be 'taken over', which is apparently not so uncommon; members of the government take over houses for 'urban development', which means that they build low-cost housing and sell it at vast profit.

Having an unexpected free morning, we decide to set out in search of a mechanic, but we have not gone far when we see a petrol queue! Yesterday on all the garage forecourts the pump attendants had been doing a little dance of empty hands, so this is a moment to seize, particularly as there are no more than about 30 cars (a few months ago the queues might involve a day or longer). Ruth walks home to bring the second car and more money, and I settle down into the camaraderie of life in the queue.

The black man in front tells me that he and his passengers are going to a funeral, and when I ask for whom, he replies in traditional African fashion 'my cousin-brother'. In front of him there is a large young man, a white Zimbabwean, who left the country five years ago. This is his third visit back, a week's holiday his wife told him would be a mistake and after only two days he realises how right she was. When his car runs out of petrol we all help him push it, but clearly there is more wrong with it than that, for even with a full tank it fails to start, and my last glimpse is of a dejected hunk of a man slumped under the bonnet, doubtless wishing he were back in London. Behind me there is an older white woman in a green-and-white flowery frock who is delighted to find a captive audience and leaps out of her car to catch my attention, leaving her husband sitting stoically in the front seat reading a book entitled *Moment of Truth*. She is a pensioner and therefore well and truly caught in this economic disaster. She is extremely bitter and understandably so. She feels abandoned and forgotten by Britain. 'They just shrug us off,' she says.

Her woes are genuine but her shrill voice is unrelenting and I am glad to be distracted by the cheerful sight of *sadza* being cooked over a bright open fire in a three-legged iron pot. I ask the young man stirring it if I may take a photo. He says yes, but within moments all hell has broken loose. 'Who are you? What are you doing?' A man in a woolly cap with a bottle of beer is thrusting a card into my face. He tells me that he is a war veteran. A small throng collects. He demands my name and my address; he says that I must go to the police station. My protests that I am a visitor and an artist who enjoys photography go unheeded. It gets ugly. The queue snakes slowly along and my former companions evaporate. I am allowed to reach the pumps and at this point Ruth appears and, recognising how serious it could become, tells me to give him the film. I start to wind it back and when it jams, as it often does, I open the back of the camera in order to speed things up. This simply furnishes him with proof that I am destroying the negative to hide my ulterior purposes. He seizes me by the arm with his one free hand, the other still clutching his bottle, and telling me I am under arrest, marches me off to the police station. I am put in a small room while Ruth goes home to find my passport. There is nothing to do but wait. I'd had the good sense to empty my bag of virtually everything and to slip my notebook into the glove compartment of the car. When at last my passport arrives the war vet disappears and I am allowed to walk free – but deeply embarrassed and concerned at adding yet one more burden of anxiety to a friend who is already sufficiently overwhelmed by life in Mugabe's Zimbabwe.

I've been acutely aware of the level of personal suffering underlying the economic and political situation here. At home we read the statistics about HIV/Aids; here I am faced by its reality. I now feel so ashamed of how easily I could write 'grandmother' in such a light-hearted way when here the grandmothers are often the only ones left to bring up as many as nine or 10 grandchildren. I also learn about 'intermediate mothers', the informal

township mothers for the Aids orphans they find roaming the streets, sleeping in burned-out cars or on rubbish tips.

Douglas, a member of the creative writing group I am meeting with, tells me earlier this year, under the initiative of an Ndebele woman and with two Swiss volunteers, he helped take two busloads of Aids orphans to a camp. Older teenagers who had themselves been Aids orphans have become counsellors for the younger ones, since only those who have themselves been through this can know the devastating loneliness, the sense of shame and of being cut off. There is singing, dancing, gospel music. But they also learn to overcome difficulties. In groups of 10 they are taken through the woods to a 15-foot wall and then left to figure out how to scale it. When they do they have learned that there's nothing in life too big to conquer – and they have learned to trust one another. ❏

Esther Moir *is a writer and lecturer. The second part of her 'letter from Zimbabwe' will appear in the next issue of* Index

Harare: Shona sculpture of grandmother and child. Credit: Esther Moir

WWW.INDEXONCENSORSHIP.ORG
CONTACT@INDEXONCENSORSHIP.ORG
TEL: 020 7278 2313 • FAX: 020 7278 1878

SUBSCRIPTIONS (4 ISSUES PER ANNUM)
INDIVIDUALS: BRITAIN £32, US $48, REST OF WORLD £42
INSTITUTIONS: BRITAIN £48, US $80, REST OF WORLD £52
PLEASE PHONE 020 8249 4443
OR EMAIL TONY@INDEXONCENSORSHIP.ORG

Index on Censorship (ISSN 0306-4220) is published four times a year by a non-profit-making company: Writers & Scholars International Ltd, Lancaster House, 33 Islington High Street, London N1 9LH. *Index on Censorship* is associated with Writers & Scholars Educational Trust, registered charity number 325003 **Periodicals postage:** (US subscribers only) paid at Newark, New Jersey. Postmaster: send US address changes to *Index on Censorship* c/o Mercury Airfreight International Ltd Inc., 365 Blair Road, Avenel, NJ 07001, USA